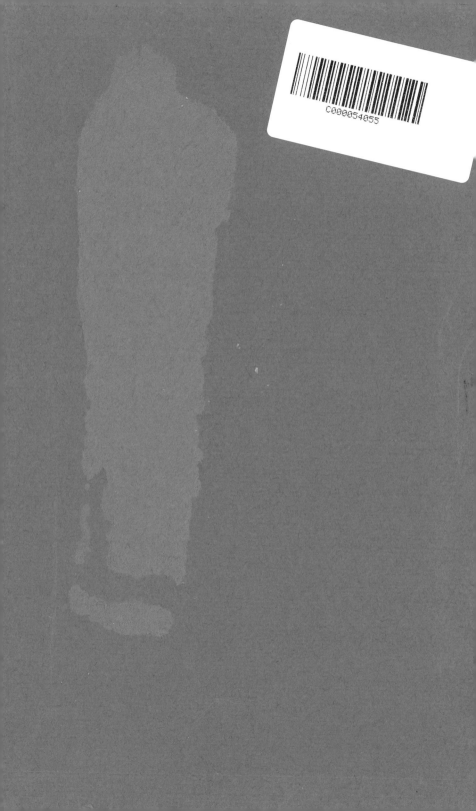

C000054055

THE CENTRE FOR ENVIRONMENTAL STUDIES SERIES

General Editor: David Donnison

SWINDON: A TOWN IN TRANSITION

This book is one of a series edited at the
Centre for Environmental Studies and published
on its behalf by Heinemann Educational Books
Ltd. The series will present work in the fields
of planning, and urban and regional studies,
The Centre is an independent research
foundation charged with the furtherance and
dissemination of research in these fields. Further
information about this series and the Centre's
work can be obtained from the General Editor.

Swindon: A Town in Transition

A Study in Urban Development
and Overspill Policy

MICHAEL HARLOE

 Heinemann: London

Heinemann Educational Books Ltd

London Edinburgh Melbourne Auckland Toronto
Hong Kong Singapore Kuala Lumpur
Ibadan Nairobi Johannesburg
Lusaka New Delhi

ISBN 0 435 85300 7

© Centre for Environmental Studies 1975

First published 1975

Published by Heinemann Educational Books Ltd
48 Charles Street, London W1X 8AH

Reproduced and printed by photolithography and bound in
Great Britain at The Pitman Press, Bath

Preface

Michael Harloe's book is one of a series of studies begun at the London School of Economics and Political Science and completed at the Centre for Environmental Studies with the support of a grant from the Social Science Research Council. This work has produced two other books: *The Organization of Housing*[1] by Michael Harloe, Ruth Issacharoff, and Richard Minns, and *Government and the Planning Process*[2] by Peter Levin, and many shorter papers.

A great deal has been written about new towns, but the expansion of older towns like Swindon under the Town Development Act has been almost entirely neglected by researchers. Harloe shows that Swindon's expansion, like all major development projects, was a complex and essentially political process. Local government played a central part in the story. The development was led by the late Murray John, a great Town Clerk, and carried through by a small and frequently overburdened team of officials, working loyally with a Town Council deeply rooted in the life and industries of the town. Railwaymen in the Labour party were the original political core and continuing supporters of the expansion scheme. The central government, the London County Council, and an initially hostile Wiltshire County Council also played important and sometimes conflicting parts in the story, so did private enterprise of many kinds. But it was the Swindon Council and their remarkable officials whose persistent and imaginative determination sustained the

---

[1] London: Heinemann, 1974.
[2] London: Allen and Unwin, 1975.

impetus of development to which others were able to contribute, or compelled to react.

Harloe concludes with an appraisal of the gains and losses resulting from Swindon's expansion, and the lessons the rest of the country may learn from it. The human outcome — and it is rare for social research to produce such clear conclusions — was in most ways successful. A rather stagnant railway town, on the brink of sinking into decay, changed what appeared to be the irrevocable course of its history. Before long Swindon had gained more jobs, fewer unemployed, higher wages, better houses, more opportunities for women, and wider cultural opportunities — and still had lower rates of delinquency than the rest of the country. Swindon's expansion, though undertaken for the benefit of its own people, also gave more help to ill-housed Londoners than an equivalent investment in new towns. Other towns and other people have a great deal to learn from Michael Harloe's revealing account of this achievement.

> David Donnison
> Centre for Environmental Studies
> January, 1975

Contents

Acknowledgements

This book originated during my employment by the Borough of Swindon between 1967 and 1969. Working as a social planner in a team of officers preparing a feasibility study for the further development of the town, I realized that I had a unique opportunity to piece together the story of how Swindon had become the largest town expansion scheme in Britain. I was in a position where I had privileged access to decision makers and their records; with these I could chart the progress of a major piece of planning from the 'inside'.

With the benefit of hindsight I now realize that many employers, especially local authorities, would have automatically refused the request I made to my chief officer, the Town Clerk, to be allowed the freedom to examine the Council's achievements and failures but typically I was allowed to go ahead, with every assistance I required. More recently the successor to the Borough Council, the Thamesdown District Council, has in its turn helped to make publication of this book possible. At no time has there been any attempt to restrict my access to records or to censor anything I have written. Both authorities have encouraged me to complete this study and I am deeply grateful to them.

However, my greatest debt must be to 'the TC' as he was always known. I regret that my repayment, with this book, must be a posthumous one. David Murray John died in 1974, a few weeks after he had retired from the office he had held since 1937. Swindon, to whom he gave a lifetime of service, owes him more than can be expressed in a few lines. He more than anyone else rescued the town from oblivion. Mistakes were made, as he would readily admit, but the great mass of Swindonians are better housed, better fed, and lead a better life today than they would have done without Murray John's efforts. I came to work for him at the end of his long career but found that there was no thickening of his intellectual (or

political) arteries; he was still scheming and working as hard
as ever for Swindon's future. He had a rare ability to be able to
listen to ideas, even when they came from a raw recruit to
local government, and to back them if they made sense.
Behind his shy, unassuming manner—and the inevitable
cigarette—there was an extremely sharp intelligence laced
with a dry wit. Murray John taught me more about politics
and policy making than I had learnt before or have learnt
since. He was an outstanding local government officer and a
fine person.

One of Murray John's qualities was his ability to attract and
retain a strong team of officers. I owe a particular debt of
gratitude to two of them, Bill Cairns who was Deputy Borough
Treasurer and latterly Controller of Development, and the
late John Moulton, the first neighbourhood worker and
latterly the Community Services Assistant. Both these men
taught me a great deal about Swindon and town development,
and this book would have been poorer without their help.
Barbara Morgan, the Chief Executive's Personal Assistant, has
also been a constant source of encouragement and help.

My colleagues at the Centre for Environmental Studies have
also given me much help, especially David Donnison and
Richard Minns. Juliette London and Judy Lawes coped
patiently and efficiently with the thankless task of typing
successive drafts. Finally I must thank the Swindon Public
Library, the British Museum Newspaper Library, and the CES
Library for their help.

Michael Harloe
London, December 1974

For Judy, Ruth, and Titus

Introduction

British social policies have been subjected to close analysis and criticism in recent years. However, some areas have escaped attention. Foremost among these are the measures which sought to deal with urban squalor and the inter-regional imbalances of population and employment, by exerting a greater control over physical planning and industrial location. Four acts of parliament laid the framework for these policies, the Distribution of Industry Act 1945, the New Towns Act 1946, The Town and Country Planning Act 1947, and the Town Development Act 1951.[1] While location of industry policy has begun to receive critical attention, the system of town and country planning has been subjected to relatively little criticism.[2] The few available new town studies tend to fall into two well defined classes. The first are written by those who have either worked in or on these towns, and are more propagandist than critical. The second are detailed studies of particular aspects of the towns, valuable but limited in scope.

The expanding towns, i.e. towns which grew by using the Town Development Act to receive overspill population and industry from the conurbations, have been completely ignored. Only three works have been published on them in the twenty odd years in which the policy has been in existence. Of these, one is a formalistic guide to planning procedure in such towns with a minimum of analysis and comment, one a

---

[1] A good summary of the background to this legislation is contained in Ashworth, W. *The Genesis of Modern British Town Planning* (London: Routledge and Kegan Paul, 1954).

[2] Since this was written Peter Hall and his colleagues have published the first major evaluation of the post war planning legislation. See Hall, P. *et. al. The Containment of Urban England* (London: Allen and Unwin, 1973).

detailed study of the economic problems of the expanding town of Basingstoke, and the last, to which particular reference will be made later on, a highly personal and selective study of the expanding town of Swindon.[3] This study also takes the town of Swindon as its subject but the object is to illustrate some of the problems of implementing the social policy objectives that inspired the post-war physical planning legislation.

The form of this study has been determined by the view that, despite their undoubted value, statistical measurements of the output of social policies are no more than preliminary to a more fundamental evaluation of their operation. By measurement we may discover how much benefit accrues to the population from a given policy, and even what the distribution of this benefit is. However we can learn little about really interesting questions, such as why were the benefits less than or different from those expected, or why were they distributed in a particular way. But unless we can begin to answer such questions, we cannot suggest ways in which policies might be altered in order to achieve aims. All we can derive from a narrow, statistical approach are recommendations which are either totally condemnatory — 'abolish it altogether' — or are partial, incoherent, and possibly inconsistent — 'there is a gap — let's plug it with a new bit of policy'. Both sorts of suggestions have in fact been made about town development policies.

In order to achieve the more satisfactory understanding that is required, we have to study in detail the process of implementation of social policies. Any new piece of social legislation, such as the Town Development Act, promises certain benefits to a variety of different groups. In doing this it also requires certain other, or even the same, groups to incur certain costs. The extent to which the various participant groups in the implementation process are forced into it, and the extent to which this is a voluntary response, varies from measure to measure, and even within the confines of a given policy. But, even after this association takes place, the degree

---

[3] Seeley, I. H. *Planned Expansion of Country Towns* (London: George Godwin, 1968). Dunning, J. H. *Economic Planning and Town Expansion* (Southamption W.E.A. 1963). Hudson, K. *An Awkward Size for a Town* (Newton Abbot: David and Charles, 1967).

to which any group can maximize the benefits it receives and minimize the costs will depend on the skill and effectiveness with which it operates during the implementation process. So it will not be possible to forecast the outcome of a policy measure if sole attention is paid to the model of the implementation process and the formal policy goals. Of course, these are important because they often define the extent to which groups can manipulate the situation to their own advantage. However we also need to study the various groups which are parties to the policy, in this case the town development process. Given the diverse goals and ideologies of the participants, what we shall be studying are processes of conflict, compromise, bargaining, and the management of these processes.

The Town Development Act is permissive, not mandatory legislation. So, in each case where it is used, somebody (or bodies) has to initiate the process. In the case of Swindon it was the Borough Council, which remained the prime mover in the scheme. Therefore it is inevitable that this Council's actions take the centre of the stage. Much of this study concentrates on that authority's efforts to overcome or to manage the constraints which prevented, or threatened to prevent, it achieving its goals, and the ways in which these goals were modified or abandoned in practice. Therefore most of the relationships we shall be examining are those which existed between the Borough Council and those on whom it had to rely for economic, social, or political support.

Seen in political terms the town development process consists of a series of interacting bodies. However, the exchanges that take place between these parties are concerned with concrete entities. To use an economic analogy, the main factors of production in town development are people, houses, and jobs. The town development process requires complex organization, the purpose of which is to combine these factors in a satisfactory way. All these factors are in scarce supply, including the skills required to set up and manage the operation. Therefore, apart from the study of political processes, we have to account for those elements in the situation which the participants cannot determine, but which nonetheless, together with those elements that they can determine, affect the outcome of a town development scheme. Thus an examination of factors such as the national economic situation, trends in industrial location, and social patterns must be integrated into the study.

Before going further, it is necessary to outline the Town Development Act and the major participants and processes in any scheme carried out under it. The Act was a product of the rethinking of national planning policies, stimulated by the publication in 1940 of the report of the Royal Commission on the Distribution of the Industrial Population (Barlow Report). This report addressed itself to the twin problems of urban squalor and of industrial congestion. Apart from several recommendations which contributed to the Town and Country Planning Act, the New Towns Act, and the Distribution of Industry Act, Barlow also suggested that industry and population could be decentralized to 'small country towns'. These were places whose economic base and population were in decline, and would benefit from an inflow of people and jobs.

The Act itself is short and simple. In essence it allows a bargain to be made between the two major parties to a town development agreement. Large cities, who cannot satisfactorily accommodate all their industry and population (the 'exporting authorities') can offer them better conditions in the expanding towns ('the receiving authorities'). The receiving authorities, in providing a solution to big city problems, are also regenerating their economic base. Naturally few of the receiving authorities can offer to meet the full costs of this operation, so the Act makes the exporting authorities pay a subsidy to the receiving authority for each family housed in the expanding town. It also enables the exporting authorities to help with certain costs, but these are open to negotiation between the two parties. In Swindon's case the exporting authorities only paid their statutory contributions, but in many other schemes far more financial and technical help was given.

Apart from this, the Act enables the Minister to make grants to help the receiving authorities. In theory, these could cover a wide range of operations; in practice, they have been restricted to cover 50 per cent of the capital cost of any new sewerage, water and drainage works, and, in latter years, amenity provision. County boroughs and county councils in whose areas the schemes take place are also empowered to contribute, and some have given financial and technical help.

However, in the period this book covers the Wiltshire County Council, in whose area Swindon is located, did not do so. The Act also contains various other powers. The most important is the power to acquire land by compulsion for town development purposes, even though it is not designated by a development plan for such acquisition.

We have now outlined the policy with which this study is concerned. From the brief details of the Town Development Act which have been presented, we can begin to see what the process of town development involves, what the central bargain is, and who the main parties to the bargain are. As these elements together provide the basic subject matter which we shall be dealing with, they are now examined in more detail.

The main parties to any town development agreement are obviously the receiving and the exporting authorities. Their agreement to operate a scheme is a purely voluntary one, based on calculations of the advantages that each will gain from the bargain. On the one hand, the city hopes that it will find an additional way of relieving housing pressures and industrial congestion at reasonable cost.[4] On the other hand, the receiving authority hopes that the incoming firms and workers will bring new jobs and prosperity to the town. This will enable it to improve public services, while providing greater job opportunities and higher incomes. It also hopes to achieve these ends at minimal cost to its existing inhabitants, i.e. without rapid and large rate increases. Therefore, it wishes to get the maximum financial assistance from the exporting authority and central government, and also to gain from the new and enhanced rateable values created by growth.

However, despite the fact that the initial bargain is struck between these two authorities, other bodies are also involved in a rather more involuntary way. Typically, they are forced to incur costs on behalf of a project initiated by others, over which they only have a limited degree of control in exchange for benefits which may be far less tangible than those gained by the receiving and exporting authorities. The two main

---

[4] In an era when the big cities are increasingly worried about their loss of industry, it is the former rather than the latter aim which is the main reason for overspill.

bodies which come under this heading are the Ministry itself, and the country councils in whose areas the schemes have been carried out. The Ministry promotes town development as a part of a national planning policy, and makes funds available for it. However, this policy has to compete with others for resources. The Minister, and through him the Treasury, will be concerned to set some upper limit on their liability for town development grants. There will also be concern that the parallel policy of steering new employment to the development areas in order to bolster up their declining employment, income, and population is not severely affected by an unduly high proportion of mobile industry deciding to go to expanding (and new) towns rather than to the development areas. Similarly, those departments of central government concerned with the social services and transport will also want to limit the liabilities they incur. Therefore, the Ministries will try to set the amount of resources being committed to town development at a level which safeguards other policies while enabling the schemes to go ahead. However, as the operation of the schemes is mainly in the hands of the receiving and exporting authorities, the Ministries only have indirect and partial control.

Rather similar arguments apply to the county councils. As the providers of certain services, particularly education, health, welfare, and roads, they find themselves committed to heavy expenditures to meet the needs of the incoming population. But they often do not have full control over the pace at which the receiving authority is pushing ahead with its scheme. Pressure will come from the other county districts, who feel that a disproportionate amount of resources is going to one area. Counties have varied in their reactions to town development, some have become deeply involved from the beginning, hoping no doubt to gain an additional measure of control over the scheme by this process. Others, such as Wiltshire in the period we consider, have avoided direct involvement and limited themselves to providing the statutorily required services. Of course town development can be advantageous to the county as well as the district, it generates new rateable value and jobs, the benefit of which is not confined to the area of the receiving authority. However these benefits are less visible and immediate and therefore less politically acceptable outside the reception area. Furthermore they do not flow from a decision taken by the county authority, but from one taken by a constituent district, which nevertheless commits the county to certain actions.

Many other bodies find themselves committed to take action by the existence of a town development scheme. These range from statutory bodies such as regional hospital boards, which may need to provide new or expanded hospital services, to churches and local voluntary organizations, which have to expand their activities. In the case of Swindon, the two surrounding rural district councils were the most significant of these bodies. As is so often the case, there had been a long history of mutual suspicion and rivalry between the rural districts, with their distinctive political and social traditions, and the urban area with its radically different history and outlook. Town development rapidly affected the rural areas. Swindon's expansion threatened their boundaries and finally the expansion of industry and population spilt over into their areas, forcing them to take action to deal with the situation. So changes were induced over which they had little control. Of course expansion brought benefits but these were ones which they had neither sought, nor in many cases saw the necessity for.

So far, we have sketched in the effects of expansion on the main units of government involved in the process and their attitude towards it. However, in the final analysis, town development creates costs and benefits for individuals, and we must now bring this element into the picture. Money, land, jobs, houses, and other services and facilities are the main physical components of the process. The bargain between the receiving and exporting authorities is reflected at the individual level of the inhabitants of these two bodies. The newcomers exchange the social, economic, and recreational benefits of the big city, such as closeness to kin, wide job choice, and range of entertainments, for better housing and a better physical environment in the expanding towns. The existing inhabitants hope to gain the benefits of improved investment in their town such as renewal and extension of public services, wide job choice and higher incomes, in exchange for accepting an influx of 'foreigners', with the resulting social and physical disruption. The problems of ensuring that this equation is achieved to the benefit of both sides presents the receiving authority with a series of problems.

The major ones analysed in this book are those of ensuring that firstly sufficient new jobs of the right sort are obtained at a reasonably rapid pace; secondly the social changes which occur are acceptable to newcomers and natives alike; thirdly land is acquired as and when required; fourthly the necessary housing and other services are made available; and finally an organization is evolved which is capable of achieving all these goals in a satisfactory and coordinated manner.

What we have outlined is a complex process involving many individuals with similar, complementary, or contradictory goals. They therefore stand to gain (or lose) to differing degrees from a town development scheme. As we have already suggested, everybody will try to act so as to minimise loss. We shall study how this process occurred in Swindon. Many of the bodies involved were *reacting* to circumstances. The Swindon Borough Council was by far the most important agent actually initiating change; probably, it had most to gain. Therefore the book concentrates on examining how the Council attempted to exercise power by persuasion, bargaining, and coercion, in order to achieve its goals in an environment which gave it certain advantages, but which also contained many serious obstacles to success. We shall see how some goals were achieved, some modified, and some abandoned on the way. What we are describing is the nature and outcome of a complex *political* process. Such a process underlines and determines the outcome of any social policy which depends on the involvement of a whole series of individuals and organizations for its outcome. Large-scale planning activities, because of the wide range and diversity of the operations and interests they of necessity involve, are a particularly worthwhile and interesting class of policies to analyse in this way. This is because of the high degree of uncertainty that results from such complexity. Therefore there is often a wide gap between the formal plan or statement of goals in the initial stages and the final outcome. The reasons for this are only understandable if the process of implementation is analysed. It follows that the remarks we made at the start of this introduction about the need to understand the implementation process, if we wish to evaluate social policies, applies with particular force in the case of town planning and its associated activities.

The book is divided into three parts. The first part contains an account of the events leading up to the town expansion in Swindon, and briefly charts the progress of the scheme. The first chapter describes the social, economic, and political character of the town. It shows how the desire and the need to expand were consequences of the declining economic future of the town, and shows how a tradition of progresive activism on the part of the Council had grown up. It also shows how the social composition of the town made it a likely candidate for the reception of working-class families from London. The chapter also discusses the important differences in social, economic, and political character between the town and its rural hinterland, differences which were to be a source of conflict throughout the expansion process. In short this chapter contains the essential background to an understanding of the environment in which town development took place. The second chapter gives an account of how the decision to expand was taken, and it gives basic facts and figures concerning the build-up of population, industry, housing, and the changes that these developments brought about in the social structure of the town. In the course of this account reference is made to many of the problems which form the subject matter of the second part of the book.

The second part of the book looks in detail at the most important aspects of the town development process which have already been mentioned in this introduction. There are separate chapters dealing with social development, industrial development, estate development, and organization and finance. These chapters analyse how the Council attempted to achieve its goals and describe how problems were dealt with. Naturally the aims and actions of the other parties to the scheme play major roles in these chapters, as does a consideration of the wider factors which have already been mentioned, such as national economic and social trends, professional practices, and political policies.

The final part of the book returns to the theme of this introduction, looking at the town development scheme as a whole. Chapter 7 draws on the previous chapters in order to describe the political process which underlie expansion. By comparison with the history of a similar scheme in Ashford, it demonstrates one of the main contentions of this study, that the outcome of major planning actions is only explicable if they are seen primarily in terms of an analysis of organizations which, by exercise of power, seek to attain their goals. This chapter brings together conclusions concerning the major elements of tactics and strategy adopted by Swindon in order to circumvent the obstacles outlined in Part Two, which the other parties to the scheme and the national trends and policies put in its way. It concludes with some reflections on the importance of political analysis in understanding the operation of planning schemes, and therefore of the need for such knowledge, both on the part of the planners and on the part of those who evaluate planner's actions.

The claim has been made that the examination of the course and outcome of social policies in terms of the model and methods of analysis used in this study is not only intellectually enlightening, but a powerful tool by which these policies can be evaluated. The last chapter is an attempt to substantiate this claim. Firstly it discusses whether the Swindon expansion was a success or failure; as we shall see this is a complex question to answer but one which, given the analysis of the previous chapters, can at least be formulated and begun to be answered in a meaningful way. Then the chapter moves a step back from the specific case of Swindon, drawing on the conclusions of this case study in order to discuss what appear to be the crucial determinants in mounting viable town development schemes. Finally, given this understanding of the town development process, the chapter attempts to look towards the future, and discusses what the likely future role of this element in national planning policy and briefly compares some aspects of it with the new towns programme. The relevance of both of these policies to the problem that they were meant to help solve, urban squalor, and some of their relative strengths and weaknesses in achieving this aim are the main topics for consideration.

Part One

The Town Development Solution

Chapter One

Prelude, 1840–1952

The coming of the railway

' . . . this country is generally a vast continued body of high
chalky hills, whose tops spread themselves into fruitful and
pleasant downs and plains, upon which great flocks of sheep
are fed, etc. But the reader is desired to observe that these hills
and plains are most beautifully intersected, and cut through
by the course of divers pleasant and profitable rivers; in the
course, and near the banks of which, there is always a chain of
fruitful meadows, and rich pastures, and those interspersed
with innumerable pleasant towns, villages, and houses, and
among them many of considerable magnitude; so that while
you view the downs, and think the country wild and
uninhabited; yet when you come to descend into these vales
you are surprised with the most pleasant and fertile country in
England.'[1]

This is how Daniel Defoe described the county of Wiltshire
in his *Tour through England and Wales,* published in 1724. In
many respects the present-day visitor to this county would have
little difficulty in agreeing with the picture that Defoe drew.
It is true that the Industrial Revolution and the succeeding
years have brought many changes — for example the decline of
the woollen industry, 'the basic and traditional manufacture
of Britain',[2] which had been firmly established in West
Wiltshire by the fourteenth century, and the spread of

---

[1] Defoe, Daniel, *A Tour Through England and Wales* (Everyman
Edition) (London: Dent, 1962) vol. 1, page 192.

[2] Hobsbawm, E. J. *Industry and Empire* (London: Weidenfeld and
Nicholson, 1969) page 12.

enclosures. But even today the county is one of the most rural in England, a county of rolling farmland, chalk hills and downs, small market towns, and ancient monuments. Although much has changed, the continuities are even more striking and visible. 'From the settlement patterns initiated in Wiltshire some 1500 years ago and virtually complete by the time of the Doomsday Survey there has been no significant departure since. The contributions to the age of coal and steel are manifest and devasting elsewhere, but even the coming of the railways to Wiltshire left its fundamental geography substantially identical with what it had been in the phase of protohistory. The map retains the imprints of the past . . .'[3]

And yet if one takes the road from prehistoric Avebury running north and climbs up to the top of the Marlborough Downs, still much as Defoe described them in 1724, one will see in the plain below an industrial town of some 120 000 people, set down in the midst of that 'most pleasant and fertile country'. The town is Swindon, and there can be no better way of appreciating the uniqueness of its physical situation, and of beginning to grasp the interest of its history and present development than this dramatic view from the downs.

As Wooldridge states, the settlement pattern in Wiltshire has hardly been disturbed since Doomsday. Indeed the town is mentioned in the Doomsday book, its first footnote in history, although the settlement certainly has an earlier foundation.[4] But it remained an obscure village for the next 800 years. Defoe does not even mention it in *A Tour Through England and Wales,* although he refers to the surrounding towns of Faringdon, Marlborough, and Cirencester. This is not surprising for, according to the Census, there were only 244 houses and 1198 people in Swindon in 1801. It was smaller than neighbouring towns such as Chippenham with 3366, Cricklade with 1333, Purton with 1467, Highworth with 1493, and even Wootton Bassett with 1244. At the beginning of the nineteenth century Swindon was a small market town. It was

---

[3] Quoted in Bracey, H. *Social Provision in Rural Wiltshire* (London: Routledge and Kegan Paul, 1952) page 5.

[4] Tallamy, H. S., in *Studies in the History of Swindon* (Swindon: Swindon Borough Council, 1950). 'Swindon' may derive from 'Sweyn's Down' the reference being being to a Danish overlord or the hill where the pigs were pastured.

too far to the east to have become a part of the cloth manufacturing area of Wiltshire, and not far enough north to become, as Cirencester did, a centre for the Cotswold cloth industry. Its only industry was stone quarrying which had probably begun in Roman times, and had latterly received an impetus from the opening up of the Wiltshire and Berkshire canal through the valley below the town. But in general terms William Morris's comment is not far from the truth. 'Formerly, as well as now, a town had to possess some special advantages over its neighbours before it could hope to enjoy a greater distinction than they, the advantage of population, or of situation, or of some particular industry. But Swindon enjoyed neither of these. The town stood on a hill—that was about the most that could be said about it.'[5]

The first thirty years of the nineteenth century saw the town in a steady decline. It was noted for incessant smuggling of tea and gin, sheep stealing, and bull baiting, the quarries produced less than before and there was a massive decline in agricultural employment, especially after the Napoleonic Wars. Enclosures (which between 1760 and 1820 covered over one quarter of Wiltshire) and, more importantly, the general concentration of landholdings of which the enclosures were but a part, and the collapse of agricultural prices caused mass unemployment.[6] Swindon, which did not enforce the laws of settlement, became a refuge for casual labour driven off the land and had a high proportion of inhabitants in receipt of poor relief.[7] Thus, although the population increased to 1742 by 1831 and 2495 by 1841, the economic base of the town was stagnating.

Swindon seemed likely to remain a small, possibly declining town on top of a hill in rural Wiltshire, of similar or less importance than the surrounding towns of Highworth, Cricklade, Wootton Bassett, and Marlborough. But in

---

[5] Morris, William. *Swindon Fifty Years Ago* (1885) page 361. Morris should not be confused with his more famous namesake. He was the founder of the 'Swindon Advertiser' and the town's first Liberal.

[6] See Hobsbawm op.cit. pages 77-87 for an analysis of this decline. The collapse of the cloth industry also led to mass employment and some of the unemployment may have come to Swindon. For conditions in the county at this time see Thompson, E. P. *Making of the English Working Class* (London: Gollancz, 1963) page 525.

[7] Wells, H. B. in *Studies in the History of Swindon* page 98.

September 1840 Daniel Gooch, the Locomotive
Superintendent of the Great Western Railway Company,
wrote a letter to Isambard Kingdom Brunel, the founding
genius of that company, which resulted in the most important
decision in Swindon's 900 years of recorded history. Gooch
argued that a depot should be built at Swindon. So, early in
1841 the directors of the Great Western Railway announced
that they intended to 'provide an Engine Establishment at
Swindon, commensurate with the Company, where a change
of Engines may be advantageously made, and the trains
stopped for the purposes of the Passengers taking Refreshment, as is the case at Wolverton on the London and
Birmingham railway. The Establishment there would also
comprehend the large repairing shops for the Locomotive
Department and this circumstance rendered it 'necessary to
arrange for the building of Cottages, etc. for the residences of
many persons employed in the service of the company.[8]

The refreshment facilities were the least successful of these
provisions. Brunel stated that he always tried to avoid them
altogether, and rudely likened coffee served there to badly
roasted corn — perhaps the railways have changed little in the
last 125 years! The feature of New Swindon, that seems likely
to outlast even the railway works, is the Railway Village, the
'cottages etc.' referred to by the directors of the Great Western
Railway. This small estate of low stone-built terraces,
reputedly laid out by Sir Matthew Digby Wyatt, the architect
of Paddington Station, with its park, church, Mechanic's
Institute, and managers' houses is still standing today. It has
been described by Pevsner as 'One of the few planned
Victorian estates, small and modest and laid out without
ingenuity, but planned all the same, and architecturally as
orderly as the design of the streets'.[9] It is a dignified
monument to the Railway Age.

The inhabitants of Old Swindon, the town on the hill,
watched the growth of the new town in the valley with
apprehension, and relations between the two settlements were
uneasy. For example, in 1847 William Morris formed the

---

[8] *Ibid* pages 99–100.

[9] Pevsner, N. (ed.) *The Buildings of England — Wiltshire*
(Harmondsworth: Penguin, 1963).

Swindon Working Men's Association to fight the candidacy of
Ambrose Goddard, the local squire and Tory MP in the
forthcoming election. The outcome of this encounter was
defeat for the railwaymen and Morris as their candidate,
none other than Brunel himself, flatly refused nomination.
But the men were more successful when they defeated a
proposal that they should be levied to provide a new church in
Old Town.[10]

However the growth of the railway works had other, more
serious effects. In the decade from 1840, the population of the
town doubled from 2495 to 4876, and the average age of death
fell from 36 to 26 years.[11] This rapid population growth soon
crowded out the original estate and created highly insanitary
conditions, culminating in an outbreak of typhus in 1853,
which was followed by a government investigation of
conditions in the town. After this the sanitary arrangements
were improved, and in 1864 Boards of Health were set up in
the two towns. Earlier medical facilities had been provided for
the railwaymen and they were compelled to subscribe to the
Great Western Railway Medical Fund, set up in 1847 by the
Company as a response to the worsening conditions. The
Company also made a grant to the Fund, and the progressive
development of the services it provided continued until the
introduction of the 1948 National Health Act. The desire to
improve conditions in the rapidly growing town also found
expression in the wish, so close to the hearts of many
Victorians, for mental self-improvement. The Mechanics'
Institutes movement established itself in most major industrial
towns in the 1830s and 1840s and Swindon was no exception.[12]
It began in 1844 with 15 members and 130 books, and its aims

---

[10] Liddiard, N. *Lectures on the history of Swindon* (n.d.)
[11] Liddiard, op. cit.
[12] See Briggs, A. *Victorian Cities* (Harmondsworth: Penguin, 1968)
pages 47-8. Engels, in *The Condition of the Working Class in England in
1844* said 'these new institutes are organs of the middle classes and their
purpose is to encourage the study of those branches of "useful knowledge"
which it is to the advantage of the bourgeoisie that the workers should
possess'. Doubtless something of these motives lay behind the support the
G.W.R. gave to the Institute at Swindon, certainly this was the case of
Crewe, for which see Chaloner, W. H. *The Social and Economic
Development of Crewe, 1780-1923* (Manchester: Manchester University
Press, 1950).

included 'disseminating useful knowledge and encouraging rational amusement amongst all classes of people employed by the company in Swindon'. In 1853 another typical Victorian institution, the New Swindon Improvement Company, was formed by public-spirited citizens to provide baths, reading rooms, lecture halls, refreshment rooms, a market, and shops. These cultural and recreational provisions played an important part in the subsequent life of Swindon. Thus although the Institute was founded in 1844, only six years before the Free Libraries Act, it was the only library in the town until 1943 when the Act was finally adopted. This was only three years before Swindon became the first municipality to open its own Arts Centre.

The Improvement Company also played a major role in the education of Swindonians. There had been schools in the town before the railways came. The Free School in Newport Street was founded in 1764 and, according to William Morris, there were three other small schools in Old Town by 1830. The Great Western Railway built an elementary school in 1850, attached to St Marks, the railway church. However the major demand that the works generated for technical education was borne by the Improvement Company until 1891, when a Technical Educational Council was established.[13] By 1900 there were fifteen major schools in the town and one technical school.

The expansion of population continued at a fast rate throughout the nineteenth century, as may be seen from the decennial census returns shown in Table 1.1.

Table 1.1

Population of Swindon, 1801-1911

Year	1801	1811	1821	1831	1851	1861	1871	1881	1891	1901	1911
Census return	1198	1341	1580	1742	4876	6856	11 720	19 904	32 838	45 006	50 751

This growth of population, which was particularly rapid in the forty years from 1861 to 1901, was stimulated by the addition of a rolling mill for rails in 1860, and the opening of

---

[13] Wells, H. B. op.cit. page 119.

the carriage works in 1868. The establishment of the rolling mill caused an influx of Welsh iron workers, and generally the area became a magnet for labour from far and wide. In particular, as Wells points out, labour was attracted from the North of England and Scotland, areas where the requisite skills for the railway works were in plentiful supply.[14]

During the last part of the nineteenth century Swindon rapidly assumed the appearance of an industrial town, and the physical, social, and cultural character of the town developed in ways which sharply distinguished it from the surrounding rural areas. As we shall see, these differences were to play an important part in the genesis and development of the expansion scheme. The railway works ran like a great wall to the north of New Swindon, three miles long and half a mile across at its widest point near the station. It is still only crossed by three roads, to the north-east and south-west of the station, giving access to Gorse Hill and Rodbourne respectively. Because of this, development began to the south of the railway line, although there were isolated areas of building in the Gorse Hill, Mannington, and Rodbourne areas north of the line. One can well imagine the concern of the inhabitants of Old Swindon as they watched the steady march of redbrick terraces up the slope towards them. And yet this growth probably saved the older settlement from decay. It too shared, to a lesser extent, in the general expansion, for as the new town crept up to the old, the latter also grew along Bath Road then down Victoria Road.[15] First contact between old and new appears to have been made at Regent Circus, but by the end of the century almost the whole of the triangle roughly demarcated by the station, Old Town, and Westcott was built up. As the town expanded the number of managers, traders, officials, and other middle-class professions increased. The present day middle-class habit of living on the periphery or outside town altogether was rare at the time. Instead the prospering trader, or even the successful railwayman, settled himself in Old Town—for instance in the large stone built

---

[14] Ibid. pages 143-146. Some doubt has been expressed as to the accuracy of the figures for immigration quoted here, but the trends are correct.

[15] The historical pattern of Swindon's growth is clearly displayed in a map contained in *Planning for Swindon, 1945* issued at that time by the Borough Council.

houses along the Bath Road, looking out across the fields below to the ever-advancing redbrick terraces, the grey sheds of the works behind, and beyond that the open country uninterrupted except by the villages of Rodbourne and Stratton and the first northern extension of the town at Gorse Hill.

The two towns, which were physically connected by 1900, were also economically connected, as Old Town was irremediably dependent for population and prosperity on the works in the valley. 1900 also marked the final political and administrative integration of the two Swindons. In this year the Urban District Councils of Old Swindon and New Swindon (which the two Local Boards had become in 1895) were incorporated as the Borough of Swindon.[16] Significantly the Charter Mayor was G. J. Churchward, the Locomotive Superintendent at the Great Western Railway Works. Old Swindon, to its chagrin, became one ward (South) in six in the new borough. However, although it was totally absorbed administratively and economically, it still retains a distinct physical, social, and even political character of its own. It is a good example of the persistence of historical patterns, and hence the importance of appreciating these patterns when describing the contemporary situation.

The period from 1900 to 1914 really marked the beginning of the end of the railway era and the start of the chain of events that led up to the town development decision. At home the railways had reached their zenith. As Savage says, 'On the eve of the first world war the British-railway system enjoyed supremacy as the principal means of long distance land transport'.[17] Yet the peak period for profits had already passed, as Table 1.2 shows.

We shall consider the reasons for this decline in a later section of this chapter. It is sufficient to note here that in the long run the decrease in profitability could only mean a decline in investment. In turn this resulted in a decline, or at best a stagnation, of output and employment in the capital

---

[16] There had been discussion of this move for over twenty years. Old Swindon objected to it for longer than New Swindon. Wells, H. B., op.cit. pages 130-4.

[17] Savage, C. I. *An Economic History of Transport*, (London: Hutchinson, 1959).

Table 1.2

Percentage of net receipts to paid-up capital

Year	1860	1870	1880	1890	1900	1910	1912
%	4.19	4.41	4.38	4.10	3.41	3.59	3.55

Source: *Railway returns 1860–1912 quoted in Savage, C. I. op.cit. page 83.*

goods industries connected with the railways. In 1928 one commentator wrote, 'The history of the Great Western Railway is inseperably linked up with the modern history of Swindon. The two have gone forward hand in hand, the prosperity of the one has found its reflection in the prosperity of the other, "for better or for worse" they are connected in a partnership which, as far as the human ken is able to fathom is absolutely indissoluble'.[18] With the benefit of hindsight the historian can see that the ultimate prospect was less rosy than the writer suggested, and the 'indissoluble' partnership was to become a debilitating bond rather than a profitable liaison.

Social and economic character

The decision to expand Swindon and its effective implementation is only understandable when set in the context of its social character and economic structure. These factors in turn are a product of historical events. In the absence of revolutionary changes, social patterns take many years to mature or to decay. Failure to consider the past or the possible future evolution of these patterns has often led sociologists, especially those concerned with the study of communities, to false or premature conclusions.[19] A good deal of Swindon's social character as it existed in the second half of this century was determined in the period from the advent of the railway

---

[18] *Swindon Advertiser*, 28 September 1928 (special issue to mark the extension of the borough boundary).

[19] For example Wilmott, P. in *The Evolution of a Community* (London: Routledge and Kegan Paul, 1960), showed in this study of Dagenham that older social patterns re-emerging in a new community over a long period of years might lead to substantial modifications in conclusions that sociologists had drawn from the study of similar communities over a shorter period.

works in the 1840s to its zenith at the time of the First World
War. The coming of the works and the subsequent growth of
the new town left but the merest relics of the old order, based
on church and squire, substituting the social patterns of an
industrialized society (though, as will be seen, these patterns
were of a somewhat unusual nature). These patterns altered
only slowly with the passage of time. This was because as long
as the Great Western Railway remained the major source of
employment in the town, the underlying industrial and
economic realities which the social structure largely reflected
remained almost constant. And when these realities did alter,
as happened increasingly in the interwar period, social
attitudes and relationships took somewhat longer to adjust.
Therefore the brief sketch of the history of Swindon to 1914 is
an essential preliminary to the following discussion of the
socio-economic character of the town, which must itself form
an important part of any satisfactory understanding of the
town's current development.[20]

A number of sociologists have remarked on the close
connections between certain types of industrial organization
and the surrounding communities. Particular attention has
been paid to what are called traditional working-class
communities.[21] There are several accounts of this concept but
they seem united in suggesting that there are two main types of
working-class traditionalism. Firstly, as shown by some of the
inhabitants surveyed at Banbury, the employees of (typically)
small businesses, who identify themselves with their employers
and who tend to be religious, thrifty, and socially and
politically conservative.[22] These people have been called
'deferential traditionalists'. The second form of traditionalism
has been called 'proletarian traditionalism'. Its character is
most clearly outlined in this passage from a recent study.

---

[20] The following account is by no means intended to be a complete one,
but merely gives the essential background to the history of the last twenty
five years.

[21] e.g. Denis, N., Henriques, F., and Slaughter, C. *Coal Is Our Life*
(London: Eyre and Spottiswoode, 1956); Klein, J. *Samples from English
Cultures* (London: Routledge and Kegan Paul, 1956); Liverpool
University, Department of Social Science, *The Dock Worker,* (Liverpool
University Press, 1954); Tunstall, J. *The Fisherman,* (London:
MacGibbon and Kee, 1962).

'The most highly developed forms of proletarian traditionalism seem to be particularly closely associated with industries such as mining, docking, fishing, and shipbuilding; that is with industries which tend to concentrate workers together in solidary communities and to isolate them from the influences of the wider society. Normally most of the workers in such occupations have a high degree of job involvement, and close attachments to primary work groups that possess a relatively high degree of autonomy from technical and supervisory constraints. Pride in doing "men's work" and an awareness of shared occupational experiences make for a strongly developed industrial *camaraderie* which is frequently expressed through a distinctive work culture. Thus primary groups of workmates not only provide the elementary units of more extensive class loyalties, but work associations also carry over into leisure activities, so that workers in these industries usually participate in what are called occupational communities. That is to say workmates are preferred leisure time companions, often also neighbours, and not infrequently kinsmen. The existence of such closely knit cliques of friends, workmates, neighbours and relatives is indeed the hall mark of the traditional working class community. The values expressed through these social networks emphasize mutual aid in everyday life and the obligation to join in the gregarious pattern of leisure, which itself demands the expenditure of time, money and energy in a public — and present — oriented conviviality and inhibits individual striving "to be different". As a form of social life, this communal sociability has a ritualistic quality, creating a high "moral density" and reinforcing sentiments of belonging to a work-dominated collectivity. The socially isolated and endogamous nature of the community, its predominantly one class population, and low rates of geographical and social mobility, all tend to make for an inward looking society and to accentuate the sense of class identity that springs from shared work experiences.' In a footnote, the authors add that 'the one-industry town with its

---

[22] Stacey, M. *Tradition and Change (a Study of Banbury)* (London: Oxford University Press, 1960). Stacey simply refers to them as 'traditional working class', Goldthorpe and Lockwood have suggested that these people be called 'deferential traditionalists' and this suggestion is followed in the present work.

dominant occupational community would seem to produce the most distinctive forms of proletarian traditionalism. Such a community tends to be highly radical and class conscious, and there tends to be a history of considerable conflict between labour and capital'.[23]

While these models of two widely differing types of traditional society have considerable validity in many situations, Swindon would seem to have a social structure which corresponds to neither of these models but incorporates elements of both of them. In particular the town has been characterized by a mixture of dependence and independence, of radicalism and conservatism, of prudence and progressiveness that underlies and partially explains the outcome of its subsequent development. It is therefore appropriate to examine these characteristics in some detail.

As we have seen the growth of the town went hand in hand with the growth of the Great Western Railway works. Estimates of the total employment at the works at any time vary slightly, but according to one source it stood at 4600 in 1875, 6000 in 1885, and had reached 11 000 by 1901.[24] The peak figure of about 12 000 was reached in 1908. These figures do not include the clerical and managerial staff. If these are included the numbers employed at the works probably rose to about 15 000 in the first decade of this century. In addition the 1911 Census notes that over 1000 men were employed on 'railway conveyance'. (These footplatemen and guards also came under the control of the Locomotive Superintendent in charge of the works, but were not themselves a part of the works establishment.)[25] The total occupied population of Swindon at the time of the 1911 Census was 21 315. So it can be seen that the Great Western Railway employed a high proportion of the economically active population, and the proportion of the town's economically active males employed at the works was even

---

[23] Goldthorpe, J., Lockwood, D., Bechofer, F., and Platt, J. *The Affluent Worker—Political Attitudes and Behaviour* (London: Cambridge University Press, 1968) pages 74-5.

[24] Derived from issues of the North Wiltshire Directory.

[25] Eversley, D. E. C. in *The Victoria County History of Wiltshire* (London: Oxford University Press, 1959), vol. 4, page 215 puts this figure at 3000.

higher. Therefore the majority of families were directly dependent on the railway works, and almost everybody else, such as shopkeepers and professional workers, was indirectly dependent on the continued success of the works. In fact the level of employment at the works grew steadily with few exceptions. There was some slight contraction in the late 1880s, and a more serious one in the last five years before the First World War, but in general the employees of the Great Western Railway could expect a lifetime of secure employment. Indeed the consternation that was felt during the latter depression highlights this expectation.[26]

According to one authority, at the end of the nineteenth century the works was probably the largest undertaking in the British industry, if not in Europe.[27] This massive complex employed a high proportion of skilled metal- and woodworkers. Examination of census data and the reports of the Board of Trade into the cost of living of the working class suggest that well over half the employees were skilled men.[28]

The works was split up into a number of different shops. These were virtually self-contained units, and it was almost unknown for a man to be transferred from one shop to another during his working life. Eversley has suggested that this was a considerable barrier to effective trade union organization.[29] The whole complex was controlled by the Locomotive Superintendent,[30] Sir Daniel Gooch being the first and most famous incumbent of this office. One historian has likened the structure of control within the railways works to that of an army in which the Locomotive Superintendent was 'an autocrat more absolute in his sphere than the Lord Chief Justice'.[31] The railway companies were some of the most successful early exponents of a positive industrial relations policy. The outlines of this policy were broadly similar in all

[26] Liddiard, N., op.cit. remarks that there were 1000 empty houses in the town in 1909-10 and talks of it as a 'dying town'.

[27] Eversley, D. E. C. op.cit. page 215.

[28] Board of Trade, Reports of an Enquiry into Working Class Rents, Housing and Retail Prices, 1905 and 1912.

[29] Eversley, D. E. C. op. cit. page 218.

[30] Renamed Chief Mechanical Engineer in the First World War.

[31] Ellis, C. H. British Railway History, volume II, 1877-1954 (London: Allen and Unwin, 1959). Chapter 8.

the main companies, although judging by the record the Great Western Railway seems to have been more successful than most. The negative elements were strict discipline and departmentalization.[32] Also the establishment of the various works in previously isolated country settlements, so that they became the major employer in the town, gave management an overwhelming control. However it is the positive side of this policy that really distinguishes the railway companies from others of the period and is of particular interest in the current context. The provision of educational and religious facilities provided effective institutions of social control. As we have seen in Swindon the school, the Mechanics Institute, and the church were all either provided by the Great Western Railway or promoted via the company's good offices. The reasons for this policy (in this instance referring to religious provision) are described by Kingsford in the case of the London and Birmingham Railway thus: 'The motives were probably mixed, as with education. A sense of responsibility for religious needs, particularly in the new railway towns, was accompanied by a realization of the value of well behaved servants. The directors were "like ordinary millowners bound to do for their population that which the millowners did," but they were also urged that "the scheme deserved to be taken up in a worldly point of view, putting aside all Christian feeling . . . since it was calculated to exalt the character of the London and Birmingham" (London and Birmingham Report, half yearly meeting, 7 August 1840). The objectives of the policy are if anything brought out even more clearly in this passage, "we are beginning to find more fully the economical result of the establishment at Wolverton. Attendance at the places of worship and the schools is most satisfactory and numerous. The result is more important than the mere comfort of the company's servants there. It has a result which not only acts on our profits but also most materially on the convenience and safety of the public. You will reap the benefits of this, for I am sure that there is not a single person attached to that establishment who would not willingly and gladly come forward and perform extra services in order to

---

[32] On the railways' labour policy see Kingford P. 'Labour Relations on the Railways 1835-1875', *Journal of Transport History* vol. 1, no. 2.

meet occasional emergency". (Chairman, London and Birmingham railway, half yearly reports, February 1843, and February 1844).'[33]

The provision of welfare benefits was another important way in which the railway company consolidated its hold upon the men. In Swindon, membership of the Medical Fund was compulsory. Large numbers of the employees were also members of the Sick Fund. Receipt of benefits was dependent on continued employment by the Great Western Railway. Thus, besides being a town which had a remarkably high standard of public health and education, these facilities also served to tie the employee to the Great Western Railway. These factors, taken together with the fact that a high proportion of the employees were skilled men and thus a part of the 'labour aristocracy'[34] which was chiefly characterized by its conservatism, made for a work force and indeed a whole community that was sober, industrious, unified, perhaps a little cautious, and which, by and large, was prepared to agree that 'what was good for the company was good for Swindon'.[35] Nor should one underestimate the special position that the Great Western Railway held among the railway companies and the men's pride in a sense of identification with this position. Hamilton Ellis describes it thus, 'the Great Western Railway had an unbroken tradition and a proud awareness that it was different from other railways. In prestige this

---

[33] Quoted by Kingsford, op.cit. He also says that the benefit of this policy, for the companies, was felt most fully in the railway towns where the provision was most ample.

[34] Apparently some doubt surrounds this concept (see Pelling, H. *Popular Politics and Society in Late Victorian England* (London: Macmillan, 1968) chapter 3) but it has its defenders (e.g. Hobsbawm, E. J. *Labouring Men* (London: Weidenfeld and Nicholson, 1964) chapter 15) but both authors mentioned here at least agree that the term could be applied to engineering craftsmen, the basis of Swindon's 'labour aristocracy'. But though sharing the attitudes which Hobsbawm characterizes as those of the labour aristocracy, the Swindon men did not share the high wages which he feels is possibly the main criterion of a labour aristocrat.

[35] The Board of Trade Report for 1905 (referred to on page 25) said, 'Employment tends to be steady and less subject to fluctuation than in towns which depend on some single general industry. Distress is consequently rare and there is an absence of all extreme poverty. Wages are not very high . . .'

railway led easily. Certainly its long distance services were very fine indeed, and in spite of a speciously patronizing style which distinguished some of its publications, it had a public which swore by it'.[36] Furthermore, while the railwaymen did not repeat the mistake they made when they assumed that Brunel would be prepared to represent their interests against the local landowners, even the most class-conscious among them spoke of, and to, the Great Western Railway with a special tone of voice. For example a resolution from the newly formed Swindon Trades Council in 1891, 'resolved that we, the Swindon and District Trades Council representing the majority of your servants at Swindon respectfully beg to convey to your Honorary Board our sincere thanks and gratitude for your kindness in granting us the privilege of the farthing a mile; also the still greater boon of three days holidays per year without deduction of wages, as stated by your Honorary Chairman at the last half yearly meeting of shareholders, and we humbly pray you would give us the said holidays at our Annual Trip which would greatly relieve the difficulties arising by the long forced holidays'.[37]

The success of the company's policy was helped by the fact that it rarely interfered in the affairs of the society beyond the factory gates. Of course the Great Western Railway was a highly important factor in that society, but it did not attempt to impose its will directly. This helped to prevent class divisions in the town becoming acutely realized, and when a self-consciously working class element did emerge, with the formation of the Trades Council in 1891 and then the Labour Party, the aim of these bodies was to gain position and status for themselves within the existing society, rather than trying to overthrow that society. Of course a considerable number of managers served on the Local Board and then the Borough Council[38] but the railway company never provoked the antagonism that occurred at Crewe.[39]

The distinctive pattern of industrial relations established by the Great Western Railway, had, in combination with other

---

[36] Ellis, C. H. op.cit. page 316.

[37] Trades Council Minutes (T.R.C.) 16 March 1891.

[38] e.g. Churchward, earlier Gooch was M.P.

[39] See Chaloner W. H. op.cit.

factors, important effects on the development of the society and politics of the town. One of the most spectacular results of the economic stability and the pervasive ethic of sobriety and thrift encouraged by the Great Western Railway was the unusual and possibly unique degree of owner occupation that developed in the town. In the words of the North Wiltshire Directory for 1884, 'another sign of the times may be quoted in reference to New Swindon, and that is the large number of working men who occupy their own houses. We have no statistics at hand but we venture to say that there is no place in the kingdom where the ratio of dwellers in their own houses is greater than at New Swindon. This is due, in great measure, to the operation of building societies, which have encouraged habits of thrift'. The first building society was formed by the manager of the rolling mills, Thomas Ellis, in the early 1860s, and by 1870 there were five societies doing considerable business. By 1900 about 60 per cent of the town's houses were owner-occupied, probably the highest percentage in the United Kingdom at the time. This high proportion of owner occupiers persisted until the Second World War.[40] It was estimated that approximately 70 per cent of the houses in the borough were owner-occupied in 1938, a remarkable figure for a working-class industrial town.[41]

There was also a multitude of friendly societies in Swindon at the end of the nineteenth century. The North Wiltshire Directory for 1901 shows that the two largest of these, the Oddfellows and the Foresters, had over 8500 members between them. Fourteen others were also listed. It is clear that the values of thrift and self-help were firmly embedded in the community. There were also a number of well-supported temperance societies, and most of them had close links with the wide range of nonconformist churches in the town. These churches proliferated in the town in the second half of the nineteenth century. In 1840 when the Great Western Railway first came to Swindon there were only two chapels in the town, one Congregational and one Wesleyan, but the influx of railway workers from all over the country led to a period of

[40] Hudson, K. *The Early Years of the Railway Community in Swindon* (Transport History, Newton Abbott: David and Charles, 1967) pages 130-52.
[41] Borough of Swindon, Record of Administration 1947.

intense religious activity in the town. The primitive Methodists were especially active during the 1880s and 1890s, and we learn that a 'great revival' took place in the town in 1880-1.[42] The influence exercised by these denominations (in favour of sobriety and self-help) reinforced the effects of the railway company's policy. However the distinctive contribution of nonconformity was the emphasis it placed on individual initiative and the free combination of individuals to achieve desired ends. Thus money was quickly raised from the communicants of the various sects to build their chapels at the same time as many of the individuals were buying their houses in the town.

For these reasons newcomers soon began to have an interest in the town's development and, side by side with a continued dependence on the Great Western Railway, the railwaymen began to take an independent attitude to the wider affairs of town government, for they could rightly say that while the works might belong to the company much of the town belonged to them. But the very fact that many of the workmen had this stake of ownership in the town tended to reduce the likelihood of their adoption of extreme political attitudes. The effect of house ownership on political militancy in this period was noted by John Burnett in 1872. He wrote of an organizer of the period, 'the chances are that had Gourley been allowed to remain at Jarrow, he might very possibly have got a house through the medium of the Factory Building Society, the possession of the house would have kept him quiet at Jarrow (the possession of a house having that effect on a man)'.[43]

By the end of the nineteenth century there was a small nucleus of trade unionists in the town[44] who were determined that proper attention should be paid to the interests of labour in the town. Many of the people who formed the backbone of the Trades Council when it was formed in 1891 had close connections with the non-conformist movement, and the

---

[42] I am indebted to Miss Elizabeth Crittall for this information.
[43] Burnett, A. *History of the Engineers Strike in Newcastle and Gateshead. The Nine Hours Movement* (1872), quoted in Jeffreys J. B. *The Story of Engineers* (London: Amalgamated Engineering Union, 1945) page 85. See also Pelling op.cit.
[44] There had been craft unions in the works since the 1860s; they were not recognized by the Great Western Railway.

social and individual values taught by the church were also applied by them in the industrial and political sphere. Thus ministers were sometimes invited to speak from Trades Council platforms or to sponsor their meetings,[45] and the Council also expressed support for temperance movements. At first it confined its attention to purely trade union issues, such as recognition and the payment of trade union rates, and it soon decided to put up working-class candidates for election to local bodies to achieve these aims. It was not until very much later that the Trades Council decided to affiliate to the Labour Party. The decision to form a Divisional Labour Party and sponsor a parliamentary candidate was not taken until 1916. Meanwhile working-class representation on the Borough Council grew steadily, as Table 1.3 shows.

Table 1.3

Structure of Swindon Borough Council 1900-1950 (percentage)

	1900-01	1900-10	1919-20	1930-31	1940-41	1949-50
Professional	69.0	56.5	44.0	29.0	31.0	22.5
Workers	25.0	29.0	44.0	42.0	44.0	58.5
Retired	4.0	12.5	6.0	21.0	10.0	4.5
Miscellaneous	2.0	2.0	6.0	8.0	15.0	14.5
Railway employees	23.0	30.0	40.0	40.0	33.0	61.0

Source: *S. J. Hill and A. T. Hudson in 'Work, wages and pastimes of the people of Swindon', 1950.*

This growth of working class representation ended the Liberal-Conservative division which dominated town politics before the First World Wat. It was replaced by a Labour-Independent division after the War. During the twenties and thirties Labour formed the official opposition on the council, eventually taking control in 1945 and retaining it until 1969.

There were very few Conservatives on the Council in the period we are concerned with, and the resultant lack of national politics at local level was an important factor in the politics of expansion.

---

[45] e.g. T.R.C. 5 February 1902, when 'Canon Ponsonby as curate and Rev. Williams' are invited to a social and to address a gathering.

However the early efforts of the trade unionists to organize their fellow workers were less successful than their efforts in the political sphere, as the figures in Table 1.4 for the period before the First World War demonstrate. By 1937 the Trade Council claimed to speak for 10 000 trade unionists.[46] However, as late as 1937, the then Chairman of the Trades Council could say of the situation in the town that, 'inside the railway factory matters are not so good as they might be. Outside the factory it is a perfect example of what trade unionism might not be'.[47]

Table 1.4

Number of Trades Unionists affiliated to Swindon Trades Council

Year	1894	1895	1896	1897	1898	1899	1900	1901
No.	1800	1905	1767	1600	1776	1706	1831	1954

Year	1903	1904	1905	1906	1907	1908	1909	1910
No.	2071	1600	2550	1900	1382	1152	2500	2000

Source: *Board of Trade Labour Department Returns 1896–1910 (ex. inf. Swindon Council).*

Perhaps the majority of the working people in the town would have agreed with a prominent member of the Trade Council, who was also a councillor, when he said that 'in future Trades Unionists should make more use of their political power and avail themselves of the political machinery by returning more of their own class to Parliament. There would be no need for strikes in order to improve their conditions if they returned their representatives to Parliament to pass just laws'.[48] In any event the lack of militant trade

---

[46] T.R.C. 26 August 1917.

[47] T.R.C. 27 July 1937. Alfred Williams, writing in 1915, had this to say: 'The trade unionists are usually as well agreed as the others to work extra time, there is but very little difference discovered between them. No matter how loudly they disclaim against the system and advocate the abolition of overtime, should the order be issued the community obey it with alacrity'. *Life in a Railway Factory (1915)* (Newton Abbott: David and Charles, 1969) page 293.

unionism probably contributed to the lack of a clear class base
to politics in the town and a tradition of consensus rather than
conflict. As we shall see these were ideal conditions for town
development to take place in.

The history of social service provision in the town illustrates
the practical results of this consensus. While the foregoing
analysis has attempted to show the evolution of specifically
working-class organizations in the town and the way in which
they attempted to gain improvements via political
organization, the growth of progressive attitudes in the town
was not limited to the labour and trade union movement.
Although the Labour Party was in opposition on the council
until 1945, by this time Swindon had gained a reputation as a
highly enlightened local authority in many fields.[49] The two
outstanding examples of this progressive approach were health
and education. The influence of the Great Western Railway's
early provision of these services must have had much to do
with encouraging their improvement and extension to the
standards well beyond those that the local authority was
legally obliged to provide. For example, in 1914 the Council
expressed its intention of providing a full maternity and child
welfare service in the town and started to implement the policy
in advance of legislation which made this an obligatory duty.
The service was then continually developed up to the passing
of the National Health Act after the Second World War.
Judging by the fact that the infant mortality rate in this
predominantly working-class town only exceeded the national
rate for four years during the period from 1901 to 1946, this
provision was effective. In 1899 the Swindon School Board
retained a doctor to inspect sick children, several years before
school medical inspections were provided for by law and the
school medical service subsequently underwent continual
alteration and improvement. These, and the many other

[48] T.R.C. (Newspaper cutting insert dated 20 May 1917). The Swindon
division was formed in 1918. It was Conservative until 1929 when it
returned Christopher Addison (the former Liberal Minister) for Labour.
He lost the seat in 1931, regained it in 1934, and lost it again, to a
Conservative in the following year. The seat has been held by the Labour
Party since 1945. It was lost to the Conservatives in 1969-70.
[49] See Swindon Borough Council, Record of Administration 1947, for a
full record.

developments that took place in the health service, gave
Swindon, in the opinion of W. A. Robson, the best local
medical service in England.[50]

Educational improvements matched those in the health
service. After the passing of the 1902 Education Act, the
Borough virtually took over control of higher education within
its boundaries from the County Council. A special rate was
paid to enable the town to have a higher standard of provision
than the surrounding area. Among these extra benefits were a
far greater number of free places in borough secondary
schools, the payment of training grants to student teachers, a
higher standard and wider provision of technical and evening
classes to meet the industrial requirements of the town, and
the early establishment of a juvenile employment service.
Swindon's attitude towards education is also illustrated by the
fact that in all but two years from 1921 to 1938 it spent more
per child on elementary education than the national average,
and more than the County Council in every year during this
period. There were also many developments in youth work, for
example the appointment of a full time youth officer in 1929,
ten years before the government suggested that this should be
done.

The extent of these progressive measures and the lack of
political discord concerning their implementation, suggest
that the Swindonians' involvement with town affairs was
matched by a concern for the quality of the town's social
institutions and life. There was a very definite sense of
community which at base rested on the common factor of
employment at the railway works. Although there were
differing social groups, the most distinctive being the railway
and other workers, the managers, and the (mainly small)
shopkeepers, all these groups were in one way or another
dependent on the same industry. Furthermore all shared, to a
greater or lesser extent, in the same progressive attitudes
outlined in the preceding paragraphs. This sense of
community persisted until the coming of town expansion in
1952. Indeed it is still a potent force in the town today, long
after many of the original factors leading to its existence have

---

[50] Robson, W. A. *The Development of Local Government* (London:
Allen and Unwin, 1931).

decayed. The following passage, written in 1945, is an over-idealized picture of the community but it errs in degree rather than substance: 'To be employed in the Great Western Railway works is to be, in the Swindon phrase "inside". This means that everyone "inside" knows everyone else, or at any rate something about everyone else, so that the town becomes rather like a big family. The disadvantages are outweighed by the advantages . . . [the passage goes on to recall how, in the depression of the thirties, those in work aided those out of work] . . . and the big family "inside" is made of individual families, most of them owning their own houses . . . Swindon is a town of few council houses . . . and many of these families have a Great Western tradition of more than two generations . . . Moreover the daily occupation of most of the railway people of Swindon gives about as satisfying and full a life as an industrial one can be in this part of the century. Mothers and wives can take pride in houses that are their own, sons and fathers work in a species of industry which is as yet far removed from the soul destroying chain-belt system associated with mass production. Most of the jobs in the works require skill, craftsmanship and intelligence . . . Outsiders have commented on the drab appearance of much of Swindon, especially the industrial parts, and though good architecture is rare in Swindon the good life is less rare. From this railway town came sturdy individualists . . . and vigorous institutions such as the Swindon branch of the Workers Educational Association and the various musical, operatic, artistic, learned, and sporting clubs which are known outside the town itself. The majority of the parish is "inside" and meets both at daily work and at public worship. It is not considered odd for some senior official in the works to ring up a subordinate in another department to tell him that he is wanted to serve Mass at St Marks or St Saviours, St Lukes or St Johns on the following morning. Nor is it odd for the reverse to happen.'[51]

So far the analysis has concentrated on factors internal to Swindon's social and economic structure, but the town's relations with the outside world must now be described. Many observers have noticed that the coherence of a social group relates to the strength of the barriers that separate it from

---

[51] *St Marks, Swindon — 1845-1945*, (n.d.) page 1.

other surrounding groups. The high degree of geographical, economic, and social isolation of Swindon strongly affected its social attitudes and political outlook. Therefore it is important to study these factors if we are to understand the course that the town subsequently took and the obstacles that it faced.

Swindon is geographically isolated, there is no town of comparable size within thirty miles. Oxford, thirty miles to the north-east, is the nearest large town to which Swindonians have had easy access. However such journeys are hardly an everyday affair for the majority of the people even today, still less during the railway era. The area surrounding Swindon which lies in the counties of Wiltshire, Berkshire, Gloucestershire, and Oxfordshire forms part of some of the most rural countryside in Southern England. Swindon is the largest town in Wiltshire, and the Swindon conurbation contains between a quarter and a fifth of the local population of the county.

Table 1.5

Population 1901-1966

	1901	1911	1921	1931	1939	1951	1961	1966
Swindon Municipal Borough	45 006	50 751	54 920	62 401	61 000	68 670	91 739	98 410
Highworth and Cricklade Rural Districts	25 636	26 141	24 612	26 833	27 000	36 910	45 603	56 240
Wiltshire County Council	271 008	286 429	291 687	303 193	310 500	386 692	422 985	471 350

Sources: *Census reports, 1901-66. 1939 estimate for Swindon from* Planning for Swindon 1945, *other 1939 estimates from the 1951 Census.*[52]

[52] N.B. The 'conurbation' referred to in the text comprises Swindon Municipal Borough, Highworth Rural District Council, and Cricklade and Wootton Bassett Rural District Council. An examination of census returns by parish has shown that the major increments of population in the rural districts, especially in the postwar period, have been in parishes adjacent or close to Swindon Municipal Borough and any attempt to measure the effects of Swindon's expansion must take this fact into account.

But the numerical predominance of Swindon is far less important than the fact that, ever since the coming of the railway, there has been a sharp contrast between the economic base of the town and that of the surrounding countryside. Before 1840 Swindon was a market town dependent for a living on agriculture. Since that time it has been an industrial town, dependent at first on the railways and latterly on a wider range of industries. This sharp economic difference brought in its wake equally acute social and political differences. After the initial period when labour was recruited in part from the surrounding countryside, the expanding railway works depended on skilled and semi-skilled labour recruited from all over the country. Naturally much of this labour came from the established industrial areas of Great Britain, in the early years from the North and Scotland. Then, on the opening of the rolling mills in the 1860s, there was an influx of Welsh steel workers. Finally, during the last part of the nineteenth and the first decade of the twentieth centuries, greater numbers began to come from the south east and London.[53] The immigrant nature of the town was remarked on by the Registrar General as late as 1911 and J. H. Thomas, himself a Welshman of course, describes Swindon as 'a town whose population was singularly blended of English, Scottish, Irish, and Welsh with, probably, the Welsh predominating'.[54] These immigrants brought their own attitudes and institutions with them and these had little in common with the customs of rural Wiltshire. The impact of the immigration on the religious composition of the town has already been noted. Also the political independence that the working men began to show contrasts sharply with the continuing subservience of the agricultural worker to his employer. Nor was there any likelihood that the newcomers would eventually integrate themselves with the surrounding country communities because the town continued to have radically different interests from those of the rural areas. Instead the community evolved a way of life of a rather distinct nature, recognizably that of an industrial community

---

[53] Wells, H. B. op.cit. Again doubt has been expressed as to the accuracy of the figures, but the trends are correct.

[54] Thomas, J. H. *My Story* (London: Hutchinson, 1937) page 17. Thomas spent most of the first decade of this century in Swindon and served on the Council and the Trades Council. He is buried in the town.

but at the same time, because of the isolation of the town, rather inward looking.[55] For this reason, and the others which have been outlined, it was cautiously progressive rather than radical, closely unified rather than split into a number of clearly defined groups, rather sober and industrious, and even, according to Alfred Williams, somewhat subservient industrially if not politically.

In these circumstances it is hardly surprising that the gulf between the county government and society and that of the town has been a constant factor in the history of Swindon. On several occasions the town has attempted to break away from the political control of the County Council altogether by being constituted a county borough. Since the last war two attempts have been made but without success. On these occasions the longstanding and wide-ranging differences between the two authorities have been revealed. For example, the Borough felt that it had always been far more progressive than the County Council in developing the social services. The county for its part wished to preserve rural interests and ways of life in a predominantly rural area. Any further extension of Swindon's autonomy might threaten these interests. The differences can be clearly seen in the political sphere; the majority of parliamentary and county council members are Conservative while in recent years Swindon has mainly had Labour members.

To conclude, there are fundamental and longstanding differences which have increased the internal coherence of Swindon's social structure, have served to heighten its isolation from many influences, and have intensified its sense of independence. Of course these same factors have also tended to increase the suspicion, and at times the downright hostility, of the rest of the county. In this context town development was one of a long line of issues which served to highlight the division.

The decline of the railway works

We have already referred to the confident assertion by a local paper in 1928[56] that the fortunes of Swindon would

---

[55] Williams, A. op.cit. says that the inhabitants took little interest in anything outside the town.

continue to be inseparably linked with those of the Great Western Railway. There was apparently no reason to doubt this prediction as the town and the works emerged from the First World War into the prosperity of the early twenties. Prewar employment had reached about 14 000 by 1905 but had dropped slightly by the outbreak of war. After the war, during which the railway stock had been depleted, there was a great deal of re-equipping to be done, and employment reached an all-time peak of 14 369 in May 1925.[57] The works had not expanded physically since the first decade of the century but Eversley had suggested that this was a deliberate decision of the Great Western Railway directors, dictated by the increasing difficulties that the Locomotive Superintendent had in coordinating the operations of the sprawling industrial complex. Alfred Williams, in his book *Life in a Railway Factory*, complains bitterly that the administration and methods used in the works were old-fashioned and out of date, and that the directors had lost touch with the men. Thus he tends to confirm the suggestion that the works had become too large for effective control to be exercised,[58] but there seemed to be no reason why the works should not continue to maintain its maximum output for many years to come.

However there were factors underlying this optimistic picture which soon resulted in a sharp and permanent contraction of the enterprise. The most immediate factor was the economic depression that began at the end of the 1920s. The course and causes of this depression are well known. They caused a world wide drop in the demand for railway equipment and a reduction of employment at the works. However, in the long run it was the expansion of motor car manufacturing, one of the few growth industries of this period, that did most to affect Swindon's future history.

Table 1.6 gives an idea of the phenomenal growth of the road transport industry during the interwar period.[59]

The railways found themselves unable to cope with the greater speed and convenience of motorized transport. This situation was made worse by the companies' costing policy

---

[56] Savage, C. I., op.cit.
[57] Eversley, D. E. C., op.cit. page 218.
[58] Williams, A. op.cit. *passim*.
[59] Savage, op.cit. pages 145, 174.

Table 1.6

Number of motorized goods vehicles in the U.K. in 1904–39	
1904	4 000
1914	82 000
1920	101 000
1930	329 794
1939	488 000

Number of buses and coaches in the U.K. 1926 and 1938	
1926	40 118
1938	53 005

Total number of motor vehicles in the U.K. 1911–38	
1911	192 877
1920	650 148
1930	2 273 661
1938	3 084 896

Source: *Basic Road Statistics.*

which determined the price for the transport of goods by the value of the load, rather than its bulk or weight. This policy encouraged industrialists to send low-value commodities by rail and high-value goods by road. Many of low-value commodities, for example coal, are very bulky and require special rolling stock for their carriage. However, as the charge for them was tied by law to their value, the profits accruing to the railways were miserably small. On the other hand, the road hauliers were free from the restrictive controls imposed on the railway and were able to charge on a cost plus basis.[60] According to Walker and Savage,[61] the outcome of these developments was that, particularly after 1930, the railways were caught between the twin disadvantages of falling traffic and rising costs. The magnitude of this change can be seen from Table 1.7.

So the interwar years marked the end of the railway system's supremacy as the principal means of land transport. Nor was it at all easy to divert production of engines and rolling stock into export markets. A combination of high costs and a great increase in protective tariffs abroad meant that the chances of increased trade were slight even where the internal combustion engine had not yet begun to supplant the railway engine. Some idea of the magnitude of this loss of overseas

[60] Savage, op. cit.
[61] Walker, G. and Savage, C. I. *Inland Carriage by Road and Rail* in Burn, D. (ed.) *The Structure of British Industry, Vol. 1* (London: Cambridge University Press, 1958).

Table 1.7

Railway statistics 1913 and 1920-38

Year	Net revenue (£m.)	General merchandise (m. tonnes)	Passengers carried (excl. season tickets) (millions)
1913		67.8	1 199.3
1920		68.7	1 579.0
1925		59.7	1 232.6
1930	38.5	53.2	844.3
1935	33.7	45.3	856.2
1938	29.8	44.3	848.9

Source: *Railway Returns.*

markets can be gained from the fact that exports of iron and steel, and goods manufactured in these materials, fell by about one-third in volume between 1929 and 1937.[62]

All this inevitably meant that employment at the railway works began to decline during the thirties. By 1936 employment had shrunk to 11 500, and by 1939 to 10 500.[63] Although this was a very serious situation, the minutes of the Trades Council bear eloquent testimony to the suffering and indignity that the unemployed had to endure especially in the early thirties,[64] the extent of the distress was never on the scale of that experienced by certain other one industry towns such as Jarrow or Sunderland. Two factors helped the town to avoid this fate. Firstly, unlike shipbuilding for example, there were still some orders and, even more importantly, stock and track continued to need repair and replacement. Therefore there were still many jobs available at the railway works. Secondly, Swindon is only thirty miles away from the car works at Cowley near Oxford and employment in the car, cycle, and aircraft industries rose from 245 000 to 410 000 between 1930 and 1938.[65] The university town of Oxford was deficient in the industrial skills that Lord Nuffield required for his enterprise

[62] Youngson, A. *The British Economy 1920-57* (London: Allen and Unwin, 1958).

[63] Eversley, D. E. C. op.cit. page 218.

[64] e.g. 'This Council registers its vehement protest against the present Government's Unemployment Scheme. We consider such legislation as Salutary Fascism and liken it to sentencing millions of our fellows of the working class to permanent semi-starvation. We demand that a humanitarian legislation be introduced as becoming a civilized country'. T.R.C. 6 December 1933.

[65] Youngson, op.cit. page 107.

but Swindon had these skills to spare. As a result many workmen commuted on special trains to Cowley during this period, and this served further to diminish the prospect of mass unemployment.[66]

But if the town did not die it certainly began to wither. For the first time since the beginning of the railway age the upward trend in its population levelled off and then began to fall. The drop between 1931 and 1939 was small, from 62 401 in 1931 to 61 000 in 1939, but the underlying trend was more significant because the town was gradually losing its young population. Apprentices finishing their time at the works and finding themselves unemployed had to leave Swindon in search of work in the expanding light industries of the South East and even school leavers were forced to follow the same course.

There was very little that could be done to reverse this situation. Although the Council made some attempts to induce new industries to move to the town, these efforts were fruitless.[67] Furthermore the little government aid that was available had been reserved for those areas in the North, Scotland, and Wales where the problems were far more serious. Thus by the outbreak of the Second World War Swindon was squarely faced with the problem of being a declining one-industry town. It was luckier than some as the decline was, as yet, a slow one but people realized that if prosperity and progress were to continue, new factories must be established and industrial diversification achieved.[68]

Conditions in the town

Another important reason for seeking some way to regenerate the town was its poor environment. Not even its most loyal

---

[66] There was considerable migration to other towns as well, especially Birmingham, Gloucester, and Coventry. The numbers of unemployed left in the town probably did not rise above 3000 in the thirties.

[67] *ex.inf.* Mr C. Smith. There was a suggestion at this time that the Goodyear Tyre Company might come to the town but this did not occur.

[68] It was, furthermore, still a low-wage town. An economic survey (*The Home Market*, 1939 edn. Harrison and Mitchell) showed that the income groups, in 1931, were as follows:

   4.5% of income groups with an income of £10 per week and over,
   16.5% of income groups with an income of £4–£10 per week,
   40.0% of income groups with an income of £2.50p–£4 per week,
   39.0% of income groups with an income of £2.50 or under.

citizen could pretend that Swindon is a beautiful town to look at. John Betjeman has rightly said that there is very little architecture in Swindon and a great deal of building.[69] Apart from the somewhat withdrawn elegance of parts of Old Town and the charm of the original railway village, the general impression is one of street upon street of red brick terraces. In the affluent sixties many of these houses were enlivened by their owners' remarkable decorative schemes, but several descriptions of the town that exist from the inter-war period paint a rather different picture. Thus in a broadcast in 1937 Betjeman had this to say, 'the streets of the prewar [i.e. World War One] Swindon are depressing rows of two storeyed, semi-detached houses packed closely together and hardly any trees. Bay window, front door, bay window for miles. Almost every street has houses with only two storeys. Even the main shopping street contains only a few buildings above this two storey uniformity. But this would not matter so much if the houses were pleasant to look at. Even for two storey some of the roads are too narrow . . . speculators have thought of their money before other people's health and happiness. They have crowded houses on sites and spent money on outward show instead of internal good arrangement . . . this applies more forcibly to the Swindon houses built since the war . . .'[70]

The Board of Trade report into the cost of living of the working classes in 1908 noted that the work people of Swindon were almost exclusively housed in well-built brick cottages 'erected in rows of uniform character', but however drab these might be the amount of living space available was adequate. The majority of cottages were four-roomed but there were a large number with five or even six rooms. Overcrowding was rare.[71] In the twenties and, more particularly, the thirties a national building boom occurred and this had its effect in Swindon. The town had been fairly compact but now houses began to spill out along the main roads into the surrounding areas. The expansion of the Highworth and the Cricklade and

---

[69] Betjeman, J. in *Studies in the History of Swindon* (Swindon: Swindon Borough Council, 1950) page 161. Developments since 1952 have began to alter the state of affairs.

[70] Betjeman, 10 May 1937, report in *Evening Advertiser*.

[71] Board of Trade, op.cit.

Wootton Bassett Rural Districts really dates from this period. Betjeman described the results with horror, 'all the approaches to Swindon are arranged with these things called desirable residences, each of which is different but only different in some horrible little particular of outward showiness. Stained glass windows, gables, standard front doors bought cheap by the dozen and artificial beams'.[72] He also complained that housing areas were mixed up with factories and gas works, and that ribbon development stretched out towards Highworth, Crickdale, Oxford, and Rodbourne. He concluded, 'Swindon is a warning to all England to keep watch on the speculative builders'.

Accounts of the quality of life in the town during this period also present a rather gloomy view. The best description of the Great Western Railway works is contained in Alfred William's book *Life in a Railway Factory*. Williams was a poet as well as an artisan, and it is evident that he found the atmosphere in the workshop physically and intellectually stifling but it is difficult to believe that many others did not share his frustration to some degree. 'When the summer is over, when the majesty of July and August is past and gone and golden September gives way to rainy October, or, most of all, when dull gloomy November covers the skies with its impenetrable veil of drab cloud and mist day after day and week after week, with scarcely an hour of sunshine, the utter dismalness and ugliness of the place are appalling. Then there is not a vestige of colour. The sky, roofs, walls, the engines moving to and fro, the rolling stock, the stocks of plates and ingots of iron and steel, the sleepers for the rails, the ground beneath — everything is dark, sombre and repellent. Not a glint on the steel lines! Not a refraction of light from the slates on the roof! Everything is dingy, dark, and drab. And drab is the mind of the toiler all the time, drab as the skies above and the walls beneath. Doomed to the confinement from which there is no escape, he accepts the conditions and is swallowed up in his environment.'[73]

J. B. Priestley, on visiting the town in the autumn of 1933, also gained little pleasure from the experience. 'So out I went

---

[72] Betjeman, J. op.cit.

[73] Williams, A. op. cit. page 12.

to see how the people who build the best locomotives in the world enjoy themselves on a damp night in early autumn . . . The main street was singularly quiet. Now and then a pair of ladies would hail a passing pair of girls; that was all. The only lights shone from the three picture theatres of the town, from the pubs, which were poor places, and from a fish-and-chip shop here and there. These were not enough to take the murk out of the street which had an unfriendly shuttered look. This, I said to myself as I wandered about in the dwindling rain, is one of the penalties inflicted upon you if you live in these small industrial towns, where you can work but cannot really play . . . A turning at the bottom of the main street directed me to the Playhouse. It was not a bad building, and would make an excellent Little Theatre. A depressingly small audience, which could not muster more than a dozen in the best (two shillings) seats, was watching a touring revue company.'[74] Priestley was also astonished to find that the porter at the hotel in which he stayed was dedicated to the collection of endowment policies. Evidently the desire to save, which had been such a potent factor in the building of Swindon in the past, was still active in the town in its depressed days!

These descriptions of life in the town, by two most sensitive observers, undoubtedly convey some valid impressions. This was a town with a rather sober view of life, not given to the proud display of civic monuments so usual in many of the large northern industrial towns, and its inhabitants formed a close-knit, home-centred society.

Yet there is another side to the picture. The vigorous development of local services has already been mentioned, as has the town's early establishment of an arts centre after the Second World War. Furthermore, Betjeman also had this to say about the townsfolk in his broadcast: 'The people are some of the pleasantest and most polite you can come across. They are very proud in intellect and that sort of thing. They can sing very well and are good at getting up concerts and amateur theatricals. Good church and chapel goers'. So many people in the town did get away from their own fireplaces to act, to sing, to discuss politics and current affairs, or simply to meet one

[74] Priestley, J. B. *English Journey* (London: Gollancz, 1934) pages 43-4.

another in the pub. Nevertheless it must be admitted that the facilities available for doing these things were poor and in some cases non-existent. The town urgently needed replanning and renovation. In a publication issued by the Council in 1945, the Mayor wrote , 'In this town we have a wide variety of public services of which we are justifiably proud, but of the town itself, its buildings, streets, and general appearance we have less reason to be proud'.[75] The Borough's consultant planner had this to say, 'a very substantial acreage of the borough is still open ground, many roads lack proper terminations and much of the earlier development is substandard, according to today's most up-to-date conception of what is desirable to provide a good general level of environment, and much of the general design and outward appearance of the houses is lacking in amenity value'.[76] In addition the Swindon created by the railway age, unlike the Old Town on the hill, never had a real town centre. The main shopping street, Regent Street, was little more than a row of cottages knocked into shops. Apart from this there was a Town Hall, a curious redbrick affair built in the 1890s, and in 1938 the present Civic Offices were opened. This is a handsome enough building but one that did little to enrich the leisure activities of the town's inhabitants. There were also a number of theatres and cinemas but this was about all.

The inhabitants were certainly conscious of these deficiencies, and in 1927 the Council had retained W. R. Davidge, a past President of the Town Planning Institute, to advise them. In 1928 they decided to prepare a town planning scheme for the whole of the borough. They had also started the first council housing estate in 1919 at Pinehurst to the north of the town and employed Sir Raymond Unwin to lay it out. The estate eventually contained over 900 houses. Sites were reserved for various social amenities, churches, shops, a school, and a public hall[77] but development was slow and circumstances were against the Council's endeavours. The exceedingly low rateable value of the borough meant that little money was available for improvements, and other sources of finance were not forthcoming in these years of economic

[75] Swindon Borough Council, 'Planning for Swindon 1945' page 2.
[76] Davidge, W. R. 'Planning for Swindon 1945' page 12.

stagnation. Furthermore, the view that town planning was an essential function of central and local government only gained acceptance slowly in the interwar period. The first Act of Parliament which attempted to deal with planning at all was passed in 1909 but it achieved little. A further Act in 1919 tried to compel every borough and urban district to prepare a scheme by 1926 (later extended to 1929); however there were no penalties for non compliance. The Act was widely ignored and in 1932 even this effort at compulsion was abandoned. A later act to control ribbon development was also ineffective.[78] It took ten years to prepare a draft planning scheme for Swindon but one was presented to the Council and adopted in 1938. It is doubtful whether it could have been carried out in the conditions current at the time.

Thus the town entered the Second World War with two seemingly intractable problems, the necessity to renovate its physical structure and the need to avert the steady process of economic decline by diversifying its industrial structure. But the war opened up many new prospects for the country as a whole and for Swindon in particular.

Wartime developments

It is common knowledge that the war led to an acceleration in the pace of government intervention in the social and economic system of the country.[79] The 1944 Education Act and the Beveridge Report are perhaps the best known of the innovations, but the setting up of the Ministry of Town and Country Planning in February 1943 also marked an important development in the functions of government.

The assumption of wide planning powers by central and local government, subsequently set out in the 1947 Town and Country Planning Act, was strongly influenced by the publication of three reports on planning problems. The most important for Swindon was the report on The Distribution of

---

[77] Record of Administration 1947, page 68.

[78] See Ashworth, op. cit. Chapter 8 *passim*.

[79] See esp. Titmuss, R. *Problems of Social Policy* (London, H.M.S.O., 1950) Chapter 25.

the Industrial Population (The Barlow Report).[80] This
investigated the problems created in the previous two decades
by the decline of many basic industries, and the concurrent
growth of light industries in new locations, principally in the
South East. It also exposed the lack of any serious attempt to
co-ordinate housing and industrial development, or to provide
proper social and employment facilities in connection with
new areas of housing. The Report stated that while there
were considerable advantages to be gained from large
urban conglomerations, such as increased employment
opportunities, better social and other services, and more
efficient administration, there could be disadvantages caused
by congestion, bad planning, and long and costly journeys to
work. In particular, London was draining the industry,
population, and cultural life of the rest of the country. So its
growth urgently needed controlling.

The Report proposed action to decentralize and disperse
industries and population from congested areas, and to carry
out urban renewal with far higher standards of amenity in
existing urban areas. It emphasized the disadvantages of one-
industry towns: 'When an area that has concentrated over a
long period mainly on one form of specialized industrial
activity for international or other reasons encounters a severe
and prolonged depression the consequences to the work people
and indeed the population of the area as a whole are likely to
be disastrous'.[81] The solution was to set up trading estates
which would attract new industries into such areas and to
create associated areas of new housing. Excess population
should also be rehoused in a series of self-contained new towns,
and in the properly planned extensions of existing small towns
and villages.

However there were many obstacles to the implementation
of these new suggestions which the Barlow Report outlined.
Firstly, there was no overall planning machinery or strategy.
The few existing schemes were fragmented and purely
dependent on local initiative and interest. There was also the
problem of compensation and betterment. As things stood at

---

[80] Report of the Royal Commission on the Distribution of the Industrial
Population. Command 6153 (London: H.M.S.O., 1940).
[81] *Ibid*, page 87.

the time the cost of acquiring land for public use and the complexity of the procedures made comprehensive planning impossible. Finally it was thought that the risks and the costs of development on the scale proposed were too high to attract private finance, so central and local government investment would be required.

Two of the outstanding problems were examined by the Uthwatt Committee on Compensation and Betterment and the Scott Committee on Land Utilization in Rural Areas. But by far the greatest impetus towards effective town planning came from the experiences of wartime. The evacuation and relocation of population, the building in planned locations of new factories, and the destruction of cities by bombing showed that population could be redistributed and that the rebuilding and replanning of large areas would be an urgent priority after the war.

The first real step was taken when the Ministry of Town and Country Planning was established. Subsequently, acts were passed to prevent unauthorized development and to increase certain powers of compulsory acquisition. Measures were also taken to control the distribution of industry in 1945 and the 1947 Town and Country Planning Act made fundamental changes in planning legislation. Planning became obligatory and the county councils and county boroughs became the local planning authorities. They had to prepare planning schemes which were to be reviewed every five years. Local authorities were also empowered to purchase, by compulsion if necessary, land which would be required for any of their statutory functions for up to ten years ahead. The publication of the Greater London Plan in 1944, which accepted the need for planned decentralization of some of the population of the metropolis, was also significant. These changes in national policies aided the evolution of new ideas and proposals for possible solutions to Swindon's difficulties. Certain developments within the Borough also stimulated rethinking. The demands of war production finally brought some new industries into the town. There also came a flood of war workers with this expansion. The population of Swindon and the two surrounding Rural Districts increased sharply, from an estimated 88 000 in 1939 to 96 000 in 1940 and 104 000 in 1941.[82] A New Defence Regulation was passed in January 1941 to deal with the national problem of accommodating such workers. It allowed the authorities to close areas to evacuees and others whose presence might hinder accommodation of workers. The first Order was applied to Swindon and part of Highworth Rural District Council on 9 January 1941.[83]

Because of the desire to make provision for the social needs of this increased population, the Council embarked on a number of ventures which were to form the nucleus of many attempts over the following years to improve the social life of the town. These included the setting up of a public library, with the formation of a number of ancillary societies concerned with music, art, drama, and literature, the acquisition of the nucleus of a permanent art collection, and the holding of regular art exhibitions. The highly successful postwar Arts Centre and latterly a new Arts Gallery sprang from this initiative. The Council took responsibility for encouraging music, art, and drama in the town by establishing the Mayor's Community Fund to finance these activities. The fund took over the Playhouse, the theatre that Priestley had said would make an excellent Little Theatre ten years before. This venture was the forerunner of the longstanding project for a civic theatre which succeeded in 1969, after many setbacks. The establishment of youth centres and community centres also laid down new policy lines which have exercised great influence over the Council's subsequent thinking.

While this work was continuing Swindon's constant struggle for administrative autonomy was entering a new phase, during which patterns were drawn which strongly influenced the relationship between the County and the Borough Council which existed during town development. The immediate cause for concern was the proposals contained in the White Paper that formed the basis of the 1944 Education Act which involved loss of effective powers to the County Council. In October 1943 the Council issued a pamphlet containing representations against these proposals.[84] This described in detail the differences, already mentioned in this book, between the County and the Borough and set out the evidence

---

[82] Census 1951.

[83] See Titmuss, op.cit. page 366.

[84] Memorandum on the administration of education in Swindon dated 13 October 1943.

for the claim that the Borough had proved to be an efficient and progressive administrator of the education service and should be allowed to continue to run the service of the future. Much the same suggestions were made in a pamphlet concerning the 1945 White Paper on the National Health Service. The whole controversy was summarized in another document which put forward Swindon's claims for county borough status.[85]

These efforts had varying degrees of success. Thus under the 1944 Education Act the Borough became the only 'excepted district' in Wiltshire. This allowed it to have an education department which, broadly speaking, was responsible for the day-to-day running of the town's schools, but not for overall planning and finance. A combined committee of Borough and County representatives was given powers to administer the local health service in Swindon and the surrounding area. This was replaced by a committee of the Borough Council after the 1961 Local Government Act. Furthermore the hospitals in the area were administered by a Swindon and District Hospital Management Committee under the authority of the Oxford Regional Hospital Board, an arrangement that the Council had pressed for its submissions. In an agreement made in 1948 and subsequently redrawn in 1957 and in 1960, the County delegated wide planning powers to the Borough. So Swindon managed to achieve a great deal more autonomy than most non-county boroughs.[86] This independence was to play a vital part in ensuring the success of town development. However the Borough twice failed to obtain county borough status and remained quite closely dependent on the support of the County Council for the approval of plans and the provision of services. This has led to a number of conflicts and delays which will be more fully examined as they arise in the history of the expansion process.

---

[85] Memorandum on hospital policy, the National Health Service and local government dated 10 April 1945. It is interesting to note that another pamphlet on the potentialities of Swindon for industrial development was issued at the same time.

[86] In 1968 there were thirty local authorities with delegated powers in the Health Service and thirty in education. Report of The Committee on Local Authority and Allied Personal Social Services (see Bohm Report, London H.M.S.O., 1968) Command 3703 Appendix F paras. 63 and 151.

By the end of the War new proposals, which were seen as offering a solution to Swindon's problems, were made public in an important publication entitled *Planning for Swindon 1945*. This set out the conclusions which had been reached as a result of the changes in national policy and local conditions which have been mentioned. Although many of its specific recommendations proved to be unworkable in the austere period ahead or became obsolete with the passage of time, the broad objectives it laid down have never been abandoned by the Council. They were a major influence on the decision to adopt the Town Development Act in 1952.

The Plan concentrated on three main areas in order to meet what had been seen as Swindon's three main problems, the need for new industry, the need to improve the physical environment and housing, and the need to improve the physical facilities of the town. A number of war factories had been erected in and around the town, among them the Vickers Armstrong factory at South Marston, the Marine Mountings factory at Wroughton, two Armstrong Whitworth factories at Blunsdon and Sevenhampton, and the Plessey factory inside the town. The Plan stated that a new effort must be made to introduce increased and varied employment. In order to achieve this it pressed for the retention of the war factories and proposed to establish a trading estate on available land in the north-eastern part of the town. The report also stated that 'side by side with the development of Swindon as a place to work in, there should be development of Swindon as a place to live in'.[87] Many of the proposals in this sphere came together in the central redevelopment scheme which had been drawn up by the Borough Surveyor in 1943. We shall refer to this again in Chapter 5.

The increase of population caused by the war, some of which remained afterwards, had caused a heavy demand for housing. This had partly been met by prefabricated units but these would soon need replacement. In addition the need for new houses was swollen by the pent-up demand of the war years and the return home of men from the forces. So there was an urgent need for houses which forced the Council to act

---

[87] *Planning for Swindon 1945*, page 43.

in advance of any general plan for reconstruction or improvement of the town. The major part of the Corporation's energies over the next few years were occupied by the attempt to meet this demand.

Postwar policies 1945-52

As the war ended the problems of national reconstruction became apparent, as did the difficulties of carrying out this reconstruction in a situation where huge debts and the destruction of international markets meant that austere economic policies had to be pursued. But the General Election had brought the Labour Party to power. It was committed to a wide-ranging programme of social reform which it began with great speed. Moves begun in wartime to set up improved health and education services were continued. Their effects on Swindon have already been referred to. But housing was the most pressing problem. Nationally about 700 000 houses needed repair or replacement. Millions of men were due to return from the war and the marriage and birth rates were rapidly rising.[88] The government embarked on a crash programme of building and the problem of housing dominated the proceedings of the planning committees of local councils. Donnison remarks that although the housing programme was successful, little rethinking was done. Even the new towns policy did not become effective to any degree until the 1950s. In the main the government relied on rent control and the building of council housing, much of it prefabricated to bypass delays in the construction industry. In this situation the simultaneous expansion of housing, replanning of older areas, and provision of a full range of social and commercial facilities to serve these areas, which was what had been contemplated in the Swindon plan, soon became reduced to an all-out effort to build new houses.

The Plessey Company requested advice or help in the housing of workers for their new factory. They were assured of help and the Town Clerk was commissioned to prepare a report on the housing needs of the borough. The report

---

[88] Donnison, D. V. *Government of Housing* (Harmondsworth: Penguin, 1967) pages 63-7.

concluded that after the land at the Pinehurst Extension Estate had been used up, the Council would have no further land to build on. So it was suggested that land for about 550 houses (44 acres) be bought to the north and south of Moredon Road. This formed the future Moredon Estate. About 200 acres, for 1500 houses, a school, and a large recreation area were also to be acquired north of Stratton Cross Roads. This later became the Penhill Estate, the first to receive Londoners. A further area was also to be acquired around Croft Road in the south, but this proposal was later dropped. The immediate problems surrounding this course of action were shortages of skilled manpower in the Surveyor's Department and shortages of building labour. It was thought that the latter problem might be met by the importation of Irish labour and the former by an expansion of the staff of the department. This was the first of many such requests for staff and resources, which were to transform the internal structure of the departments concerned from that of a fairly small local authority to that necessary for a fast-growing town, and make possible the complex series of operations that town development entailed. Further changes soon occurred. A Borough Architect's Department was set up early in 1946, a move which was virtually unheard of in a non-county borough. A Housing Officer was appointed to head a new housing section in the Treasurer's Department (rather surprisingly a separate Housing Department was not established until 1966). This housing report also reflected future administrative and policy-forming arrangements. It was jointly prepared by the Town Clerk, the Treasurer, and the Surveyor. This inter-departmental liaison was to form the core of the machinery for carrying out all the subsequent expansion. Without it continued progress might not have been possible. We shall return to the discussion of these developments in Chapter 6.

The report was approved and negotiations began for the land. At the same time work continued on the Pinehurst Extension Estate. However during 1946 two problems which Swindon had suffered from in the past once again failed to find satisfactory solutions. These were the question of its relations with its neighbours, and the need to increase social amenities in the town. Although new community centres were rapidly set up, other schemes were not so successful. The establishment of a new technical school had to be postponed. Furthermore, the government refused to allow shops and other facilities to be built on new estates until national housing needs had been reduced. While the first priority was to produce more houses this policy seems to have been rather short sighted, especially as the housing plan was soon slowed down by the economic crisis of 1947. It was undoubtedly responsible for creating a good deal of hardship on the new estates. The Regional Planning Officer tried to promote an attempt to improve the planning of the areas into which Swindon was expanding. He suggested that the Borough and the Highworth Rural District Council engaged a planner to present outline plans for the two authorities. Unfortunately, when this proposition was put to the rural district they refused and this chance of arranging some effective co-operation in the planning of estates was not repeated. Such attitudes were typical during the course of town development.

Despite progress with the Moredon housing development the pressure for houses continued. The Ministry of Supply urged the Council to make more housing available for Vickers workers. In addition the local waiting list had risen from 1100 in June 1945 to 2530 a year later. By 1947 it stood at a high point of 3685. Adding in the Vickers requirement, the total list came to well over 4000. But there were many delays and the building of Penhill only began in 1951.

The other two schemes that had assumed first priority in the Borough's postwar plans, the creation of a trading estate and the central area redevelopment scheme, ran into even more severe difficulties. The attempt to retain wartime industries was largely successful; however these were all in the engineering sector and it was clear that diversification of employment could only be gained by importing new industries. Unfortunately the Board of Trade, which had powers to restrict the location of industry, was pursuing a policy of sending firms to depressed areas. Clearly Swindon was not such an area. This was the source of one of the major conflicts which accompanied town development, and forms a major theme of Chapter 4.

The future of the central area scheme was also in doubt, as the Regional Planning Officer had decided that the scheme was of a long term nature and incapable of speedy implementation. This being the case, approval to make compulsory purchase orders was unlikely to be given. The Town Clerk argued against this decision and it was agreed that the Corporation should put forward an interim programme for the next five to ten years. As things were to emerge, the Council were not able to make a start on redevelopment until 1955. The long and complex events which characterized central area redevelopment are reviewed in Chapter 5.

The basic reasons for these difficulties came out clearly in a meeting when the topic of the general development of the Borough was discussed. 'At a conference some twelve months previously, the Regional Officer of the Ministry of Labour had stressed the acute labour shortage in Swindon, and expressed the opinion that the new firms established in the district should be absorbed before the further establishment of new firms was considered. The Town Clerk submitted that, while the view taken by the Regional Officer of the Ministry of Labour was unobjectionable on the assumption of the Ministry, it could be strongly argued that in the interests of the diversification of industry and the securing of a balanced community, substantial further immigration of firms should take place. Further, the Town Clerk pointed out that the policy of new towns was being proceeded with, and that one could achieve the same result without opposition locally and at much less cost, by building up Swindon to the extent of another twenty or thirty thousand population. Mr Waddell stated that he could assure the Corporation that the need and claims of places like Swindon, and of Swindon in particular, were very much in the minds of the Ministry, but that as a short-term policy the Ministry must concentrate on taking industries to the development areas where there was unemployment. Mr Waddell added that the Corporation need not despair of appropriate action in the interest of Swindon being taken by the Ministry as soon as conditions permitted.'

A long-term outline plan was submitted in accordance with the agreement at this meeting. It underlined the disadvantages that Swindon possessed a heavy reliance on the Great Western Railway, a lack of female employment, low rateable values, and substantial areas of bad layout and obsolete development.[89] For the first time, it clearly laid out the objectives in concrete terms: 'There should be ensured by every means possible a steady growth in the size of the town to the optimum figure visualized for Swindon as an urban community of 80 to 100 thousand. The essential services for this population are already available, or can be made so without difficulty, and the fullest economic use of the services and amenities already provided is reasonable and proper. The securing of a balanced community should be constantly pursued, and as part of the effort to achieve this it is felt that there should be located in the town a section of a Government Department or some such comparable body of workers. Broadly, it is considered that a policy comparable with the New Towns policy should be followed in regard to Swindon, and the existing town used as a nucleus to be expanded so that its planning, social and economic defects can be remedied. After most careful consideration, it is felt that the outstanding defect in the town is the sense of a worthy and pleasing Centre . . .'[90]

Despite these representations, apart from rather grudging approval to purchase and plan (but not commence) part of the trading estate at Rodbourne Cheney and a similar tentative start on improving the sewage system, the 'short-term' policy of favouring development areas, and to a degree new towns, persisted for the next five years. The possibilities of 'appropriate action in the interests of Swindon being taken by the Ministry' remained remote. Meanwhile the increasing cost of providing and maintaining the ever-growing stock of council houses, in a situation where there was little increase in

---

[89] The lack of sufficient female employment had been a problem as far back as the First World War. After 1914 a few firms (usually clothing concerns) came into the town, but the position was still bad after the Second World War. Thus an investigation of 157 English and Welsh towns having in 1951 populations of 50 000 and over found that Swindon, with 26.8 per cent of the labour force being female, ranked 138 in order. (Moser, C. and Scott, W. *British Towns* (Edinburgh: Oliver and Boyd, 1961) pages 144-5). In 1947 about 46 per cent of the rateable value came from dwelling houses. Of this 37.7 per cent came from houses of up to £14 rateable value, a further 16.7 per cent from houses of £25 rateable value and over (*Long Term Outline Plan*, 1947).

[90] *Long Term Outline Plan*, Town Clerk's Office, Civic Offices, 7 February 1947 (typescript).

[91] The contribution made to the rates by industry was severely reduced by the derating of the railway works, the only substantial industrial concern in the town, and the nationalization of the borough's electricity generating station which reduced its rate payment.

industrial and private rates to offset these costs, threatened to put a stoppage to operations.[91] There was a very real danger that the town would become one with an impossibly high burden of council houses to maintain and with an increasingly heavy rate burden[92] and be unable to afford the desired development and expansion.

Conclusion

This account of the 'pre-history' of the town has shown how many of the factors which inspired the decision to adopt the Town Development Act arose; factors which were also to play a major role in determining the nature and outcome of the subsequent development process. Patterns, customs, and conflicts which were a product of the railway town were carried forward into the new era so that much of the history of this period is inexplicable without an understanding of the earlier time.

Within the town the lack of sharply-perceived class division, the strongly-held values of thrift and sobriety, and the social and geographic isolation resulted in a unified community, with many attitudes shared by all sectors of the population. Much of this was a result of the total dependence of the town on the railway works for continued employment and prosperity. On the other hand the nature of the employment at the works produced an occupational community that had a good deal in common with communities dependent on such industries as mining, docking, fishing, and shipbuilding. And as in these communities there emerged a distinctive structure of progressive working-class politics. However, in Swindon this was not paralleled by a history of sharp conflict between labour and capital. The desire for improvement was taken up, doubtless for widely differing motives, by the whole community and applied vigorously in the processes and provisions of town government. It is this combination of lack of serious dissent, progressive intent, and sturdy independence with regard to the outside world that underlay the large

---

[92] The possibility that the town would continue to have a rather narrow social composition was another reason for not wanting an over high proportion of council houses.

measure of unanimity with which Swindon embarked on its second planned expansion, shortly after the end of the Second World War. The motive force behind this decision was the existence of fundamental weaknesses in Swindon's economic, social, and physical structures. The town's attempts to remedy these and the difficulties it encountered have all been described in this chapter.

However we have already seen that, regardless of internal features which made it a suitable and willing candidate for expansion, the town faced an external environment which was likely to create certain difficulties. At a local level the sharp differences between the industrially based social and economic character of the town and the rurally based character of the county created political and cultural divisions and conflicts. The further growth of Swindon would increase its domination of the hinterland. This was likely to be resisted by people who preferred their own rural way of life to that which Swindon seemed to offer. At the national level the competition from the depressed areas for industry and the government's desire to concentrate its attention on their problems had effectively prevented a start being made on the plans to regenerate the town. It was in such a situation that the Town Development Act seemed to offer a unique opportunity to the Council.

Chapter Two

Expansion, 1952–66

Town development

In the last chapter we saw how the fear grew throughout the thirties and forties that Swindon would become a town in decline. However, much of the effort to deal with the problem was thwarted by national policies and legislation. Alteration of such constraints could not be achieved by a single municipal borough. It was not until a wholly different set of national pre-occupations from those held by the borough council led to new policies and legislation that the local stalemate could finally be broken. The motive forces behind the Town Development Act were the continuing concern with conditions in the conurbations, and a growing anxiety about the cost and pace (or lack of it) of the new town solution to these conditions.

By the end of the 1940s it was clear that the new towns programme would not quickly provide the large-scale relief to the housing problems of the conurbations, particularly London, which it had been designed to achieve. By 1950 fifteen new towns had been designated, eight of them surrounding London, but they had built very few houses due to difficulties of finance, land acquisition, and slowness of building up an effective administrative organization.[1] So planners began to turn to the other proposal of the Barlow Report, which was that population from the conurbations should be accommodated in suitably expanded county towns.

The Town and Country Planning Association, which had long advocated and supported the new towns policy, formed a Country Towns Committee to investigate these ideas. Their conclusions were received with much attention at Swindon. The T.C.P.A. concluded that 'there is general agreement as to the need to expand suitable country towns as a part of the policy of decentralization and dispersal from the big cities; most country town authorities appear willing to cooperate and yet so far little has been achieved. In the main we are satisfied that this is due to the financial difficulties which face these authorities once they embark on planned expansion and, to a lesser extent, to shortcomings of government policy affecting the distribution of industry . . . many local authorities though willing in principle seem disinclined, in practice, to embark on town expansion by accepting other authorities' overspill population. These receiving authorities probably have an acute housing shortage, rates are high (and tending to rise) and they are, in many cases, in arrears with services, such as schools, open spaces and municipal buildings; sewage and water supply may only suffice for a very limited increase of population, whilst the layout of the central shopping and business areas of many of these older country towns will almost certainly require to be modernized and made more spacious . . .[2] The report also pointed out that these improvements were essential if industry and population were to be successfully attracted and retained, and that a measure of political agreement in the towns concerned would be essential.

Soon after these proposals were made the Conservative Party won the 1951 election. They had not been happy with the cost of the new towns policy and adopted town development as an alternative, announcing almost immediately that a Town Development Bill would be brought before Parliament. Unfortunately it seems that this was regarded as a method of getting decentralization on the

---

[1] Orlans in his book on Stevenage gave a graphic description of these problems as they affected the first of the new towns in its early years. See Orlans H. *Stevenage: A Sociological Study of a New Town* (London: Routledge and Kegan Paul, 1952).

[2] MacFarlane and Kirk, *Expansion of Country Towns*, 22 March 1950 (typescript).

cheap. The Act which emerged was considerably less effective than it might have been if it had offered help on the scale that had been suggested by the T.C.P.A. and others. In addition the political problems of town expansion blocked its implementation in several places so the policy only had a very limited impact. But in Swindon there was a very wide measure of agreement on the need for expansion and a willingness to carry it out, even though the resources available to do it were slim.

Even before the Bill was presented to Parliament the Town Clerk had consulted the Ministry of Housing and Local Government and had, with its approval, contacted Tottenham Borough Council with a view to receiving population from this borough. There was no prospect of firms moving from the area but this was not of immediate importance as there were vacancies at Vickers at the time. A scheme would, however, enable the new sewers to be built and the land available in the Walcot area of Swindon to be opened up for development, and as these houses became available, it would doubtless be possible to attract decentralizing industry from other areas. While this new estate was being built Londoners could be housed immediately on the Penhill Estate, which was then being built. These ideas received approval from the Town Council and more detailed studies were rapidly undertaken. The subcommittee appointed to carry out these studies reported to the Council in January 1952 that, subject to agreement with the local planning authority, the Minister of Housing and Local Government was prepared to accept that Swindon should be expanded to receive population and industry from London. The Council resolved to approve the policy of expansion for Swindon and approved, in general terms, an outline plan for twenty years and an initial six year plan that had been submitted by the committee. It also decided to write to the Wiltshire County Council, the local planning authority, to ask for their agreement to an expansion of the size indicated in the plans. These plans had suggested that some 1200 acres within the Borough at Walcot plus another 1500 acres outside the Borough be developed, to give the town a total population at the end of twenty years of somewhere around 120 000. This figure was desirable because it was calculated that it would enable the engineering sector of the town's economy to be so diluted that it would not provide more than one-third of the total employment available. The programme aimed at an eventual building rate of 1000 houses per year.

The extent of this programme and the speed at which it had been advanced created a furore outside the town, although there was a wide agreement on its wisdom within the borough. In particular the County Council felt that it had been ignored and the following few months were taken up with difficult negotiations with it. While these were occurring, preliminary physical plans were produced and visits were made to new towns to find out what their problems were, how they managed to attract industry, and on what terms factories were sold or leased. The Town Clerk talked to several large building firms and got assurance that they would be willing to build in the town. Approaches were made to the L.C.C. for the eventual export of people and firms from their area. At the same time a draft agreement was worked out with Tottenham under which Swindon would build houses for the London borough and seek re-imbursement for the cost incurred from the Ministry of Housing or, failing this, Tottenham would pay. Housing allocation and rents would be fixed by Swindon in consultation with Tottenham, who would also have the right to nominate such tenants as both parties to the agreement thought fit. This was to be the first of many similar agreements with London boroughs.

Following Swindon's letter to the County Council, the matter was put before the appropriate committee of the planning authority and little more was heard for some time. Eventually, after several anxious inquiries at the Ministry of Housing by Swindon, the Minister sent a letter to the County in June in response to their request for guidance, pointing out that he had approved the decision to expand in principle but had not approved any specific location or size for the expansion because this was a matter for the two councils to decide. Before giving final approval he wanted to hear the views of the County Council but remarked that it would be of benefit if the town expanded in order to diversify. This would also enable it to make a significant contribution to the problem of overspill. In view of the fact that he was replying to a request from the County for guidance, however, he mentioned that discussions had taken place with the Board of Trade and other departments and it was considered that an increase of population totalling about 26 000 overall giving a town of some 95 000 would be reasonable and involve the minimum of interference with agriculture. The letter also made it clear that the town was likely to attract yet more engineering industry because of its existing industrial structure. However the Board of Trade would also try to encourage other concerns such as chemical, food, and clerical firms to come to the town.

On 21 October 1952 the Clerk of the County Council sent a letter to the Town Clerk which finally gave consent to the expansion but on a reduced scale. The resolution of the planning committee was as follows, 'The Committee, having consulted Swindon Borough Council and the Highworth Rural District Council, are of the opinion that the ultimate population of the Borough of Swindon should be limited to 92 000 or such less figure as can be accommodated within the present borough boundary and that the building of houses by the Borough Council outside their boundary should be opposed.' The Borough Council replied that they had decided to proceed with the development on the scale allowed by the County but they could do no other than demur at the restriction imposed by the planning committee and were not disposed to argue this aspect of the matter at that time. They then resolved that 'Subject to satisfactory financial arrangements with the Government Departments expansion proceed within the boundary and in due course consideration be given to making any necessary objections when a detailed examination has been made of the County Development Plan.'[3] After this examination had been carried out the Council resolved that it would not object to the Development Plan at that time but it reserved the right to submit further expansion proposals if necessary in future.

This exchange was to set the tone for relationships between the Ministry, the County, the Rural Districts, and Swindon concerning town development. The Ministry, anxious to pursue town development but not at the cost of an outraged rural population (plus its Conservative M.P.s)[4] acted as mediator and tried to arrange a compromise. The County disliked expansion but felt that they had to bow to the

---

[3] Swindon Borough Council minutes. 28 October 1952.

inevitable, without giving way altogether. So far as the Rural Districts were concerned, at first theirs was an attitude of outright opposition, both to growth in itself and also to the possible extension of Swindon's boundaries that it implied. As we shall see the former of these attitudes was modified as the Rural Districts themselves began to benefit from growth. Swindon's attitude was clear. The Ministry was mainly motivated by the problems of the big cities but this was not Swindon's main priority. Town development offered the only hope of remedying the town's problems. The relief it gave to London's housing problems was valuable but it was, from Swindon's point of view, of secondary concern. The Town Clerk, who did more than any other single person to promote expansion, summed up the town's attitude to expansion. In a talk to a local group, he said 'To seek the advancement and prosperity of our town is a worthy ambition and deserves our best endeavours' and a few years later he described the motive which led the town to adopt the scheme as 'enlightened self interest'. In conclusion it is clear that attitudes to the scheme were to a large extent going to depend on the perspective of those who were making the judgement.

Population trends

As we have seen the shadow factories which settled in Swindon during the Second World War formed the basis for its postwar growth. This new employment stemmed the population decline which had occurred in the thirties. By the 1951 census the town showed a modest population increase over its 1931 level. However it was with the reception of families from London under the town development scheme that the second period of rapid growth in the town's history really began.

Table 2.1

Population growth: Swindon Municipal Borough 1931-66

Year	1931	1951	1961	1966
Population	62 401	68 670	91 739	98 410

Source: *Census Reports.*

---

[4] The Local Conservative MPs tried to lobby the Minister of Housing and Local Government to halt the Swindon scheme and also raised the matter in the Commons.

The population grew at an average annual rate of 3.3 per cent from 1951 to 1961, compared to a rate of about one per cent for Wiltshire and half a per cent for England and Wales. In the second intercensal period, from 1961 to 1966, the borough grew at an average annual rate of 1.4 per cent, the rates for Wiltshire and England and Wales respectively being similar to those in the preceding period. These statistics suggest that Swindon's expansion can be divided into two phases, an initial period of rapid growth and then a period of slackening growth. Examination of the Registrar General's mid-year estimates of population growth for these years clarifies this pattern. Growth was slow in the four years from 1951 to 1955, under 3500 in total during this period. Then, with the influx of newcomers, growth increased during the years 1955 to 1963 to an average annual figure of just over 3000. From 1963 onwards the population increased slowly, if at all. The period from 1955 to 1963 was the time when most of the newcomers arrived. This was the peak period for the development of the new local authority estates which housed them and much of the industry that employed them. By the end of this period there was very little land left within the then existing boundaries for any further public or private housing development or for the location of new industry. By 1961 Swindon had almost reached the limit that the County Council had placed on its future growth in 1952. As the Borough Council had never accepted that this limit was binding for all time and wanted to continue growth, they either had to extend their boundaries or promote growth outside them. The complex and difficult problems that this raised are discussed in Chapter 5.

The 'overspill' growth in the sub-region, here defined as the surrounding rural districts of Highworth and Cricklade and Wootton Bassett (see map, Figure 2.1), followed a rather different pattern.

Here the population grew at an average annual rate of 2.3 per cent during the fifties but at double this rate, 4.6 per cent during the first half of the sixties. Examination of data at ward level confirms that the growth of population in both periods was closely associated with the growth of the borough. Heavy population increases were mainly confined to those rural wards which had a common boundary with the town. Highworth Rural District, lying to the east of the town,

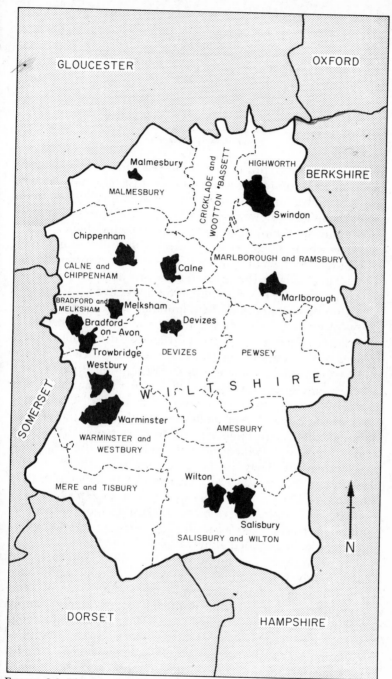

FIGURE 2.1 The location of Swindon, Highworth, and Cricklade within Wiltshire.

Table 2.2

Population growth: Highworth Rural District and Cricklade and Wootton Bassett Rural District 1951–66

1951	36 910
1961	45 603
1966	56 240

Source: *Census Reports.*

increased at the fastest rate. Within this district the parish of Stratton St Margaret showed major growth. Much of the new industry and a large amount of new housing is located here. After the initial inflow of population into the borough, mainly into public housing, there was a later demand for private housing which could not be met within Swindon's own boundaries. So new private estates were built just outside the town. This explains the accelerated growth of these areas in the latter part of the period which this book covers.

Within the town most of the population increase has been in the peripheral areas, where most of the newcomers settled. The pattern for the early period differed in detail but is likely to have been generally similar. There was very little clearance and housing redevelopment in the existing built-up area. Nor are there any signs that the already existing housing stock was used any more intensively because of expansion. Occupancy rates in the central areas of the town fell during the period, although there were some signs in the late sixties that young owner occupiers were moving into these areas. This development is likely to be accelerated by the Council's declaration of General Improvement Areas under the 1969 Housing Act. The central areas were found, in a special survey done in 1967, to have very high concentration of old people. This might be expected from the facts derived from the survey of population mentioned above.

The promise of a new house and a new job is likely to appeal most strongly to the young, in particular to couples who have started having a family or who are about to do so and consequently face all the problems of obtaining family accommodation in the metropolis. All the new and expanding towns have had an intake in which young families predominated and they have all experienced rapidly increasing birth rates, falling death rates, and therefore a large 'natural' population increase. This situation creates particular problems concerning the development of the social services. The difficulties that Swindon faced are discussed in Chapter 3. Table 2.3 shows that the birth rate in Swindon, initially only slightly above that for England and Wales, increased sharply through the fifties. Note that the really dramatic rise did not occur until after 1955, when the town development scheme was well under way. This rise then levelled off in the sixties, after the main period of expansion within the borough had ceased. In this latter period the rural districts had birth rates which were as high, or higher, than Swindon, as the following table shows.

Table 2.3

Swindon and surrounding areas: crude birth rates 1961-66 Live births per thousand population

Year	Swindon M.B.	Cricklade and Wootton Bassett, R.D.	Highworth R.D.	Wiltshire C.C.	England and Wales
1952	15.2	18.2	16.5	15.3	15.3
1953	16.8	21.3	17.8	16.4	15.5
1954	16.3	17.8	16.5	15.9	15.2
1955	16.1	19.2	16.1	15.8	15.0
1956	18.6	18.0	16.6	16.0	15.7
1957	20.0	19.7	16.1	17.0	16.1
1958	19.9	18.3	18.5	17.4	16.4
1959	21.2	18.0	18.6	17.7	16.5
1960	22.6	17.9	20.1	18.9	17.2
1961	21.8	17.6	20.8	19.1	17.4
1962	22.4	17.3	22.0	19.6	18.0
1963	21.3	20.9	22.8	20.2	18.5
1964	21.8	18.4	24.2	20.2	17.5
1965	20.7	19.4	24.6	19.7	17.3

Source: *Registrar General's Annual Returns*

Apart from the youthful nature of the population caused by the high birth rates there is also the fact, already mentioned, that immigrant parents are themselves young. No statistics are available to show this for the first period of expansion but since 1961 the Ministry of Housing and Local Government has collected details of migrants to new and expanding towns. Table 2.4 compares Swindon with four other expanding towns. The time periods are not identical but this is unlikely to affect the figures materially.

Table 2.4

Immigrant Structure: Swindon and other areas - local authority tenants

Age	Swindon	Haverhill	Banbury	Wellingborough	Andover	England and Wales
0-14	37.3	37.8	40.7	36.1	35.1	23.0
15-24	23.8	21.0	16.8	21.4	18.5	13.2
25-39	30.4	29.2	31.3	27.0	37.0	19.7
40-64	7.9	10.6	10.0	13.8	8.9	32.2
65+	0.6	1.4	1.2	1.7	0.5	11.9

Source: *Swindon Development Study No. 4: Population.*

Table 2.4 shows à preponderance of young immigrants and a lack of the older age groups. Swindon is very similar in the composition of its immigrant flow to the other four expanding towns. If anything it has a slightly younger composition than the others but too much should not be made of these small differences because of the varying time periods involved. According to the G.L.C., available evidence suggests that the peaks of imbalanced age structure are even sharper in the expanding than in the new towns. However studies of migrants to new towns in recent years (done for the proposed expansion of Ipswich) suggests that these towns had a preponderance of movers in the 20-24 age group.[5] Further examination of the Swindon data shows that it too had such a concentration, 20 per cent of all movers were in this age group. The Ipswich report found that there had been a shift in the composition of movers to Crawley. The greatest number of adult movers is now found in the 20–24 group whereas in earlier years it was the 24–29 group. This change was accompanied by an increase in the number of children under five and is attributed to the national trend towards earlier marriage and bears out the contention that the onset of marriage and children is a prime incentive behind the move to a new or expanded town. It seems likely that broadly similar trends took place in Swindon.

One advantage that an expanded town has over a new town is that the former usually has a large existing population. The heavily imbalanced age structure of the expanding town is therefore less evident than that of the new town. We will

---

[5] Source as for Table 2.4

return to this topic later but it should be mentioned here that the benefits of such a more balanced overall population composition may be largely illusory if all the younger people are concentrated in one or more areas within the town. Table 2.5 shows the overall age structure of Swindon's population in 1951, 1961, and 1966.

Table 2.5

Age Structure - Swindon Municipal Borough 1951, 1961, and 1966

Age Group	1951 %	1961 %	1966 %
0-14	21.9	27.2	27.0
15-25	12.1	12.3	13.0
25-39	21.9	22.5	18.0
40-64	32.3	28.1	29.0
65+	11.5	9.9	10.0

Source: *Census Report.*

The 1951 data show an age structure which is fairly close to the national average at that time. In contrast the figures for the two following censuses show that the percentage of children had increased quite considerably by 1961 and that this high level was maintained until 1966. Swindon was almost completely built up by 1966. The persistence of a high birth rate caused some surprise at this time because it was expected that the new families who had come to the town would stay where they had originally settled. Thus the proportion of children on the new estates would begin to fall. In fact many of the first families left the local authority estates after a few years and new families came into their vacant houses with their growing families. This process became very important as town development continued. We will discuss its implications further below.

Apart from the people who were housed in council dwellings a town such as Swindon which is growing also has to house considerable numbers of people in the private sector. These are mainly the senior and managerial staff of firms that move and also others, especially skilled men, who come to areas of major employment opportunity on their own initiative in order to find employment. The rapid growth in private

housing in the latter part of the expansion was partially a
result of this type of migration. It also grew because many
people moved into the owner-occupied sector from local
authority privately rented accommodation. As we have stated
much of this housing is located outside the borough, especially
in the Highworth Rural District and, to a lesser extent, in
Cricklade and Wootton Bassett Rural District. Census data
gives some clues as to the size and nature of the resulting
movements.

The 1961 Census only had migration tables covering those
who had moved within the last year. These showed that, even
at that time, the rate of immigration to Swindon was fairly low
at 66 persons per thousand population, compared with
Highworth and Cricklade – 106 and 109 per thousand
respectively. The outflows from Swindon and Highworth were
also low, 49 and 43 thousand respectively, but high from
Cricklade (85 per thousand) due to the movements of forces
personnel in that area. The migration balances for Swindon
and Cricklade, at 17 and 24 per thousand, were low but that
for Highworth was far greater, at 63 per thousand. By 1966,
over a five year period, Swindon was actually losing
population at a rate of 3 per thousand over the period.
(Comparison with the 1966 one-year data suggests that this
was an accelerating trend. Cricklade was gaining population
at a rate of 101 per thousand but the really outstanding
growth was in Highworth, which increased by 233 per
thousand. This was over twice as fast as any other county
district in Wiltshire. The rate of immigration to the rural
district was over twice the county average as well.

In 1961 about one-third of the immigrants to Swindon came
from Greater London, a similar proportion from the
surrounding counties (including the rest of Wiltshire), and
another third from elsewhere in England and Wales. Many of
the immigrants to Cricklade were in the army and came from
some distance but, even at this stage, almost half Highworth's
immigrants came from Greater London and a similar
proportion from other parts of England and Wales, excluding
the surrounding counties. Over a third of the people leaving
Swindon moved to Highworth and a smaller proportion went
to Cricklade. By this stage just over 50 per cent of Highworth's
immigrants came from Swindon. However, few of the
newcomers to the rural districts came directly from London. It

seems that the normal pattern has been a move from some distance to Swindon, followed by a shorter move out of the borough to the rural areas after a few years.

Table 2.6

Swindon Further Expansion Group: Household Survey 1970 - Tenure of Movers

Present (1)	Owner (2) %	Council rented (3) %	Private rented (4) %	Forces (5) %	Tied to job (6) %	Other (7) %	All movers (8) %
Present tenure by previous tenure							
Previously owner	43.0	8.2	8.3	—	9.5	28.6	27.6
Council	30.4	51.1	13.1	—	14.3	14.3	37.1
Private	17.6	31.6	70.5	—	19.0	14.3	25.5
Forces	2.5	1.8	—	—	—	—	2.1
Tied to job	3.5	3.5	4.9	—	52.4	14.3	4.4
Other	2.9	3.6	3.2	—	4.8	28.6	3.3
Previous tenure by previous but one tenure							
Previous but one owner	51.9	8.2	11.2	16.7	8.4	16.7	
Council	20.3	36.7	8.7	—	16.7	50.0	
Private	21.5	45.9	67.5	33.3	41.6	16.7	
Forces	1.3	—	2.5	50.0	—	—	
Tied to job	2.5	6.1	8.7	—	33.3	—	
Other	2.5	6.1	1.3	—	—	16.7	

Unfortunately the census does not give details of the tenure changes of movers but the 1966 census does show that 84 per cent of all those who moved into Highworth in the five-year period were owner occupiers, the figure for Cricklade is 49 per cent, whereas only 32 per cent of the movers into Swindon were owner occupiers and 54 per cent moved into local authority housing. A survey of households in Swindon and the surrounding areas helps to confirm the patterns of movement outlined above. This work was done in 1970 but questions were asked about moves within the previous nine years. The survey shows that considerable numbers of immigrants who came to the area through the official G.L.C./L.C.C. channels had ended up, some years later, in private housing (28.8 per cent). Rather more of those who had moved with their firms, 39.2 per cent, owned their houses. This might be expected, as this latter category included management. Incidentally the sample found that twice as many people had moved to the town with

their firms as had come through the official scheme. Questions
about their previous tenures were also asked for those people
who had moved into the area within the past nine years and
had since moved at least twice. Table 2.6 sets out the results.

The total sample consisted of 61 per cent owner occupiers,
32 per cent local authority renters, 6 per cent private renters,
and 1 per cent other tenures. Of these 36 per cent had moved
at least once in the previous nine years. By comparison with
column 8 of Table 2.6 it can be seen that disproportionate
numbers of council tenants and private renters made a move
and far fewer owner occupiers moved than would be expected
if one assumed that all tenures had an equal propensity to
move. The high rate of movement among private renters is no
surprise. In a town such as Swindon, where this sector is small,
it serves as a temporary device for housing newly married
couples and new arrivals waiting for local authority housing or
to buy their own homes. Table 2.6 shows that 17.6 per cent of
those who moved to their own homes came from this sector
and that 31.6 per cent of those who moved into council
property were previously private renters.

The local authority movers are more interesting; 30.4 per
cent of all those who bought their own homes came from the
council sector. The survey does not trace distances or
directions moved within the area but it is likely that a high
proportion of these former tenants moved off the Swindon
estates into the surrounding rural districts. Eight per cent of
the sample had moved twice. Again substantial percentages of
those who then moved into their own homes came from the
council and privately rented sectors (20.3 per cent and 21.5
per cent respectively). These movements had important
implications for the social structure of the town which we shall
refer to in more detail later.

Housing development

Table 2.7 sets out the housing record for Swindon from 1953-5
to 1965-6.

The outline housing programme which had been proposed
when expansion began bore little relationship to what actually
happened. The programme aimed at gradual build up of
local authority housing to an annual output of 1000 houses by

Table 2.7

Swindon Housing Record

Year	1953/4	1954/5	1955/6	1956/7	1957/8	1958/9	1959/60
Local authority houses	589	700	754	1197	778	478	560
Private houses	87	149	196	194	364	317	326
Total	676	849	950	1391	1142	795	886

Year	1960/1	1961/2	1962/3	1963/4	1964/5	1965/6
Local authority houses	507	693	312	393	611	27
Private houses	436	359	268	139	65	30
Total	943	1052	580	532	676	57

Source: *Swindon Borough Council Records*

1957. This rate would then be maintained for five years, by which time all the expected overspill would be housed. In fact the expected output was exceeded in 1956/7 but production then dropped well below the expected levels in succeeding years and never again reached the 1000 mark. Of course housing output was tied to the inflow of population and this in turn to the new jobs coming to the town or being created by the growth of existing industry.

It is the management of this relationship which is at the core of any town development scheme and is therefore a major theme of this study. The initial programme could only be an idealized picture of possible future progress. The national economic recessions in 1957/8 and 1961/2 affected the rate of increase of jobs in the town and led to a reduction in housing output. As Table 2.7 shows this effect only became apparent about a year later in each case. Also the fall in railway employment (in the 1960s) meant that many of the new jobs went to existing inhabitants of the town who did not of course, require new houses. Because of the time it takes to build, a reduction in starting new houses only reflected in a fall in completions some time afterwards. Reduction in the rate of private housing completions may also be noted in Table 2.7.

The outline programme was for a total of 7750 local authority dwellings by 1961. In practice only 5563 houses were built in this period and only about 13 000 of the 19 600 people that it was proposed to take from London had been housed. This target was not reached until the end of 1965. At this point the programmed number of local authority houses was also completed. The delay was primarily due to the rate at which it had been possible to create new jobs for Londoners in the town. At the expected occupancy rate of 3.5 persons per house the plan proposed to accommodate 27 125 persons from all sources during the expansion, i.e. from London via the I.S.S., key workers from London, and elsewhere, and local applicants. The statistics suggest that far more people than this were actually housed by the local authority stock though. Apart from the 19 600 Londoners housed by 1965, there were 5552 key workers housed from elsewhere and approximately 22 000 persons were also housed from the local list. So approximately 47 000 people were housed in a stock of council housing originally intended for some 27 000.[6] The reason for this apparent contradiction was that a large number of the houses were let several times over to successive tenants. To some extent this phenomenon should have been recognized as a possibility when the initial plan was drawn up, although the number of relets in the existing stock at that time was minute, but the sharp rise in the rate of relets (percentage of relets to total dwellings rose from almost nothing to over 8 per cent at the end of the period) could not have been foreseen. It was this change which made the need to increase the local authority stock of declining importance as expansion proceeded. It will be referred to again in Chapter 3. This unexpected growth in the stock available for letting was one of the main reasons why an important change occurred in the Borough's housing policy in the early sixties, when the emphasis moved away from the production of more family housing for rent towards the replacement of temporary housing and building more for special and local needs, especially old people.

---

[6] These calculations are based on local authority estimates made for the Registrar General's Annual Population estimates.

The acquisition of the whole of the Walcot area for development marked the start of the first phase of policy, a rapid acceleration of the already large programme of public housing for overspill and local needs. The area was divided up into three neighbourhoods for local authority tenants, Walcot, Park North, and Park South. Each contained between 1500 and 1950 houses and they were cut off from two areas of private housing, the Lawn and West Walcot estates, by a major spine road, Queens Drive (see map, Figure 2.2). This road acted as an effective social and physical barrier between tenants and owner occupiers. Despite the concern the Council expressed about the integration of Londoners and Swindonians on the local authority estates it was unwilling to attempt to mix the classes, as some new towns had done.

At the completion of the Penhill estate in mid-1955 the contractors moved on to Walcot, followed by Park South a year later and Park North one year after that. The mounting of such a large programme presented special problems. Apart from the difficult nature of the terrain, being blue clay it became easily water-logged and unworkable, and there were endless problems of labour supply. The need for very close coordination between the builders, the direct labour site works force, and the statutory undertakers was paramount if houses were to be handed over in time to meet the growing demand from industry. Great flexibility was also required as the demand for houses rose and fell with changing economic conditions. Three major contractors built for Swindon at the start. However only one of these, John Laing and Co, could consistently meet the demands placed upon them and so they did an increasing proportion of the work. Their main house type, the Easiform house, is a rationalized traditional design made by pouring concrete into metal shutters erected on site and then building within this shell an inner wall of breeze blocks. Attempts were made to vary this style by the use of brick fronts etc, and also by building some traditional brick houses and multi-storey flats and by varying lay-outs, but the need for speed dictated the process and is probably responsible for a certain monotony in some parts of the estates today. Also the Ministry insisted on extensive use of non-traditional building — two-thirds of all Swindon's postwar housing is of this type — and would only allow a very limited degree of variation in designs in any one contract.

Partly because so many of the families housed were with children, or likely to have them soon after moving in, production was concentrated on three-bedroom houses. The argument was that 'compared with a two-bedroom dwelling the additional cost of providing an extra bedroom is outweighed by the social benefit that this confers'.[7]

Table 2.8

*Swindon Municipal Borough. Characteristics of the total local
authority housing stock 31 March 1966*

Type	Numbers	Percentage	Bedrooms	Numbers	Percentage
Houses	7745	77	1	804	8
Flats	1793	18	2	2746	27
Maisonettes	195	2	3	6397	63
Purpose built Old People's Dwellings	367	4	4	153	1.5

Source: *See footnote.*

The small number of one-bedroom houses was justifiable at a time when families were being housed but it meant that single people and couples, be they old or young, had a rather poor chance of being housed. This became a matter of some concern, especially when the number of old people in the town grew. The very small numbers of four bedroom houses available was always a problem but one that seemed difficult to solve in a mass production housing programme.

The vast majority of movers to Swindon and local applicants preferred a house to a flat but rather a large proportion of flats were built, for a number of reasons. Most of these flats are in low-rise three- or four-storey blocks introduced onto the estates in order to raise densities and also because they were quick to produce at a time when demand was high. In addition some multi-storey blocks were put up for the above reasons and also because of a belief that something was needed to add drama and a focal point to large areas of low housing. Unfortunately these flats have been less appreciated by their occupants than by the architects.

---

[7] Swindon Expansion Project Joint Steering Committee. *Swindon. A Study For Further Expansion* (Swindon, 1968) page 108, para. 21.16.

By about 1960 the first neighbourhood to be started, Walcot, was nearing completion and Park South and North only had about two years' building work left on them. In 1959 industrial demand seemed to be recovering and the need for more land for council houses and jobs became a major issue. At the same time the two private enterprise neighbourhoods, Walcot West and Lawn, were virtually full up and more land was needed for private housing. The subsequent negotiations to open up the land to the east of the borough are described in Chapter 5. By the time this was becoming available the council's housing policy had changed. The recession of 1966 slowed down incoming industry and the rising rate of relets in council housing meant that the reduced flow of newcomers could be housed in them with increasing ease as time went on. As Table 8.2 shows there was also a growing number of houses available for local needs. The most pressing demand was for more private housing. Eventually, the land to the east (North Dorcan) was used for this purpose and for the new Greenbridge industrial estate.

This changed situation first became apparent to the Council in 1962. At the same time two domestic problems faced them. The first was the existence of a number of old wartime temporary buildings on sites within the borough. These had tended to be used as a dumping ground for problem families and this had not improved their already dilapidated condition, nor the situation of many of these families either. Another problem was the growing number of old people who needed small and sometimes purpose-built accommodation. The renewal of the town centre also began to displace people, many of whom were aged. In the first hectic phase of expansion there had been little chance to clear unfit housing or build more for the old but now the housing programme could concentrate on doing these two things. Neither of them required the use of new land outside the borough, as they involved the redevelopment of existing sites and a certain amount of infill.

At the same time the Council resolved to take what measures they could to encourage owner occupation. This would meet the already apparent demand and would also, if the Council could help marginal buyers, release more council houses for newcomers. The development of the Nythe Estate on the North Dorcan area from 1963 onwards by speculative builders helped to meet the demand from those who could afford the normal deposits and repayment terms required by the general run of building societies. The houses built varied from fairly expensive and well-designed ones down to the cheapest that private enterprise could produce, with standards well below the Parker Morris level. Even these houses were beyond the means of many would-be buyers and so two new policies were introduced to help the situation.

Ever since 1924 the Council had advanced money for house purchase, at first under the Small Dwelling Acquisition Acts and later under various Housing Acts. From this time until 1963, 1500 loans costing £1 360 000 had been given and at the end of the period there were 570 outstanding accounts. These figures show that only moderate use had been made of this scheme but in the early sixties the number of loans granted rose rapidly as more people began to own their own houses in and around the town. Thus well over a third of all the loans granted under the Housing Acts were made available in the three years 1960-63. The amount lent doubled during this period and further increases were expected. At first this rapid growth in lending worried councillors who had had a long history of financial prudence. Despite the fact that there had only been one repossession, as long ago as 1929, they asked the Treasurer to report the possibility of imposing a limit on future advances in case the then current downturn in employment led to a series of mortgage defaults. On the contrary the Treasurer argued that the risks to the Council were minimal, as the property could always be resold or let at no loss to the Council. He urged an expansion of the scheme in line with the new housing policy of the Council, which was to encourage owner occupation. 'A scheme of housing advances is, however, only one element in the solution of the Council of its problems as a housing authority, and members will be aware that each loan made for house purchase means in effect one less house to be built by the Council for letting, and each house built brings an additional burden on public funds for subsidy which would rise substantially if too many houses to let are provided. The Housing Committee at their meeting on the 12 June 1962 decided to revise their policy in relation to the provision of houses for letting and to place emphasis on the provision of houses for sale. Furthermore it was suggested that there should be improved facilities for obtaining advances on mortgage.'

The Treasurer's advocacy changed the Committee's mind and the scheme was liberalized to allow for thirty-five years repayment periods and maximum advances of 99 per cent on cheaper property and 90 per cent on more expensive property. The subsequent rapid expansion of housing loans can be judged from the fact that £1 116 000 was allocated to this purpose from the end of 1963 to the end of 1965.

The most novel departure in policy was the decision to, in effect, make the Council into a private enterprise developer. The officers had always opposed the sale of council houses (an issue raised by councillors in the early fifties and again now) but, instead, suggested this new policy. The idea was that the Borough should commission firms of builders to erect for them an estate of houses on an area of North Dorcan, to a layout and specifications drawn up by the Council's planners and architects. The Borough would then market these houses. Anyone who was a tenant, paying maximum rent and therefore able to afford the cost involved, or an applicant on the housing waiting list who appeared to be similarly qualified or who would be eligible to be a tenant under the town development scheme, could apply for one of the houses. If successful, they could deposit as little as £25 and repay over thirty-five years. Perhaps surprisingly this example of a local authority taking the place of private enterprise was approved by the then Conservative Government and a first stage of 156 houses went ahead. Because the scheme was done under the Housing Acts and the loan sanction and debt formed a part of the Housing Revenue Account, the Ministry insisted on a higher standard for the houses that the private developer would have required. However, because the Corporation did not aim to make a profit and because it combined the roles of several of the middle men in the private enterprise process, the houses could actually be offered at a lower price than those available from private builders. Naturally these could be expected to object if the policy was carried out on a large scale but in Swindon they accepted that there was a need that they could not meet and did not object to a modest scheme. The public reaction was wholly favourable. There had to be a ballot to allocate the first houses as there were 788 valid applications for the 156 houses. The prices varied from £2250 for a semi-detached two-bedroom bungalow to £2725 for a three-bedroomed semi-detached house. In addition a wide

range of extras was available. The houses were arranged on
the Radburn pattern around a twelve-acre park and the
designs selected were produced by a builder who was expert in
providing for the private rather than the local authority
market.

The policy satisfied a number of requirements. It reduced
the length of the waiting list by providing a viable alternative
for some of those on it. It also freed some council houses for
other applicants and it met a growing demand from those
newcomers, mainly skilled workers, who could afford to buy
on moving to the town. In the view of the Borough Architect
and the Planning Officer the quality and layout of some of the
new private enterprise housing on the Nythe Estate was
appalling and they felt that the new houses would, by their
example, help to raise standards. The scheme was self-
financing and a provision that if people left before they had
occupied their house for five years they must offer it to the
Council at the price they paid, plus the cost of improvements,
so that it could then be resold at current market value under
the same terms to a new purchaser, meant that it would even
produce a small profit for the ratepayers. The purchasers got
good-quality housing at minimum price, and if at any time
they could prove hardship, arrangements were made for them
to pay only the interest element of the loans until their
problems were resolved. The first scheme proved to be such a
success that further stages were started. By 1969, 850 houses
were sold and the Covingham Estate was completed.

The impact of Swindon's development on the surrounding
areas was most evident in the case of housing. Much of the new
private housing required by those working in the town was
built in the rural districts. On the other hand most of the new
local authority houses were in Swindon. Of the 9358 local
authority houses erected in the subregion between 1953 and
1966, 7527 were in Swindon. Of the 9614 private houses built
in the same period only 2981 were in Swindon and 4797 were
in Highworth Rural District.[8] This distribution of public and
private housing reinforced the level of social and political
polarization between the town and the surrounding areas

---

[8] Swindon Expansion Project Joint Steering Committee. *Swindon. A
Study For Further Expansion*, Appendix D. Table 5, page 148.

which, as we have seen, was so much a feature of Swindon's past.

Industrial development

Reference has already been made to the attempts by the Council to diversify the industrial structure of the town in the immediate prewar and postwar periods and the reasons why these efforts met with little success. The Distribution of Industry Act 1945 implemented the recommendations of the Barlow Commission and instituted, via the system of industrial development certificates, control over the location of mobile industry. So unsuccessful was Swindon in obtaining industrial development certificates that, by the time expansion started in 1954, the Corporation's Cheney Manor industrial estate presented the following picture.

Total area of the estate	74 acres
Stage 1 development	34 acres
Sites available	75 acres
Sites disposed	3 acres

The situation was not as gloomy as these statistics might suggest because the factories which moved to the town during the war, or had expanded then, had an unsatisfied demand for labour. The result was that at the start of 1954 there were about 1000 male jobs available in the town. Therefore it was possible to start receiving overspill population before any new firms had agreed to come to the town. The subsequent development of the industrial structure of the town can best be followed by reference to Table 2.9.[9]

We have noted already that the history of the expansion seems to divide into two periods, from the early fifties to the end of that decade and then a second phase in the sixties. The first phase contained the really rapid expansion of the town and the second phase was mainly one of consolidation. A

---

[9] Table 2.9 is based on records held by the local employment exchange rather than census data. It covers the area of that exchange which included Swindon and its subregion and therefore presents a more realistic picture of the employment available in the area than a census-based table which would only cover the town itself. Additionally the alterations made in the occupational classification between 1951 and 1961 make it difficult to compare census data from those years anyway.

Table 2.9

Employment Structure, Swindon Exchange Area, 1949, 1959, and 1965

Industries	1949 Nos	%	1959 Nos	%	1965 Nos	%	1965 % Great Britain %
Extractive	2920	7	2906	5	2305	3	5
Metal manufacturer		0	47	0	1	0	2.7
Engineering and Elect.	3905	9	8394	15	11 721	17.3	9.8
Metal Goods (other)	34	0	21	0	610	1	3.4
Total eng. and elect.	3939	9	8462	15	12 332	18.3	15.9
Vehicles	12 494	29	16 886	30	14 690	21.8	3.7
Food, Drink, Tobacco	1603	4	1241	2	1497	2.2	3.5
Chemicals	4	0	95	0	73	0.1	2.2
Textiles	163	0	281	0	151	0.2	3.3
Leather and Fur	4	0	72	0	95	0.1	2.3
Clothing and Footwear	1083	2	923	2	1124	1.7	
Bricks	227	1	147	0	194	0.3	1.8
Timber and Furniture	231	1	245	0	853	1.2	1.3
Paper and Printing	202	0	377	1	579	0.9	2.7
Office Manufacture	77	0	301	1	420	0.6	1.5
Total other manufactured goods	3594	8	3682	6	4986	7.3	18.6
TOTAL ALL MANUFACTURED GOODS	20 027	46	29 030	51	32 008	47	38
Construction	2330	5	2888	7	5058	7.5	7.2
Gas, Electricity, and water	679	2	977	2	1191	1.8	1.8
Total	3009	7	4865	9	6249	9.3	9
Transport and communication	6307	14	4402	8	2737	4.1	7
Distribution	4256	10	4868	9	7686	11.4	12.8
Other services	7107	16	11 070	19	16 127	24.2	28.2
TOTAL SERVICES	20 679	47	25 205	44	32 799	49	57
Not classified	80	0	8	0	341	0.5	
TOTAL INSURED POPULATION	43 706	100	57 149	100	67 453	100	

Source: *Employment exchange records*

rather similar picture emerges from the study of industrial development in the town. The initial period, when jobs were available at existing firms, enabled a start to be made on expansion. However this was no long-term substitute for the attraction of new industries. The attempts made at this time to persuade firms to move were time consuming and largely fruitless. After some initial confusion, when it appeared that the Board of Trade had no specific policy for expanding towns, industrial development certificates were available for London firms who wished to move to Swindon. Unfortunately very few of them were prepared to move so far away from their previous location. In 1957 the Town Clerk prepared a list of twenty-two firms that had been introduced to the Council by the L.C.C. in the previous three and a half years. Of these only two finally decided to move to the town. The Clerk concluded by noting that L.C.C. representatives had visited the town in October 1956 and were 'pressed for further industry but no prospects held out'. By this time economic conditions were beginning to worsen so the few firms that might initially have moved from London were no longer likely to do so.

The original goals of the Town Development Act were to reduce population and industry in London and other cities. Because of the difficulties which have been referred to the Swindon scheme never really made a contribution to the second goal. The firms that moved to the town came from other areas, or they were new branches of firms which already existed elsewhere and were expanding. Existing firms in the town also expanded and provided new jobs. The crucial breakthrough came in 1955 when the Pressed Steel Company decided to site their new car body plant on the Parsonage Farm site, an area immediately to the west of the town in Highworth Rural District Council (see Figure 2.2). The firm had arrived at this decision by themselves but Swindon put pressure on the Board of Trade to agree to the move and the town development scheme was used to provide workers and houses. Plesseys also set up three new processes in factories on the Cheney Manor Estate during this period and Vickers continued to expand their aircraft works at South Marston as well. These three firms formed the hard core of the new expansion and diversification of Swindon's industry. In their wake many smaller firms followed. Some of them, such as the firms which packed and transported the car bodies that

Pressed Steel produced, were tied to one or other of these three large companies. Others were attracted by the fact that workers were readily available and they could move into new specially designed factories. They could build factories themselves, lease them, or buy them on mortgage from the Corporation. It needed a decision by one or two large firms to locate in Swindon before the smaller ones would take the risk. However, after Pressed Steel came and Vickers and Plesseys began to expand, the next few years were ones of rapid expansion.

Comparison of the years 1949 and 1959 in Table 2.9 (page 84) shows the effect of these developments on the industrial structure. Although Swindon was an engineering town in 1949 these skills were almost entirely concentrated in the Great Western Railway works. Only 9 per cent of the area workforce was in the engineering and electrical sector in 1949. In contrast in 1959, because of the influx of firms mentioned above, there had been some diversification of engineering employers and 15 per cent of the workforce were in this sector. The Great Western Railway workshops still employed about 12 000 people but the number of employees, though not the percentage, in the vehicles sector had increased because of the arrival of Pressed Steel and the Vickers expansion. Originally it had been thought that much of the new industry, which it was assumed would come from London, would be in the 'other manufacturing' sector. Industries such as timber and furniture, paper and printing, food, drink and tobacco, and chemicals were expected to move to the town. As can be seen this did not happen. The two other major changes in the ten-year period were an expansion of construction, because of the increased rate of building in the area, and a fall in the percentage of workers in the transport and communications industries. This latter change was a result of the first phase of reduction of railway activity. There were far fewer operating staff in Swindon in 1959 than in 1949. Service industry in the town was particularly under-represented. The changes brought about by expansion in the first period actually increased this imbalance so that, by 1959, the percentage of the workforce in manufacturing had risen to 51 per cent, from 46 per cent in 1949.

Most of the new industries, apart from Pressed Steel, were located on the Cheney Manor Industrial Estate. By 1959 almost 800 000 square feet of factory space had been built. Twelve firms were in operation and a further three were about to start operation. In all almost one million square feet of factory space was built or in the pipeline. This meant that approximately four-fifths of the available space was used up and there was an urgent need to open up new estates. As in the case of housing, industrial development was spreading over the boundary into the rural districts.

After Pressed Steel bought their site at Parsonage Farm the rest of the farm, of about 48 acres, was offered for sale at auction. Swindon's chance of getting the Ministry to agree to issue loan sanction so that the town could buy this land was non-existent as Cheney Manor was at that time (in 1955) far from full. Therefore a decision was made to buy the land out of revenue with the hope of getting the necessary sanctions to install basic services at a later date. This succeeded because the Ministry, despite the fact that its hand had been forced, eventually allowed the land to be developed. It was quickly sold or leased to three large firms, two of whom were connected with the packing and transporting of the car bodies produced by Pressed Steel on the adjacent site. Parsonage Farm, which was also of course outside the borough, could not therefore make any further contribution to solving the problem of shortage of industrial land which arose at the end of the fifties.

It was at this point that the negotiations over the land to the east of the borough referred to in the section above occurred. Eventually a site of 84 acres on the northern boundary of this site (see Figure 2.2) was designated for the new Greenbridge industrial estate. This provided the location for a great deal of the growth of the town during the second phase of expansion in the sixties. This growth differed from that which had gone before. Much new employment continued to be created by the expansion of firms which had moved to the town in the fifties. However no firms came of the size of Pressed Steel. The new firms that did come were of a rather different nature.

Table 2.9 (page 84) shows the changes that occurred between 1959 and 1965. During these years economic conditions were unsettled and the declining fortunes of some of Swindon's industries created major problems for the town. Many of the new jobs which came to Swindon were needed to replace old

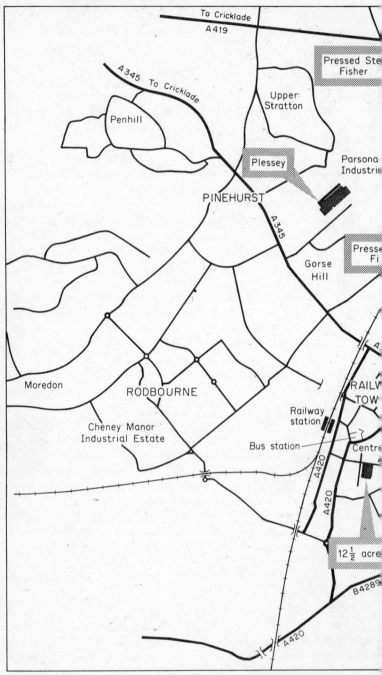

FIGURE 2.2 Swindon and surrounding districts.

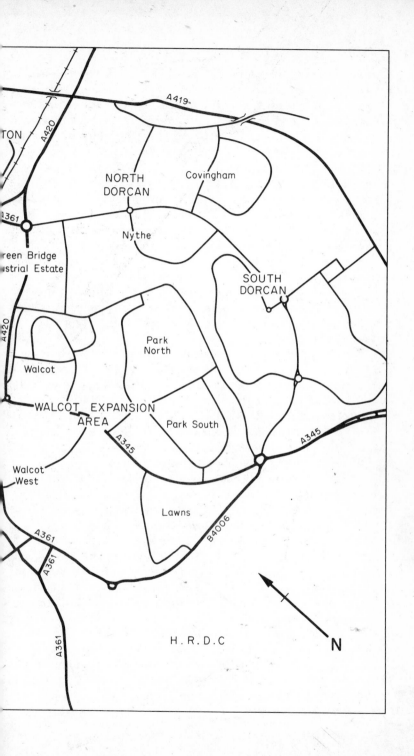

ones that were vanishing. These changes will be discussed in more detail in Chapter 4 but the two main changes deserve mention here. With the run down of the defence industry there were fears of heavy redundancies at the Vickers works. In fact this was avoided by the phasing out of aircraft production at the works and a rapid diversification into more general engineering. Eventually, in 1967, the works was reclassified under engineering rather than vehicles in official statistics, but the actual change occurred before this date. For many years Garrards had been making record player turntables in the town and they continued to expand steadily throughout the whole expansion period, latterly as a subsidiary of Plesseys. So by 1965 there had been a further modest growth in the engineering and electrical sector. Apart from the greater measure of stability this introduced, it could be argued that one of the goals of expansion, that of offering a wider range of employers for the skilled engineering workers, was being achieved.

By far the most serious problem in these years was the long awaited rundown of the railway works. As a byproduct of the Beeching Plan to rationalize British Railways operations, the works were re-organized in 1963/4 and railway carriage production discontinued. This resulted in the loss of 4000 jobs in a very short period, about two years. Despite the fact that some of the older workers retired early many new jobs were still required for the younger men. In this situation the importation of new workers from London under the town development scheme had to take second place. Unfortunately the railway's rundown coincided with the beginning of the period of national economic crisis that lasted into the 1970s, so conditions in other industries in the town were also difficult. In 1964 and 1965 there were some redundancies in the other industries in the town and also short-time working, for example at Pressed Steel. The fact that many of the major firms were only branch factories added to the general instability. When trade conditions were difficult the tendency for management to make efforts to rationalize and switch production round between factories in different parts of the country intensified. Labour was often redeployed but redundancies were also quite frequent. Also the growth of take-over bids and subsequent rationalization sometimes created unemployment.

The Greenbridge Estate mainly supplied jobs for those made redundant because of the trends outlined above. It also provided work for the large numbers of school leavers, the product of the young immigrant families, who were coming on to the job market for the first time. The new firms were difficult to attract, because of the uncertain economic conditions. Few were prepared to move and those that did were more heavily pressurized than ever before by the Board of Trade to move to development areas. A number of smaller engineering firms and some technologically advanced electronics firms came to the estate. Distribution firms began to show a greater interest in the town. Swindon's position, on a north/south route between the Midlands, Liverpool, and Southampton, and the imminent extension of the M4 motorway from London to Wales, made it a natural centre for their activities.

The result of all these changes can be seen in Table 2.9. In contrast with the previous period there was only a modest increase in the engineering and electrical sector and a decline, because of the railway redundancies, in the vehicles sector. Other manufacturing industry showed very little change from its share of employment in 1959 or 1949. Construction employment expanded numerically, but not as a percentage, and there was a further decline, related mainly to the railways again, in the transport and communications industries. The major developments occurred in distribution and other services. A great deal of the increased activity in these sectors was caused by the increased population which needed more shops, more local and central government officials, and so on. Between 1959 and 1965 the percentage of employees in the distribution and other services categories rose from 28 per cent to almost 36 per cent, far closer than Swindon had ever been before to the national average for these categories.

Social changes

We have seen how expansion affected the growth of population, housing, and industry in Swindon and referred in passing to some of the important features of these processes and some of the problems that will form the focal points of the following chapters. But how did all these changes affect the social structure of the town?[10]

Some of the basic features have already been mentioned, such as the age structure of the newcomers and the high birth rate that resulted. The typical pattern was revealed by a survey carried out by the Council in 1970. Most of the newcomers had small families, and the average size on arrival was 2.9. Then, over the next four or five years, the family grew rapidly, on average to slightly over four persons per household. It then stayed at this level for perhaps as long as ten years, by which time the eldest children were beginning to leave home. In social terms this meant that there were a large number of housebound mothers on the new estates and a large number of young children, although at first there were very few teenagers. We shall explore the implications of this situation in the next chapter.

One might expect that this biased immigration would result in significant changes in the overall distribution of household sizes in the town. Table 2.10 sets out the figures for 1951, 1961, and 1966 respectively.

While there was a slight growth in the proportion of medium-sized families, the most noticeable trends are some growth in the proportion of large families and the increase in one person families. This gives the clue to what happened.

---

[10] Only fragmentary sources are available for this section and for part of Chapter 3. Apart from census data, which contains little of real interest and is further nullified by the lack of comparability between 1951 and 1961 data, much reliance has been put on interviews with local officials, the files of the Council's social development section, and other documentary sources.

Interviews of key individuals were helpful but they usually added little to what could be gained from these sources. Most people do not keep personal records of what is happening to them and are only able to recollect past events in very general terms. Very often one would hear an identical and inaccurate story from several different sources which also suggest that, after some time, an accepted version of events evolves and differences which may actually have existed get forgotten. What is lacking is any real knowledge of how face-to-face social relationships were altered, if at all, by development. In some other expanding towns there was considerable conflict created by the changes that occurred; in Swindon there is very little evidence that this happened beyond a handful of discontented letters to local newspapers on the basis of which it is not possible to make any generalizations.

Table 2.10

Household size Swindon Municipal Borough 1951, 1961 and 1966 (percentage).

Year			Household size (persons)			
	1	2	3	4	5	6 or more
1951	7.8	29.5	26.5	19.5	9.5	7.5
1961	8.1	27.9	23.6	21.7	11.1	7.5
1966	10.0	28.0	22.0	21.5	10.3	8.2

Source: *Census Reports.*

The influx of young families was offset by the growing numbers of old people in the town as a result of a naturally ageing population structure. This demand was added to, after some years had passed, by overspill families who wanted council accommodation for their aged parents, so that they might move from London and be near their sons and daughters. The proportion of old people in smaller households rose especially quickly towards the end of our period. Thus the percentage of one- and two-person households which contained persons of pensionable age or over rose from 49.7 to 55.1 between 1961 and 1966. This ageing of population went almost unnoticed for many years while the Council, as we shall see in the next chapter, concentrated on the immediate problem of trying to satisfy the social needs of a young and growing population.

Turning now to the effects that expansion had on the social class and socio-economic structure of the town, Table 2.11 compares the social class distribution in 1951 and 1966.

In 1951 Swindon was overwhelmingly a town of skilled workers, as one would expect given the dominance of the engineering industry in the town. In a sense the social structure was highly concentrated, being mainly upper working class. It was particularly lacking in the professional middle class or, indeed, the less well-qualified and lower earning members of that class. By 1966 there had been some changes in this picture. Although the predominance of skilled workers remained, the percentage of the upper middle class had almost doubled. Many firms had arrived in the town, bringing not only new manual workers but new managers and professional workers as well. Also the growing town required many new people in this group to carry out the sort of work that the smaller railway town did not generate.

Table 2.11

Social class distribution of economically active males, Swindon Municipal Borough 1951 and 1966 (percentage)[11]

Social Class	1951 Swindon	1951 England and Wales	1966 Swindon	1966 England and Wales
1. Professional	1.8	3.2	3.4	4.1
2. Intermediate	10.1	14.3	9.8	14.6
3. Skilled	62.1	53.4	54.1	49.1
4. Partly Skilled	12.4	16.2	23.1	22.3
5. Unskilled	13.6	12.9	9.6	8.0

Source: *Census Reports.*

There was also a decline in the unskilled working class. This was very much in line with declining opportunities for such people in the national economy over this period. Swindon also shared a national trend towards a blurring of the skilled/semiskilled distinction. Many of the new industries no longer required the old form of apprenticeship training, stretching over several years and producing a skilled man at the end of the process, but only gave some rather limited form of job training. While the unskilled still tend to have less status than anyone else, there is also no sign, in the Swindon context at least, that the semi-skilled/skilled distinction has much social or economic reality any longer. In this respect the town has probably changed because, when the railway was the only

---

[11] The social class distribution — which has been a feature of successive censuses since 1911 — is simply a regrouping of the occupational classification into a smaller number of broad groups. The basic criterion on which the allocation is made is 'the general standing within the community of the occupations concerned'. According to the Registrar General the 1966 groupings follow the same general lines as previously 'although the allocations of occupations to the five groups have varied from census to census in accordance with changes in economic conditions and with the intention of preserving the gradient rather than the literal continuity' (Office of Population Censuses and Surveys. *Classification of Occupations 1970* (London: H.M.S.O., 1970) page 10). Given the large element of subjectivity involved in the classification it would not be wise to regard it as giving a very reliable picture of changes in the social structure of the town during expansion. However it is the only measure we have that enables a comparison to be made over the whole period of growth and so some cautious conclusions will be drawn.

major employer, the hierarchy of skills and earnings that it created were known to all and tended to be reflected in social valuations outside the working situation. This sort of change in attitude cannot be measured; one has to rely on the evidence of those who lived in the town before and after these changes occurred. However there seems no doubt that the recognizably small-town atmosphere, described by Birch and his associates and Stacey, which imposes a certain degree of uniformity and narrowness on people, was present in Swindon and has been greatly reduced by the coming of town expansion.[12] Of course the more traditional outlook and attitudes still persist, especially among the older inhabitants. Even the Town Clerk, who played so large a part in bringing about expansion, admitted to a twinge of regret as the old patterns of life disappeared. Nevertheless there seem to be very few who would actively wish for a return to the old days.

As we have said there are a number of drawbacks to the social class data which limit the confidence that one can have in conclusions drawn from them. The socio-economic group classification is a much more reliable source of data. Unfortunately the whole basis of the classification was changed in 1958 and so no useful comparisons can be made from an earlier period. However comparison of tables from the 1961 and 1966 census confirms the pattern of changes derived from the study of social class data drawn from the 1951 and 1966 reports. In addition it shows that the expansion in the upper middle class was mainly due to an increase of professional workers. There were also more managers in the town after expansion. These were mainly shop managers rather than industrial executives. Of course senior and middle management was required for the new firms but they tended to live outside the town.

Conclusion

In this chapter we have followed the pattern of growth through the years from 1952-66. We have shown how this fell

---

[12] Stacey, M. *Tradition and Change (A Study of Banbury)*. (London: Oxford University Press, 1960) and Birch, A. H. *Small Town Politics* (London: Oxford University Press, 1959).

into two rather distinct periods — first a time of rapid growth
within the town, coinciding with the arrival of many
Londoners and several major new firms, and then a period of
consolidation, when there was far less growth within the town
and reduced immigration. The main change in these years was
the build-up of private housing and industry outside the town
and within it the absorption of the redundant railway
employees.

From this picture we can abstract many of the themes of the
subsequent chapters. For example, the need to cope with the
social problems of rapidly expanding population, the problem
of obtaining sufficient employment, the necessity of obtaining
land for development at the periphery and for the
redevelopment of the obsolete central area, the finance which
was required for all of this, and the scale and complexity of the
organization needed to cope with the process. Apart from the
problems which such requirements would inevitably raise in
any situation, we have seen in Chapters 1 and 2 how, at the
political level, the environment in which town development
took place was a highly uncertain one. Apart from uncertainty
about the extent to which the Ministry of Housing would in
fact support Swindon's aspirations and the necessity for key
contributions from other ministries, such as the Board of
Trade (who clearly had other preoccupations), the County
Council and the surrounding rural districts did not share
Swindon's enthusiasm for the project and might be in a
position to obstruct its progress. Also, despite the general
agreement within the town that expansion should go ahead,
would the consensus survive the difficulties which lay ahead,
and would the benefits outweigh the costs of development for
the town's inhabitants? The Town Clerk once described town
development as a process in which 'we ricochet from crisis to
crisis'. In Part II we shall examine in great detail some of the
obstacles which contributed towards this violent trajectory.

Part Two

Town Development: Process and Problems

Chapter Three

Social Development

Social costs and benefits

The implications of expansion for individuals who actually moved to the town, and for those who were there already, were of paramount importance regardless of the costs or benefits of town development for the various participating organizations. The Council might successfully negotiate the wider problems of town development, but unless it continued to receive strong support for its actions *within* the town the effort would collapse. So the expansion had to offer clear benefits to newcomers and natives alike, for them to accept the social, economic, and physical changes which occurred. In this chapter we concentrate on the social aspects of expansion, leaving other aspects to later chapters, although some reference to them here is inevitable.

We have already discussed many of the reasons why town development offered advantages to the existing population of the town. These were new jobs, new services, and the other benefits of growth. A specific pledge concerning public housing was also made at the time when town development began. At least 350 houses per annum were to be made available for local needs. This was more than hitherto, and the increase was only possible as a byproduct of town development. Taking one year with another, an average of about 375 houses per annum was made available for local needs. So the pledge was fulfilled. However, all these benefits might have counted for very little if the influx of newcomers had so disrupted town society that the attitudes of hostility and bitterness resulted. So it was inevitable that most of the social development programme was directed towards the newcomers, rather than towards the existing inhabitants who presumably had already achieved a stable pattern of social life in the town. In other words, the main problem thought to exist was one of integrating the immigrants into the existing way of life in the town.[1] For the newcomers adequate housing and jobs were important. However these could only be a partial compensation for the loss of the facilities of the big city and of the network of social relations that resulted from the decision to go to Swindon. The Council had the most direct opportunities for influencing the social consequences of development through integrative community work and social service provision. Neither of these was problem-free, and together they form the main theme of this chapter.

Before discussing these issues it is worth setting out in detail the most apparent costs and, benefits to the individual participant in town development. Only when these are understood is it possible to grasp the importance of the action the Council took to provide social services and community work, and at the same time the limitations of this policy.

Two surveys, made at different stages in the growth of the town, enable us to throw some light on what town development meant in social terms for the individual. The first was carried out by Cullingworth in 1960. It concentrated on discovering what appeared to be the social benefits and problems caused for the newcomers by a move to Swindon.[2] The second was a survey of households carried out by the Council in 1970.[3] Although this was made well after the period with which we are concerned, some of the results concerning migration and movement are of interest.

---

[1] The history of other town development schemes amply justifies the priority attached to this aim in Swindon.

[2] Cullingworth, J. B. and Brown, P. *Social Development in an Expanding Town* (A report to Swindon Borough Council, 1960) and 'Swindon Social Survey. A Second report on the Social Implications of Overspill' *Sociological Review* (N.S.) 9, 1961, pages 151-66.

[3] Swindon Further Expansion Group. Household Survey 1970.

The Cullingworth survey found that most of those who moved to the town came because of the opportunity to better their housing situation; 72.7 per cent came for this reason whereas only 18.6 per cent moved to get employment. However when the immigrants were divided into those who came from London and those, mainly key workers, who came from elsewhere there was a marked difference between the two samples. Whereas almost 85 per cent of the Londoners moved because of bad housing conditions, only 17 per cent of the others moved for this reason and almost 70 per cent came to Swindon because of the employment opportunities that it offered. Therefore it seems that Swindon was making a significant contribution to rehousing those in bad conditions in London. Whether these people were statistically those in greatest need cannot be assessed, but it is clear that they themselves thought that their housing was bad enough to require a move, and perhaps this should be the main criterion by which to judge Swindon's contribution. The survey attempted to estimate the extent of housing need among the newcomers, and concluded that at least 80 per cent of them had been living in substandard accommodation. However the evidence on which this was based was rather sketchy.

Housing was also the main source of satisfaction created by the move to Swindon. Fully two-thirds of the sample were pleased with their new houses, and most of them only had minor complaints. The main dislikes were the lack of amenities in the town, low wages, and high costs. The former complaint was an inevitable product of the move to a small town which simply could not afford the range and level of facilities that were available in London. However, as we shall see later, a combination of circumstances caused long delays before some of the basic services such as schools, playgrounds, and bus services, were available for the newcomers. Therefore some of the complaints were probably quite justified.

The most serious problem was the financial strain that the move imposed. Three factors accounted for a large number of families feeling worse off after their move. The first was that wage rates were generally lower than in London and less overtime was worked. It was of course, precisely these possibilities that attracted new firms to the town. Second, most people had been living in cramped conditions with little or no furniture of their own, so that they needed to buy furnishing for their new houses. The only way most could manage this was by contracting hire purchase debts. Over 70 per cent of the sample had outstanding accounts. Third, the rents of their new houses were normally higher than the rent that they had been paying in London, and this added to costs. The survey found that there were also widespread complaints that the general cost of living was higher in Swindon than in London, but the investigators could find no real evidence that this was so.

The Swindon survey, and a previous one at Worsley, were originally intended to assess the validity of Willmott and Young's conclusion that a move from London created severe social problems for the movers because of the breaking of kinship ties.[4] The Swindon survey stated that this was a problem of rather minor importance compared with the other difficulties which have been mentioned. An interesting finding was that almost 30 per cent of the sample had relatives in Swindon, which suggests that the severance of kinship links was not likely to be as complete as one might assume. It is possible that families who had successfully settled in the town were a source of encouragement to their relatives to make the move as well. In later years there was also a considerable number of aged parents coming to join their sons and daughters, as we have already noted.

Some of the most interesting findings of the Cullingworth survey concern the social aspects of employment. The researchers reported that they found a remarkably widespread feeling of insecurity. They accounted for this by pointing out that there was nothing like the same variety of employment and employers as there had been in London. Also, many felt that the working conditions were inferior in Swindon. There were fewer fringe benefits, such as tea breaks, and the employers had a less satisfactory relationship with the men — 'Here the employers don't trust the men who work for them'. Most people were very concerned that there might be major redundancies in one of the three or four major

---

[4] Cullingworth, J. B. 'Overspill in South East Lancashire'. *The Salford-Worsley Scheme Town Planning Review*, vol. 30. no.3, 1959. Young, M. and Willmott, P. *Family and Kinship in East London* (London: Routledge and Kegan Paul, 1957).

employers that together employed the bulk of the male labour force, and that school leavers would not have so wide a range of opportunities as in London. It may have been these factors, together with the lower wages, that led half of those in the sample to change their job at least once since the time that they had come to the town. It seems likely that some of these complaints were justified. Certainly the reduction of available employers as a result of the move from London was real, although the same situation could of course be seen by native Swindonians, who had previously had to rely on the railway works, as an improving one. Wage rates were lower in Swindon for a number of trades as they varied from region to region with London often getting the highest rate. Also, there is evidence that at least one of the major employers gave out rather misleading information when recruiting labour in London about the money that the firm was prepared to pay. This firm was also notorious for having very poor labour relations, and was guilty on more than one occasion of behaving in a despotic manner towards its workers. In time most of these problems were solved by trade union action and there were several bitter strikes. However, given the debts which the move incurred for many families, the disincentive to strike must have been great in the early days. Furthermore newspaper reports show that even when the men did come out they were often opposed by their wives, who had to make ends meet with very little of the communal support that they would probably have received in London.

Just over 14 per cent of the sample wished to return to London, but records suggest that it is unlikely that more than half of this percentage actually went back. Sometimes the desire to return was a passing phase. The social workers observed a common sequence of events during which the initial satisfaction with the new house gave way to an intensive feeling of homesickness for London as the problems of the new environment became apparent. More often than not this particularly affected the wife, who was alone at home all day. A return visit to London to see relatives was often all that was required to convince them that their first choice had been correct, although one housewife told the local paper that she had actually persuaded her husband to leave Swindon and get a flat in London. On their way back to Swindon to clear up she saw the queues, the fog, the cost of a snack at the station, the length of time it took to travel in the city, and promptly decided to stay in Swindon.[5] For those who really did want to return the penalties could be high. Apart from very exceptional circumstances, the authorities would not give them any help to return. On arrival in London they would have to find accommodation, having completely lost any priority they might have had for council accommodation in their original borough. While the need to move people out was paramount, it does seem extraordinary that for many years there was little attempt made to explain the implications of a decision to leave London to those who opted to move.[6]

The Cullingworth survey concluded that the reasons for wanting to leave Swindon were often intangible and indefinite. There were complaints that the townsfolk were unfriendly, but the survey found that the Londoners who said this often displayed condescending attitudes towards the locals and might themselves have created this hostility. An exhaustive search of the press covering the whole period of expansion suggests that such feelings were never widespread. From time to time there were dissatisfied letters from both sides but there was no single issue which created a barrier between the old and the new.

The financial pressures mentioned above created a pressing need for the woman to find some form of part- or full-time work. One might also guess that this would be a way of relieving the isolation and boredom that some of them felt. The remarkable increase in the number of working women in the town was one of the most striking results of expansion. According to census data, the female activity rate was under 30 per cent in 1951 but had risen to 42.5 per cent by 1966. The 1970 survey, referred to earlier, found that this had subsequently risen to 44 per cent. This was very similar to the rate for the London area, the highest in the country, and well above that for the south-west region which contains Swindon. It is particularly high, given the fact that there are above-average numbers of married women with children in the town. The railway town offered some employment for women in the shops and the clothing industry, but little else. One of the benefits brought

---

[5] *Evening Advertiser*, 1 May 1959.

[6] This lack of information has since been rectified by the G.L.C.

by expansion is that there are now many firms which require female labour, and that much of this work is available on a part-time basis. The proportion of economically active women in part-time employment has risen from 32 per cent in 1951 to 53 per cent in 1970, and the 1970 survey found that there were very few women still looking for work. This suggests that the earlier demand for female employment has been fulfilled.

The 1970 survey also revealed the patterns of movement into, out of, and within the town and its surrounding area. The three main reasons for a move were a change of employment (22 per cent), 'personal reasons' (23 per cent) and the need to find larger accommodation because of the demands of a growing family (21 per cent). Apart from this 9 per cent moved solely in order to buy their own accommodation. Forty-one per cent of the sample moved right away from Swindon and, as it seems likely that those moving for employment reasons would have been over-represented in this subsample, those moving for the other reasons stated would have been even more preponderant among those who moved locally.

To summarize, expansion offered the newcomers one great benefit which was the new housing that it provided. However, it is probable that the men earned less and had a narrower choice of employment than in London. The combination of vastly improved housing and lower incomes available for leisure created a more home-centred existence than before. This fact is commented on by many of those who came to the town from London. The move was probably beneficial for the children as well. They had a far better physical environment in which to grow up, and were likely to benefit from their parents' new way of life. On the other hand, the level of amenity provision was low and, as we shall see later, some essential services were lacking. Very little attempt was made to explain the pros and cons of a move before people arrived in the town and there was no arrangement by which those who could not manage could return to the city. In short, the vast majority benefited by the move but a few were probably left with bitter regrets. The move to Swindon seems to have set off in some families an acute desire to improve their situation still further and may, in some sense, have been a promoter of upward social mobility. Nowhere is this more apparent than in the great demand for owner-occupation.

Initially the plan was to provide for sale a quarter of all houses in the development area. This soon proved to be insufficient, and the leading local firm of estate agents reported as early as 1957 that the price of building land around Swindon was rising rapidly.[7] They also reported that the market for cheaper, second-hand houses within the town was rather depressed. The prices of prewar housing had fallen by 5 per cent in the preceding year, and the agents felt that the then current mortgage interest rate of 6 per cent had put home ownership beyond the means of many of those in the middle income groups. It was not until later that large numbers of local authority tenants began to realize that they could afford to buy, and aspired to do so. When in 1956 the Council started a differential rent system on their estate only about 20 per cent of the tenants could afford the maximum rent. Over the next few years this proportion rose rapidly as incomes increased and, as house prices were only inflating relatively slowly, the feasibility of house purchase increased.

As we explained in the last chapter this trend became apparent in the early sixties when the Council realized, in the words of one official, that by building so much public housing they were in dange of 'providing permanent solutions for temporary needs'. The subsequent changes in housing policy, including the houses for sale scheme, have already been outlined, but the importance of this movement into owner occupations was revealed in a survey of council house vacancies, carried out in 1965. This showed that 60 per cent of the tenants left in order to buy their own houses in Swindon or the Swindon area, 26 per cent left the district because of changes in employment, and 14 per cent for other reasons.

Calculations made in 1963, at the time when the houses for sale scheme was being worked out, showed that at that time houses could be provided which were within the means of people with incomes in the range £15–£20 per week. Comparison with figures from the Family Expenditure Survey for the period — which show that approximately two-thirds of the U.K. households were earning £15 per week or more in 1963 — suggest that this scheme offered the possibility of home

---

[7] *Evening Advertiser*, 1 January 1957.

ownership to a considerable proportion of Swindon population.[8]

Another analysis of the first successful applicants for the houses for sale scheme in 1965 showed that 28 per cent had incomes under £20 per week and 87 per cent had incomes under £25 per week. At this time it was possible to provide two- or three-bedroomed houses for families in these income groups to rather higher standards than private builders could produce. Also the favourable mortgage terms that Swindon made available were not matched by the building societies.

Several surveys of those who moved to the new private estates showed that Londoners had seized the opportunity to improve their housing and, of course, their social status by a move to owner-occupation. Of the first 836 houses built for sale, 301 (36 per cent) went to people who had originally come from London to Swindon's local authority estates. Similar proportions of ex-Londoners had moved into the main private-enterprise housing areas. In 1968, one firm noted that 15 per cent of the houses on one of their estates had been sold to families moving directly from London. This suggests that by this time the initial problem of low wages had been greatly reduced.

Another analysis of the first 185 families moving under the houses for sale scheme showed a further interesting tendency. 170 (92 per cent) of them came from the new estates of Walcot, Park South, Park North, and Penhill whereas 15 (8 per cent) came from the older estates of Pinehurst and Moredon—far less than a consideration of the number of people housed on them would lead one to expect. The former group of estates contained far more Londoners than the latter group. Also their age structure was younger than that of the other group. It seems therefore that the suggestion by officials that the estates were merely transit camps for those moving towards owner occupation may have concealed a more complex truth. Some of the estates were like traditional local authority housing areas, containing a majority of residents

---

[8] *Family Expenditure Survey Report for 1963*, (London: H.M.S.O., 1965), Table 2, page 26. A market research survey in Swindon in 1964 showed that the U.K. and Swindon income distributions were very similar, the Swindon mean and distribution around it being slightly higher than the U.K. one.

who made the move into council housing at an early age and stayed there for many years without displaying any aspirations for owner-occupation and the middle-class life style that often accompanies it. The other estates were very different. In terms of background and upbringing those living on them might have been similar to those who lived on the older estates, but they intended to stay in council housing only for a relatively short period until they could afford to buy their own homes. Many of those who made this move were people who originally came to the town from London or elsewhere as key workers. These were skilled workers on fairly high wages who moved to Swindon for reasons of employment rather than of housing. Although we have no definite evidence of their attitudes, this does suggest that their preparedness to move to better their economic position might correlate with a desire to improve their housing and social situation as well. These are the working-class equivalents of those middle-class families which Stacey, in her study of Banbury, found were prepared to move around the country (the spiralists) in order to improve their situation.[9] However, the desire to move out was not limited to key workers or even to those who came from London, as shown by the origins of the purchasers of the first 836 houses for sale. Many Swindonians also bought their own houses. As there was no feature of the housing allocation process which would account for the more ambitious ones being located on the newer estates, it may well be the case that the example of friends and neighbours who left to own their own houses induced a similar desire in those who might not otherwise have done this. Thus, although we cannot prove the point beyond dispute, there is some evidence to suggest that one of the main social consequences of expansion was to raise aspirations among both the newcomers and the existing population, and that a good deal of geographical and social mobility resulted. This pattern of changing attitudes and life styles posed certain problems for the Council's social development programme which were not envisaged when expansion began and which, as we shall see, it found difficult to solve. Before analysing this, however, we shall discuss another problem which has

---

[9] Stacey, M. *Tradition and Change (A study of Banbury)* (London: Oxford University Press, 1960).

already been mentioned, the difficulties of securing adequate social services for the new population at the time when they were most needed.

Social services

The new population obviously made increased demands on the social services in the area. Surprisingly little or no attempt was made before the expansion started to assess what would be required or to investigate how it could be provided. The Council was mainly responsible for, and had a great measure of control over, the physical infrastructure, but it was in a much less dominant position in other areas such as education, health, and welfare. The authorities and departments providing these and other facilities were not directly consulted about expansion. So they found themselves in the position of having to make, in some cases, very large but unanticipated budgetary allocations for developments. Also they were somewhat doubtful whether the scheme would really go ahead, despite Swindon's declared intention that it should. Many of these services were provided by the County Council and in this circumstance political factors were very important. There was strong feeling, both on the County Council and in the county districts, that Swindon was benefiting to the disadvantage of other areas. We shall discuss whether this was true or not in educational provision later, but true or false, it resulted in pressure on county politicians and officials to refuse to give the town any special priority. The problem was that the growing population required such a priority. By forging ahead with Ministry support but very little else, Swindon had taken a decision which committed itself and many others as well to a major programme of works. In short, the functional divisions between the various authorities, with the associated chains of accountability to different bodies, were disrupted in the face of a decision which, although couched in the limited terms that physical planning espoused at that time, implied comprehensive series of economic and social policies as well as physical ones.

Although not all the services required were controlled by the County Council, it was around some of these county provided services that the major conflicts arose. This was for a number of reasons. Firstly, many of the other services needed to expand only slowly and did not require large quantities of new resources at any one moment. The services of the Ministry of Labour or of the law courts are good examples of these. Also these services, and indeed some county services, such as the police and the children's services, operate to standards which are fairly tightly controlled by central government and they are not open to much local alteration. In other cases, such as the hospital service, provision is controlled by appointed bodies which may find it easier to allocate resources on the basis of need without having to take a range of other criteria into account. In the case of the hospital service, it had been accepted before expansion that Swindon needed a new hospital, and it was relatively easy to speed up the progress of this project when the population rose faster than the Regional Hospital Board had originally forecast. Swindon may also have been lucky in being in the area of the Oxford Board — a body which had virtually no connections with the Wiltshire political system. Of course, those medical services which came under the town's Medical Officer of Health were subject to county control; and in these areas of service there was, significantly, considerable argument over expanding the services to the degree required by the inflow of population. However, as much of the work of these services is done with very little equipment and in rented premises, the capital requirements are low, and the conflict centred around manpower levels. To some extent this is a flexible item; overtime can be worked and workloads can be increased so that, by operating under some strain, the service can carry on without breakdown while arguments about resources are pursued.

For the reason mentioned above, and various other factors, the major crisis occurred in the provision of education. Apart from the fact that this was a very large user of resources, both in building and manpower, responsibility for its planning was in the hands of one of the most important and powerful committees of the County Council. Besides the strains imposed by the County/Borough differences which have been a constant theme of this book, Swindon resented the fact that after the 1944 Education Act they had lost many of their responsibilities for the town's education system to the County who, they felt, could not appreciate the requirements of an industrial town. They had been left with management powers, but the major policy decisions were taken by a committee which was subject to political pressures from all other county districts. In the very nature of things this committee could not have the same single-minded devotion to improving education in the Borough that, as Chapter 1 showed, was a feature of prewar Swindon. Furthermore, other departments of the County Council were also involved in the education programme. In particular the County Architect was responsible for designing and constructing the new schools, and it rapidly became clear that his department was accustomed to working at a far slower pace than that required by the expansion.

The whole issue was further complicated, so far as the provision of buildings was concerned, by the tight control that the Ministry of Education had over expenditure.[10] Throughout most of the fifties the demand for new schools outstripped the amount of money that the government was prepared to spend on them. Furthermore, education expenditure was often an early victim in times of economic stringency when public expenditure was cut back. The problem for a new or expanding town was that it was faced with major and rapid expansions of the school population which frequently coincided with these cuts. It was obvious that some sort of priority had to be given to their needs, and this seems to have been established at an early date in the new towns programme. Initially the expanding towns did not fare so well. Firstly, they already had some schools, so a good deal of the increased demand could sometimes be absorbed by making maximum use of the existing plant. This often involved, as at Swindon, extensive use of transport by bus which created local opposition. Secondly, the expanding towns programme seemed to lead a Cinderella-like existence so far as the Ministries were concerned.[11] It is clear that the Ministry of Housing did not attach the same degree of prestige to the expanding towns as they did to the new towns, and consequently spent less time promoting the former than the latter. Lacking a really powerful advocate at national level, the expanding towns' claim for some sort of priority in matters

---

[10] See Griffith, J. A. G. *Central Departments and Local Authorities* (London: Allen and Unwin, 1966) Chapter 2.

[11] This theme will be returned to in Chapters 7 and 8.

such as roads and education took several years to establish. In the meantime they found that the relevant Ministries refused to admit that they had special needs which required special help.

The first crisis occurred in 1952, before town development was really under way. Because of the cut back in public expenditure necessitated by the Korean War, the Minister deferred the construction of new junior and infant schools at Penhill. The Ministry refused to take into account the fact that town development would add greatly to the number of children requiring schooling. They demonstrated their unwillingness to make any special allocation for this purpose by insisting that, if the new schools were built at Penhill, the County would have to reduce the number of schools they built elsewhere. The general attitude of the Ministry towards the figures produced by the Borough in support of their case was one of scepticism—'The needs of Swindon will be kept under review in the light of actual progress of the housing estates and the number of "new" children who are in fact produced by them'. They were not prepared to make any allowances for expansion until the children were actually resident on the new estates. At one point the argument seems to have reached the absurd conclusion that, as there were at that time no inhabitants living in the areas where the new houses were to be built, it was self-evident that these areas must have a lower priority than anywhere with an already existing population! It was two or three years before the Ministry were really convinced that some degree of forward planning was necessary, and the new schools were then rather easier to obtain.

However, the Penhill issue also raised other problems. It took three years to build schools in Swindon. This may seem extraordinary by modern standards, but Wiltshire had not attempted to make use of any of the system-building techniques pioneered by a number of authorities, notably the L.C.C. and Hertfordshire, which had been essential to the success of their major school-building programmes.[12] Wiltshire schools were still traditionally built in brick, to individual plans. Apart from the time it took to design them,

---

[12] Griffith op.cit. pages 156-7.

they were very expensive and they were slow to erect, especially in Swindon where there was a shortage of skilled tradesmen because of expansion. These factors combined to make the process of obtaining schools for the new estates a slow and tortuous affair. To illustrate this point the progress of schools on Penhill is shown in Table 3.4.

The first school, far from being available at or near the start of development was opened just about the same time as the last houses were completed. The other schools took even longer to arrive. Meanwhile the children had to be taken by bus to other parts of the town where there were places available. To some extent this was reasonable, but the early educational planning was so ineffective that these schools soon became overcrowded, and it is likely that the standards of education in the town were adversely affected. Table 3.5 shows the degree of overcrowding that this policy had produced by the start of the school year 1953/4.

The figures in brackets contain the national percentage for 1953. Those for 1948 are not known. The table shows that in 1953 the situation was worse in Swindon than it was

Table 3.4

	Infants	Junior	Secondary
Requested by the borough	July 1949	July 1949	July 1949
Agreed by the Ministry	March 1952	August 1952	August 1955
Starting date	1952	1955/56	1956/57
Opening	1955	1955/58	1958/59

Source: *Swihdon Education Department.*

Table 3.5

	1948	1953
Percentage of large primary classes in Swindon (i.e. over 40 pupils)	38	47 (43)
Percentage of large secondary classes in Swindon (i.e. over 40 pupils)	13	15 (4)

Source: *Swindon Education Department.*

nationally, and that the local position had deteriorated since 1948. While the Borough politicians and officers pressed the County Council and the Ministry to approve further schools so that the Walcot and Park estates would not suffer the same plight as Penhill, the residents of that estate became very angry at what they felt was second-rate education for their children, and lobbied councillors and the M.P.

By 1955 the Borough Education Officer was predicting that the education service would soon break down in the town, and the Ministry at last took some decisions which temporarily relieved the situation. A number of schools in the programme for the expansion area were brought forward and the Borough was given responsibility for building the schools on the Walcot East Estate. The Borough had been pressing the County to abandon open-tender contracts, which had often given work to contractors who were incapable of carrying it out, in favour of negotiated contracts. The Ministry now advised the County to do this, and also to switch from traditional to prefabricated construction. It was lucky for Swindon that the Minister of Education, Sir David Eccles, sat for the local constituency of Chippenham. He was aware of what had been happening to the Wiltshire school-building programme, and took a personal interest in solving the problems. At the opening of the new junior school at Penhill in 1956 he took the County to task for their poor performance. Emphasizing the need for more speed he said, '100 children of school age are moving to Swindon every month. Are the schools going to keep up with this? The timetable is very uncertain in my view. You have eight schools on the stocks but only the eyes of the rabbit are showing outside the hole. These eight schools have got to go up pretty quickly. You will need careful and efficient planning not to fall behind. I am going to watch it carefully'. He also criticized the cost of Swindon's 'palatial' schools. He noted that there was about a 25 per cent cost reduction in the school he was opening, which was built by modern methods, compared with Swindon's previous schools which were built on the old principles.[13]

At the same ceremony, the Chairman of the County Council referred to the political factors which added to the difficulties

---

[13] *Evening Advertiser*, 17 March 1956.

of providing enough schools in the town. He said that, while Swindon complained that it did not get enough, other areas complained that it was getting too much. There was some truth in the view that more for Swindon meant less for elsewhere in the early days of expansion, when the Ministry refused to admit that it should have a special allocation. However, at the time when the Chairman was speaking, they had accepted that more had to be done for the expanding towns, and so an additional allocation was made. This being so, if Swindon had not got the new schools these would not have been redistributed to other parts of the County but used in some other part of the country. However, it is unlikely that this argument impressed those who complained. It was difficult for politicians to convince local groups that there was no way in which they could get more schools in their area. Anyway the new schools did involve the County in some expenditure, for example in staffing, which could have been spent in other areas. As it was, the lack of headquarters and teaching staff in the town, and the difficulty of getting permission from the County Council to increase the establishment, was another constant source of friction between the two authorities. But the recruitment of teachers was also hindered by the refusal of the Borough's Housing Committee to provide council houses for teachers; they argued that the County should provide the accommodation. The attempt to pursue the feud with the County to this extent was a rather self-defeating process. Eventually the policy was dropped.

By 1958 the immediate crisis was over. As the Borough Education Officer wrote, 'Between 1954 and 1958, all individuals involved (Borough, County, Inspectorate, Ministry, etc.) had by trial, error and argument arrived at a formula for marrying Borough Expansion pressures with the material limitations of financial investment, building delays, staffing development of the Walcot West, Walcot East, Park North and Lawn estates'. This working arrangement relied heavily on the fact that the people involved had got to know one another and the situation well, and had evolved a practical view of the problems and what had to be done about them. Of course, the personnel involved in such a situation are unlikely to stay the same over a long period, but normally they are only replaced slowly and so newcomers can be educated in the intricacies of the situation and the same set of working relationships preserved. Unfortunately in 1958 there were a number of simultaneous changes in the Ministry and County. These changes obliterated the series of understandings which had been built up, and the old problems merged again. The Borough Education Officer wrote an exasperated memo, 'with the complete change of personnel at all levels in 1958 the situation had reverted to the BUNGLEDOM of 1948-1954. Its inability to grasp the whole picture at one time also its extent and speed: and the determination to go through the mistakes of the past: are creating, in Borough Expansion circumstances, far greater consequences than at the time of the Pinehurst, Moredon, and Penhill housing estates'.

This time the problem revolved around the abnormally high birth rates on the new estates. Because it would in the long run be wasteful to create enough permanent school places to meet the population bulge, the new schools soon became overcrowded and the Borough began to press for temporary classrooms to be attached to them. Some of the money for this would have had to come from the minor works programme and, once again, this would result in a reduction of resources for other parts of the County. As there was spare capacity in other Swindon schools, bussing was again resorted to. Naturally parents who had waited for years to see schools built in their area, or who had been given promises that the schools would be available as soon as they moved in, were dismayed and angry to see that their children could not be accommodated in the new schools that had been built in their areas. The problem became a long-term one because the age structure of the estates did not change in the way that was expected. There continued to be a young population, and what had been thought of as a bulge became a more or less permanent feature. This was caused by the development we have already mentioned, by which the estates became temporary reception areas for families moving towards owner-occupation. As they left they were replaced by other young families, so that rather than housing an ageing population the estates tended to house a constantly renewed young population and the birth rate continued to be high.

The worst problems were eventually relieved by the use of temporary classrooms. Nevertheless the running conflict between Borough and County on education matters continued, and it covered many other areas such as technical education, as well as the issues discussed here. In some other activities, such as planning, the conflicts inherent in the relationship between the two authorities was restricted to a few issues and occasions, but it was in education, where close and continuing co-operation was required, that the limitations of understanding and co-operation were most clearly revealed.

Social development

Most of the new towns had tried to ease the social problems which occurred while their inhabitants were settling into their new environments by devoting resources to what came to be known as social development. In Swindon, unlike the new towns, there was a large existing population and so, as we have already pointed out, there was real possibility that in addition to the problems the newcomers would have to contend with, there might be friction and conflict between them and the host community.

Various measures were taken to avoid isolation of the immigrants. In particular, attempts were made to avoid geographical concentrations of newcomers. In some of the expanding towns Londoners were housed in areas apart from other tenants, but in Swindon the whole stock of existing and new houses was used to house local applicants and Londoners alike. Apart from the fact that it became more difficult when things went wrong to put the blame on outsiders, this made it impossible for the claim to be made that the newcomers were the only ones who got new housing. It also enabled Londoners who preferred to live in older houses to do so.

Another important principle was that there was only one housing revenue account and that all the rents were pooled. This meant that the newer houses were subsidized by older houses built when costs were low, although to begin with there were few of these. In some towns where Londoners were segregated they were also denied this advantage, and had to pay rents based on the current cost of their new housing. In an interview a G.L.C. official responsible for town development matters drew attention to the social conflicts that were created in towns that did not follow Swindon's example of administering the housing stock in a way calculated to

promote integration. There can be no doubt that this policy
was vitally important, especially in the early days of expansion
when neither side knew exactly what the other was like, and
the chances that mutual suspicion might deepen into hostility
were great. The first estate which housed Londoners, Penhill,
had about one-third of its inhabitants from London, one-third
were key workers, and a similar proportion were locals. As
expansion gathered pace the proportion of immigrants on the
later estates increased, and it became impossible to sustain to
the same degree the policy of mixing up the population.
However the early success of Penhill and the confidence that
this had engendered made this departure from the policy less
serious than it might otherwise have been.

It was decided, however, that these measures were not
enough. Something needed to be done to help the newcomers
in a more direct way. One of the traditional answers had been
to establish on new estates community centres where formal
and informal social groupings could meet under the general
auspices of a community association to which, ideally, every
member of the estate would belong. This approach, which
often accompanied the planning goal of creating
'neighbourhood units', has been subjected to heavy theoretical
and practical criticisms, and is now discredited and plays no
part in Swindon's current development, but in the early fifties
it was still widely accepted.[14] Swindon had tried to set up
community centres in some parts of the town during the War
but they had not been a success. Few of the 'community' were
interested in joining and most of them became effectively the
private property of small and self-perpetuating cliques of
activists who resented any outside interference. This latter
point was a particularly sore one with the Council, since it
provided the finance for them and the Treasurer complained
that he even found it difficult to audit their books. So
community centres were rejected as being unlikely to succeed
socially and not subject to sufficient control by the Council.

The policy eventually adopted was decided by the rather
unlikely combination of the Town Clerk, who was personally
concerned about social development, and two officers in his

---

[14] See, for example, Dennis, N. 'The Popularity of the Neighbourhood
Community Ideas'. *Sociological Review*, 6, 2, 1958.

public relations department who had an interest in social work. One of these subsequently became Social Development Officer, and some years later when Swindon policy was the subject of widespread interest he summarized the approach they had taken to community development thus.

'It was assumed:

1. *Freedom* — that a "free" or "plural" society was the desirable end or aim (e.g. to encourage mutually exclusive groups, both political and religious; but also to remain "uncommitted" as an authority so that any one group could die naturally if it failed to secure sufficient support).

2. *Control* — that nevertheless some degree of control by the local authority was necessary if a stable community was to result. The control proposed in this respect was to retain ownership of accommodation and some degree of selectivity as to user.

3. *Stimulus* — that some stimulus would be required to encourage the most rapid community development of the new neighbourhood units by providing, during the formative periods:
(a) somewhere to go;
(b) somewhere to turn to for help.
The 'somewhere to go' was to be met by providing common rooms. The 'someone to turn to' was to be met by providing neighbourhood workers who are qualified social workers, resident on the estates during the formative years but essentially temporary in nature, working to produce a stable community from which they could ultimately be withdrawn.

4. *Integration* — that hostility should be avoided between the new communities on the new neighbourhood units on the one hand, and the existing social pattern of the railway town on the other.'

One common room was provided on each estate. They were small multi-purpose halls with ancillary rooms. They were available for letting from the Council by any of the various social, political, and religious groups on the estate. It was hoped that they would be cheap to build, and that the charges for using them would not be beyond the groups' resources.

They also provided accommodation for official activities such as clinics and public meetings, and were built adjoining the local shopping centres.

The neighbourhood workers may have been a local invention. Certainly those who formed the policy have no recollection of seeing similar sorts of social workers in the new towns they visited during this period. They had no financial or administrative responsibilities and were not attached to any of the recognized social work agencies. Their tasks were to welcome all newcomers, deal with their initial questions, give them essential information, and help them sort out any problems. They were also to play a part in encouraging and helping group activities, although they were not to become so deeply involved that the whole organization depended on them. They were to monitor the social progress of the estates, and report to the Social Development Officer so that policies could be changed if necessary, and also act as a means of relaying the views of people on the estates to the Council. Finally, they were to act as referral agents, passing to the relevant agencies people who needed specialist help. They were not supposed to supplant these agencies or get so deeply involved in case work that, as a result, their other duties lapsed. It was thought that when, after a few years, the estates were settled, they would be able to pull out and carry on their work in new areas.[15]

In many ways this policy was successful. There were very few major social problems on the estates and contemporary press accounts show that the services that the neighbourhood workers were providing were appreciated by the inhabitants. Furthermore they did sometimes act as successful advocates on behalf of new residents. They also played a large part in helping people to organize their own activities. An occasion when the first neighbourhood worker gave encouragement to some women to demonstrate outside the shop of a local trader who was exploiting his monopoly position by charging extortionate prices is a vivid example of this, but equally good work was done helping child, youth, adult, and church groups to set themselves up. The Council files contain many case

---

[15] Of course, this task of community work is a major and growing element in social work training and practice now.

histories which show that the neighbourhood workers also did useful work in helping individuals and families in trouble to sort out their problems, or where this was impossible, by referring them to the appropriate agencies.

However, even at the time when the policy first operated (which, as we shall see, was when it was at its most effective) it had several limitations. It confined its attention to the social life of the new estate and, within that sphere, mainly concerned itself with domestic, leisure, and planning issues, and complaints about inadequate council services. As we have seen, many of the most serious problems that the immigrants had to face related to their working life and to the financial problems that they encountered. Yet the social development programme never seemed to be related to an understanding of these problems. It was suggested to the author that this was because the Town Clerk was so anxious to attract industry that he was not prepared to raise issues which might affect the willingness of firms to move, but there is no real evidence to suggest that this is so. It seems as if such problems were simply not felt at that time to be a legitimate part of social development work. This is shown by the reaction to a series of complaints in 1955 and 1956 when workers claimed that, in interviews before they arrived, they had been misled by employers regarding the level of wages in the town. The Town Clerk's Department replied that it was not really their responsibility, but did talk to some of the people involved. It concluded that there was some reason to believe that one or two employers did do this but, rather inconsistently, despite the admission that the grievance was 'fairly common and persistent', the only promise was that the matter would be watched 'with the greatest attention', and that any case that could be substantiated would be taken up. With this familiar formula for inaction the matter was dropped.

This example illustrates the narrowness of the social development programme. Although it might have been difficult for Swindon to interfere in employers' processes of selection, a more comprehensive social development policy would at least have tried to ensure that potential immigrants were interviewed by Swindon's officials in London, were told about the advantages and disadvantages of a move to Swindon, and were able to ask questions which would be answered truthfully and accurately. As it was, this did not happen, and at times there is an impression that all the persons with whom the immigrant came into contact had their own interests rather than his at heart, and were not prepared to give the sort of impartial advice that should be available if someone is to take the major step of a move out of London — especially when, as we have seen, the penalties for those who wanted to return were so high. Another aspect of this lack of connection with potential movers was that Swindon relied exclusively on the exporting authorities' assessments of housing suitability. On some occasions these seem to have been unduly biased against people who would otherwise have benefited from the move. On at least one occasion the Town Clerk intervened personally when he was given evidence which showed that an unfair judgement had been made. If Swindon had had their own visitors working in London there could have been a much more satisfactory assessment, and the potential tenant would, again, have had an opportunity to learn far more about Swindon.

Another criticism of the social development policy concerns its ideological basis. Although the Town Clerk, in an interview, strongly denied the charges, to an outsider the policy seems to have been paternalistic and elitist. This is probably a product both of the men who made it and of contemporary attitudes in social work practice. The Town Clerk was a firm believer in progress, but was sure that it was a product of the enlightened minority imposing, in so far as they could, changes on an initially unwilling majority. The first Social Development Officer had trained to be a Methodist Minister and seems to have regarded the neighbourhood workers as shepherds to a secular flock. A number of writers have criticized social work for being an instrument of social control, and a device for managing conflict and assuring conformity to a set of dominant norms and values.[16] The influence of these attitudes on policy can be seen in a number of ways. Perhaps the clearest instant is the tight control the Council kept over the meeting halls, or common rooms, that they built on the estates. No attempt was made to vest the responsibility for their running in representatives of the

---

[16] Many of the criticisms presented here are discussed in a more general and theoretical way in Heraud, B. J. *Sociology and Social Work: Perspectives and Problems* (Oxford: Pergamon, 1970).

localities or the major social organizations operating in the area. Of course, the failure of the community centres influenced this decision, but the distance that this policy put between the social development department and grass roots social groups was great, and had certain unfortunate results.

The use of the social development policy to manipulate situations rather than allow the genuine emergence of attitudes which might have conflicted with Council policy is clearly demonstrated in a note from the Social Development Officer concerning what should happen when the neighbourhood workers were withdrawn from an estate after it had settled down. He discussed three alternatives: firstly that a community association should be set up, secondly that an advisory council of local notables be established to guide further social policy in the area, and thirdly that regular but informal meetings of social workers be held. The first and second options were rejected in case they led to too much interference in what the professionals wanted to do. It was suggested that the third option was best, as it would allow good work to be done without the risk of having to accept resolutions from bodies that would clash with existing interests. This policy was adopted. In a seminar the Social Development Officer made it clear that the Council had encouraged the formation of social groups but had avoided any arrangements which would allow them to come together to exert pressure on the Council. He likened his role to that of a social engineer making plans for the community, and the neighbourhood workers to men and women on the ground who applied the social engineer's selected methods to a given situation. He made it clear that a major responsibility of social development policy was to prevent the emergence of any group with broad community backing which might be politically opposed to the current council. In relation to the values that such a policy should transmit, the same officer, in a speech to the Townswomen's Guild, suggested that the new estates might be breeding grounds for delinquency but that the middle-class standards prevalent in Swindon could help the young to develop social sense and avoid this fate.[17] Apart from any moral objections that might be made to this set of attitudes, the resulting policies failed to establish social development

---

[17] *Wiltshire Herald* 19 February 1958.

work as a major element in the developing life of the estates
(after its initial and useful impact). It must be concluded that
the officials severely underestimated ordinary people's degree
of independence and unwillingness to become objects to be
engineered. One consequence of this lack of enthusiasm for
the official initiative was that it failed to demonstrate its own
importance and, instead of being able to expand and
progressively increase the value and the range of the work it
did, faded away to almost nothing after several years. We shall
now follow these developments through.

In the view of most of those concerned, the first estate,
Penhill, had the most satisfactory history of social
development. Social and political groups sprang up at an early
date, and there was no lack of people to run them. One major
problem was the difficulty of getting a meeting hall. The
Town Development Act allowed the Ministry to make grants
for town development purposes without restriction, but very
little was actually available. The social aspect of development
was disregarded by the Ministry. Not only was grant aid
refused, but when Swindon first asked for loan sanction for the
Penhill Common Room they were coolly informed that this
item of non-essential expenditure should be deferred and
resubmitted later, the Civil Service's way of saying 'never'.
After strenuous protests by the Town Clerk the Ministry
relented, but the incident clearly illustrated their attitude,
and contrasts with the much greater concern that was felt
by the same people for these matters in the new towns
programme. Meanwhile the residents had to use for their
activities a wooden hut left by the builders, and they did not
get a permanent common room until several years after the
estate had opened.

Other facilities as well were late in arriving. We have
already referred to the schools, but it was equally difficult to
get shops before the demand reached its peak, and this led to a
proliferation of door-to-door salesmen, who charged
exorbitant rates for their produce and added to the complaints
about the high cost of living in Swindon. In later years the
Council has begun to charge artificially low rents for a year in
order to induce traders to move into new estates at an early
stage because of the social benefits that this brings, but at this
stage strict financial orthodoxy prevailed. There was a similar
situation regarding corporation bus services and, as the estate

is about three miles from the town centre, the women in particular felt cut off. At this stage it was not easy for the Council to be more generous, the financial basis of expansion was shaky and very little extra help was available for social expenditure. Nevertheless some things could have been done. A glaring fault, in an area where there were so many children, was the lack of play space. The neighbourhood workers pointed out that temporary areas could have been created on vacant lots awaiting development which were left covered with weeds and rubbish (to the annoyance of residents). But departmental orthodoxy and resentment of interference by the new social development section took a hand, and the suggestion was rejected by the relevant committee. Penhill had to wait for almost ten years before it had its full complement of recreation areas. These were of a high standard and fully equipped but in the meantime a whole generation of children had been deprived.

'The worst problem on Penhill was the area known as the Valley. Because of the rejection of Swindon's first compulsory purchase order for town development land, there was a danger that the builders would run out of work, so an additional area of Penhill was developed. This was in a valley to the north of the main site. Despite the fact that it was within a quarter of a mile of the centre of the neighbourhood, the intervening hill made access difficult, and buses could not service the area. The isolation that this created caused many complaints, and does seem to have resulted in some social problems. Once again the social development section tried to persuade the planners that something needed to be done, but they came up against the same sort of opposition as they had met regarding play areas. The planners relied on physical plans, pointing out the closeness of the area to the shopping centre, and discounted social arguments. Not until the volume of local protest reached a peak were some concessions made and a few shops located in a more accessible position.

The second estate, Walcot, coincided with a rapid industrial expansion. More of the residents were semi- and unskilled workers, and more of them were immigrants. The social organization of this estate took far longer to emerge, and there was a fairly high incidence of social problems. The official explanation of this refers to the higher proportion of less skilled on this estate and, it is tacitly assumed, a consequent lack of social skills in comparison with Penhill, where there was a higher proportion of skilled workers. This seems a rather narrow appreciation of the facts, but one that is possibly in line with the attitudes and ideology outlined above. The fact that there were more unskilled and semi-skilled workers meant that earnings were lower, and so the financial stresses created by the move were greater than at Penhill. Apart from this there were fewer Swindonians on the estate, and so there were fewer people able to make the necessary connections with existing social organizations in the town. Also, these existing organizations seem to have been far less interested in extending their activities to Walcot than they were to Penhill, to which of course, some of their members had moved.

By the time Park South and North were developed the situation had changed again. Partly because of the problems at Walcot, existing organizations, especially the churches, were more willing to accept a responsibility for working in the area than they had been at Walcot. The social development section made strenuous efforts to make premises available for social activities, and a strong tenants' association and youth club emerged. Despite the fact that the Park estates had the same sort of people as at Walcot, and just as many were newcomers, the incidence of social problems was far lower than at Walcot. This suggests that it was not the lack of possession of social skills by the residents which explains the differences, but some rather more prosaic factors. The fact that by the time the latter estates had been built wage rates in Swindon had moved closer to London levels, and the financial strain of a move had lessened, underlines this conclusion.

Of course, while these council estates were being developed private house-building was also taking place nearby. The activities of the social development section were, however, restricted to the former rather than the latter areas, which had few publicly-provided facilities. As many of the people who lived there had cars and followed middle-class life styles, being less interested in neighbourhood social activities, this may well have been a reasonable way of using limited resources. There were, though, some groups which probably suffered from this policy. The private housing areas also had large numbers of children and housebound mothers, and it was not until the early sixties, when the playgroup movement and the associated gatherings of mothers began to gain strength, that some definite provision for these needs was made. In Swindon these groups first appeared on the private estates of Lawn and Covingham. Social development policy could also have addressed itself to the problem of establishing some interchange between the areas of public and private housing which, in most cases, were cut off from one another by major roads. However little was attempted or achieved here and the social division, which was deliberately reinforced by physical planning, remained.

Naturally, the main social groups which emerged on the estates were those concerned with the groups which were unable to move off them to find recreation in the town centre or outside the town altogether. These were mothers, young children, and, in later years, the elderly. The political parties also developed ward organizations in the new areas. A survey of social groups in the town, taken in 1967, showed that most of the cultural and hobby groups met in the town centre, whereas most of the preschool, childrens, youth, and old peoples' groups met on the estates. It also showed that there were far fewer of these locally-based groups in the areas of private housing, thus underlining the differences mentioned earlier between the social patterns of areas of public and private housing.

Two general factors affected the performance of many of the social organizations on the estates. Both the social development policy and the associations assumed that the focus of most of the social activities that the residents carried out would be on the estates, but this was not so. As people settled, and as the general level of affluence rose in the fifties and sixties, tenants increasingly moved off the estates for their leisure activities. The rising level of car ownership, which no one predicted in the early postwar period, helped them to do this. It was also assumed that, once settled, most of the residents would remain where they were for many years. As indicated this was not so, and many people stayed only a short time before moving into their own homes. If the areas of public and private housing had not been so physically segregated there might have been a greater element of continuity in the membership of organizations. It has been suggested that the leaders of these organizations tended to be the higher-paid residents, whether because skilled workers were more sociable or because they worked less overtime and could give more attention to outside activities is not clear. These people were most able to buy their own houses, and so the leadership of the organizations suffered from an even more rapid turnover than the membership.

In many ways the history of the social development section paralleled that of the tenants' associations. After the initial few years, when it played a useful though limited role in establishing the newcomers, it failed to develop longer-range objectives, and lost the possibility of developing a useful and continuing role in the social life of the town. Many of the deficiencies which led to this state of affairs have already been mentioned—the narrow focus of its activities both geographically and in terms of the sort of problems where it was prepared to intervene, its prevailing ideology which tended to isolate it from the community, and its weakness in the face of entrenched attitudes on the part of other better-established council departments. In the early stages of development the department had some power because it was run by an experienced and able officer, and had the support of the Town Clerk who had a personal interest in its work. It changed when this officer resigned and was not replaced, and when the Town Clerk, on his own admission, became absorbed in other aspects of expansion. In an interview the first Social Development Officer recalled how other departments, especially Education, Housing, and Health, had been hostile towards his department. After he left and the Town Clerk concentrated on other issues, all that remained of the social development policy was three neighbourhood workers. These, in the absence of central leadership, became increasingly devoted to case-work and moved away from the initial conception of their role. As independent organizations established themselves they began to build their own meeting halls, and with the increasing direction of attention away from the estates demand for the common rooms fell. The attempt to provide low-cost accommodation was eventually abandoned in the large neighbourhood centre at Park where, for reasons of prestige, an expensive hall was built despite the protests of the senior neighbourhood worker. Needless to say, it was little used by those for whom the halls were originally intended, and the public house sited next to it, which provided dances, attracted far more support. Eventually, when the new expansion was proposed in 1968, the rump of the social development section was rescued from obscurity. A new policy was instituted which benefited from the lessons which had been learnt from the past mistakes, attempting to intervene in the social life of the whole town rather than concerning itself solely with the new estates, and relying on partnership rather than paternalism.

Conclusion

Judgements concerning the social success of the expansion policy are extremely difficult to make. Apart from the lack of evidence such an evaluation is bound to be a very subjective one. However it is clear that expansion did not give rise to major social problems and that the vast majority of those who settled in Swindon benefited from the move. To a great extent this was due to the improved housing possibilities that the move produced, as there is little evidence that better job opportunities or higher wages came to those that moved from London, although there were major benefits of this nature arising from expansion so far as Swindonians were concerned.

We have also seen how the understanding of the social implications of expansion was rather narrow, and the County and the Ministry were unwilling to devote resources to social development. The story of the school-building programme and of the social development section illustrates these conclusions. An adequate approach to social development requires far more willingness on the part of the different departments and authorities to work together than was shown in the Swindon situation. This has been an insistent theme of many studies and reports in recent years and it was not recognized, or if recognized was not accepted, at the time we have been discussing.[18] However, Swindon was not alone in this respect: it probably did as much as the new towns in the field of social development, while also sharing their faults.

Many of the policies which were thought to be important proved to have little long-term significance, and some others to which more resources could have been usefully devoted were

---

[18] For example, Report of the Committee on Local Authority and Allied Personal Social Services (Seebohm Report) Cmnd. 3703 (London: H.M.S.O., 1968).

overlooked. Partly this was because the contemporary predictions about the social patterns which expansion would produce were wrong, but partly also the values and ideologies which pervaded the policies adopted were not acceptable to those they were intended to help.

The general level of help and assistance given to intending movers to the town was not sufficient to enable them to make a well-informed choice, and there is some suspicion that the various participants in the operation were so keen to persuade people to move that they obscured the truth on occasions. There can be no doubt that the opportunity of obtaining a new house compensated many for the disadvantages of life in a small town with low wages and, initially at least, a dearth of recreational and educational facilities, but the bargain was a hard one for some.

Finally, it is impossible to determine which, if any, parts of the official social development policy were really important in achieving a major population expansion without giving rise to major social problems. Judging by experience elsewhere the decision to avoid any segregation of the newcomers was decisive. It helped too, that both new and old shared in broad terms a common industrial and political culture. The neighbourhood workers also solved many individual problems but it must be doubted whether the wider designs of the social development policy, based on a faulty appreciation of future social patterns and an inappropriate ideology, were at all effective.

Chapter Four

Industrial Development

National trends and policies

A strong case can be made for the assertion that, once the political decision is taken to go ahead with town development, the attraction of sufficient employment to sustain the population increase becomes the most important requirement. This is so because, despite the fact that most Londoners moved to Swindon to gain better housing, their ability to do this depended on adequate employment being available in the town.

This chapter is concerned with the problems that the town had in attracting sufficient employment. As the Introduction states, the constraints which any authority carrying out town development faces are varied, some are local, others national; some are essentially political and others concern basic social and economic trends which are only indirectly, if at all, influenced by the political process. Many of the problems dealt with in the last chapter were locally based (e.g. integration of the newcomers) or at least had a very strong element of the local in their composition (e.g. the struggles over school provision). Such problems were often controllable by local policy makers. However the problems of industrial development present a rather different picture.

The effects of the national policy of industrial relocation were very important. Its operation during Swindon's development serves to highlight a point made in the

Introduction that policies which may seem of primary importance to local communities, when viewed from the perspective of national government, assume a lower priority. This state of affairs can he a source of conflict, as it was in Swindon's case. Apart from these policy considerations the amount and type of mobile industry potentially available to move to an expanded town will depend very much on the state of the economy and trends in the growth pattern of industry, both with respect to the type of firm which expands and the type of labour force which is required. These are factors which are totally beyond local control. Therefore a consideration of relevant national economic trends and policies is essential, before we can see how Swindon overcame these problems and what was the rather distinctive industrial pattern which consequently emerged.

Of course the rate of growth in the national economy, the location of industry policies of central government, and trends in the growth pattern of industry are not really independent factors. For example the rate of growth in an economy (or lack of it) will materially affect industrial patterns. However as the purpose here is to describe, rather than explain, these factors they will be treated separately. The first two factors, national economic trends and location of industry policies will be dealt with very briefly, but we shall have more to say about the type of industries that moved to new locations.

Figure 4.1 presents four indicators of Britain's economic progress from 1952 to 1966. The graph reveals the familiar stop-go pattern that the economy followed during this period. The immediate reason for the repeated imposition and relaxation of credit restrictions and increases and reductions in interest rates was the fluctuating balance of payments situation. As can be seen from the figure these changes correspond very closely to fluctuations in the growth rate. There is no generally agreed explanation of why these changes occurred and we shall not pursue this question here. It is sufficient to note the pattern of events.

The indicators chosen are particularly significant in the context of town expansion. As we shall show one of the basic motivations of most firms that move, whether to new or expanding towns or to the developed areas, is the need to expand output and the necessity to find a new location in order to do this. At times when the rate of growth in the

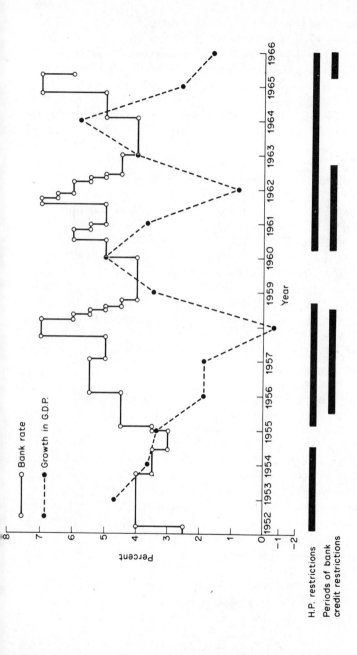

FIGURE 4.1 Bank rate, credit restrictions, and growth in G.D.P. (constant prices), UK 1952–66. Source: R. Caves and associates, *Britain's Economic Prospects* (Washington DC: Brooking Institute, 1968) chapters 1 and 2, especially tables 1.1, 1.8, and 2.1.)

economy is low they are less likely to have this need and less likely to be sufficiently optimistic about future prospects to want to move. Furthermore rising interest rates (for which the bank rate was a good indicator until recently) increases the cost of such a move and makes it less likely. The existence of restrictions imposed by the Bank of England may even make it impossible to borrow the amount of money that they require to finance a move. The imposition, at times of economic crisis, of hire purchase restrictions on consumer durables is particularly hard on the industries which produce these goods. Motor car manufacturers and their associated companies are among these industries. This was particularly significant in Swindon. Another point is that one possible explanation of the recurrent balance of payments crises of this period was that periods of rapid growth led to rises in wage costs. This then raised the prices of exports, making it more difficult to sell abroad which, in turn, ensured that exports did not rise fast enough to match the growth in imports that is a consequence of economic expansion.[1] Obviously export-oriented industries will have their growth prospects adversely affected by such a situation. This also has a special significance in the context of mobile industry.

From Figure 4.1 it can be seen that there were approximately two and a half stop-go cycles during the period we are considering. At the time when expansion started in 1953, economic growth had reached a peak and the Bank rate was 4 per cent. Despite the fact that there was soon a down turn in the rate of growth, there were successive falls in interest rates until early in 1955 and business confidence was fairly high. However by mid-1955 it was clear that a new crisis was coming and credit restrictions and interest rates rose as growth declined. From this time until the beginning of 1959 there was far less optimism and the prospects for industrial expansion were correspondingly limited. There followed in 1959 and 1960 another boom period, but this led to a further balance of payments deficit that the newly elected Labour Government faced in 1964.

Having sketched out the main changes in the economy, we now consider national policies for the location of industry. The Barlow Commission had recommended that governments

---

[1] See Caves *et.al.* op.cit. Chapter 5, pages 209-213.

should intervene in the process of relocation of mobile industry. The 1945 Distribution of Industry Act and the 1947 Town and County Planning Act gave the Board of Trade powers to do this.[2] The main purpose of the legislation was to help those areas of the country which had suffered from the decline of their traditional industries and high rates of unemployment. Its aim was to give positive incentives to industrialists to set up new plants in these areas. The Board was also given the power to prevent firms setting up new factories in the prosperous areas, such as London and the South East. It became necessary to obtain an Industrial Development Certificate for all new factory buildings of over 5000 square feet and every attempt was made to persuade firms to locate in one of the development areas. This twin policy of industrial control and financial inducement, as Cameron and Clark have called it, has remained ever since.[3] Seven subsequent Acts have also been concerned, wholly or in part, with this policy.[4] There have been many detailed changes in the legislation which do not concern us here but two changes are important. In 1964 Industrial Development Certificate control was extended to development exceeding 1000 square feet and in 1965 restrictions were placed for the first time on office developments in a number of conurbations, including London, and developers had to obtain an Office Development Permit (O.D.P.) before building new offices. This policy had not been as restrictive as the Industrial Development Certificate procedure, however, except in central London and a few other areas.

This policy is mainly intended to help depressed areas and does not contain any special provisions for other areas, such as the new and expanding towns, which also need to attract mobile industry. These towns have often complained that the Board of Trade has tried to prevent firms willing to settle in

---

[2] A good summary of the legislation is in Lee, D. *Regional Planning and the location of Industry* (London: Heinemann, 1969), Part 3, pages 13–48.

[3] Cameron, G. C. and Clark, B. D. *Industrial Movement and the Regional Problem* (Edinburgh: Oliver and Boyd, 1966) page 8.

[4] They are the Distribution of Industry (Industry Finance) Act 1958, the Local Employment Acts of 1960 and 1963, the Finance Acts of 1963 and 1966, the Control of Office and Industrial Development Act 1965, and the Industrial Development Act 1966.

their areas from doing so by persuading them to go to the
development areas instead. This is a rather inadequate
description of what actually occurred. Firstly, the policy has
been imposed with varying degrees of stringency over the
years. Comparing the dates of the legislation with the progress
of the economy outlined in Figure 4.1, it can be seen that new
government initiatives have often coincided with low points in
the economy. It is at such times, or before elections, that the
political desirability of being seen to be helping areas of high
unemployment becomes paramount. Then the pressure on
firms to move to development areas is intensified, both by
modifications and additions to the legislation and in the way
in which it is actually implemented by the Board. Secondly, as
Cameron and Clark point out, the Board was never entirely
rigid in the application of policy. It often gave in if a firm
pressed its case hard enough, or accepted a *quid pro quo*
whereby large manufacturers would be allowed some
expansion in the location that they favoured provided that
they also put some of their operations into the development
areas.[5] The Board accepted that the new and expanding towns
did have a legitimate claim to some industry and usually
allowed fairly free movement into these towns in the early
stages of development. However, as soon as the towns were off
the ground the Board became more restrictive, taking the view
that these areas had second priority to the development areas.
In practice this has meant two things, firstly that firms are
usually only allowed to go to a new or expanded town if they
have first convinced the Board that they cannot move to a
development area, and secondly, that firms already existing in
these towns have been relatively free to expand their activities
within these towns if they wish to do so. This compares
favourably with firms in London who would often not be
allowed to expand in their existing locations.

Therefore there has been considerable variation over time
in the way in which the distribution of industry policy has
affected the new and expanding towns. According to Howard,
from 1945 until 1951 the Board followed a strong policy of
directing industry to development areas. This was followed, in
the years from 1951 to 1959 when unemployment in these

---

[5] Cameron and Clark, op.cit. pages 95-96.

areas slackened, by less pressure on firms to go to them. At this time more industrial development certificates were granted for the new and expanding towns.[6] Finally, as conditions worsened again from 1960 onwards, pressure increased on firms to move to the development areas. This relationship between policies and the direction of movement has been demonstrated statistically by Sant who had shown that the new towns policy of the fifties and the increased development area incentives of the sixties were both strongly related to variations in peripheral area movement (i.e. development area movement), the former inversely and the latter directly.[7]

The final point in this brief survey of industrial location policy is that there has never been enough mobile industry to satisfy the needs of all the development areas and all the new and expanded towns. This has been made clear by a number of official sources over the years. So in applying the Industrial Development Certificate policy, the Board has not only been redirecting industry but acting to ration it out between those areas which have been competing for it. Apart from the fact that any rationing system can afford to be more generous to everyone at times when there is relatively more of the commodity available (in this case in those periods when the economy was growing faster and business confidence was high) this perpetual condition of shortage gives a certain air of unreality to some of the protests from the new and expanded towns that, but for the policies of the Board, they could have got all the required industry. As a civil servant put it in a letter to the Town Clerk of Swindon in the early sixties (after he had made just such a protest), there is a 'floating value' to mobile employment. The analogy was to the land market where 'hope value' is added to undeveloped land, this being a measure of the likely value of the land if developed in the presently existing market conditions. The point is that such a value would disappear or be greatly reduced if *all* the land to which this value is attached were actually developed because there would then be a situation where the supply was greatly increased, thus reducing the market price. So there is

[6] Howard, R. S. *The Movement of Manufacturing Industry in the United Kingdom*. (London: H.M.S.O., 1968) page 13, paras. 40-3.
[7] Quoted in Keeble, D. E. 'Industrial Movement in the United Kingdom', *Town Planning Review*, vol. 43, no. 1, January 1972, page 6.

something illusory about expecting that hope value can be realized on *all* undeveloped land. Likewise it is illusory for *all* the areas in competition for mobile industry to suggest that, but for the Board of Trade, they would have got all that they required. If there had been no rationing system some of them might have done very well. However those areas which were naturally less attractive to firms would probably have got even less employment than they did in fact receive, because of the absolute shortage of enough to satisfy everyone.

Recently researchers have investigated the pattern and type of industrial movement that has occurred since the distribution of industry policy came into effect. Keeble has reviewed the results of much of this work. His first important conclusion is that ' . . . as far as manufacturing industry is concerned, post war movement, far from embracing a cross-section of all industry, has been highly selective of the country's biggest, most rapidly expanding and most export oriented firms'.[8] As we shall see most expanding towns have not been large enough to take the biggest firms, but the rest of this conclusion applies to many of the firms that have moved to these towns. Investigation of the reasons why businessmen decide to move has shown that they are rarely willing to do so unless they are expanding and therefore wish to open a new branch factory (of course it can be argued that this is not strictly speaking a move) or rebuild to a higher capacity. The data collected by Howard puts the relationship between growth and movement beyond doubt. Using it Keeble calculated that 89 per cent of the variation in mobile employment is 'explained' statistically by variation in the volume of growth.[9]

Much of the structure of industry in the new and expanding towns is a product of this concentration of growth industries among mobile firms. The number of industries experiencing major growth in Britain in the last twenty years is limited and the number of those who were both increasing output and employment, the latter of which is essential for the goals of a new or expanding town, was even smaller. Among the major

---

[8] Keeble, D. 'Employment Mobility in Britain', in Chisholm M. and Manners, G. (eds.) *Spatial Problems of the British Economy*, (London: Cambridge University Press, 1971) page 26.

[9] Ibid., page 27. The reference is to Howard op.cit.

industries are engineering and electronics, vehicles, paper, printing and publishing, electricity, distribution and services, and chemicals.[10]

Another feature of these growth industries is that most of them require at least a hard core of skilled workers. One of the recurrent problems for firms in the South East has been a shortage of such people. Apart from the non-availability of workers this has meant that, because of competition, relatively high wages have had to be paid.[11] Therefore it is not surprising that Cameron and Clark found that a sample of firms which had moved to development areas mentioned the availability of a supply of trainable labour as the major factor which determined their choice of area to move to.[12]

Apart from this, accessibility and co-operation from the local authority were the other two main factors which influenced choices. Lower site costs in new or expanding towns or development areas are often thought to be major inducement to firms to move. However Dunning has shown, by a careful comparison of all the costs involved, that aggregate costs in new towns are only slightly lower and in development areas only slightly higher than in London.[13]

The characteristics of the firms moving to new/expanded towns and to development areas have not been differentiated so far in this discussion, but there are some differences between the two migrant flows. Keeble describes this as the dual population hypothesis of industrial movement. He writes, 'This hypothesis suggests that if local intra-urban movement is ignored, the great majority of individual moves in post-war Britain can be classified into one of two distinctive categories. Though fundamentally differentiated by distance of movement and nature of reception area, these categories also yield populations of migrant establishments which differ significantly in terms of establishment size and organizational type. In short, the dual-population hypothesis states that post-

---

[10] Beckerman, W. *et.al. The British Economy in 1975* (London: Cambridge University Press, 1965) Chapter 7, pages 201-34.
[11] The fact that many of these industries have been heavily dependent for expansion on the growth of exporting underlines the significance for them of controlling costs and remaining competitive in world markets.
[12] Cameron and Clark, op.cit., Table 8.2, page 163.
[13] Dunning, J. H. *Economic Planning and Town Expansion* (Southampton: W.E.A., 1963) page 115.

war movements of manufacturing, and to some extent office, activity in Britain may be basically divided into long-distance, large establishment movement to peripheral regions of higher than average unemployment, and short-distance, small establishment urban overspill movement around major conurbations, particularly the more prosperous 'central' regions of the country. In the manufacturing case, the former inter-regional category is dominated by the setting up of branch factories, complete transfers of existing firms being much less common. Many of the establishments in the latter intra-regional category, however, have completely transferred their activities from the central conurbations of the region.[14] Having examined the evidence Keeble comes to the conclusion that this hypothesis is substantiated by detailed studies. A G.L.C. survey confirmed that most of the overspill industry was small-scale. The average size, at the time of movement, of manufacturing plants to expanding towns (up to 1966) was fifty-nine employees. The average size of the few service-sector firms which had moved up to that time (mainly wholesalers and distributors) was ninety-six employees. But 90 per cent of the jobs which had moved to the expanding towns by 1966 were in a manufacturing industry, as service employment tends to follow manufacturing employment to the towns after a gap of some years.[15]

Keeble suggests that large firms prefer peripheral areas because these are the only areas where there are the really substantial supplies of available labour that they require. Apart from this the Board of Trade undoubtedly made great efforts to persuade firms which can make a big contribution to relieving unemployment to go to these areas, rather than new or expanding towns. The Board do not press the smaller firms so hard. Anyway many of these firms are unlikely to take the risk that a move such a long distance away from familiar markets and suppliers may involve. Managements' personal preferences are also important. It is one thing for the London headquarters to set up a new branch in Scotland which does not involve a move for top executives, but the smaller firms will want to take their management with them and, in this

---

[14] Chisholm and Manners, op.cit., pages 42–43.

[15] G.L.C. Town Development Division, Research Note, *Employment in Expanding Towns, Movement Analysis, 1969* (London: G.L.C., 1969).

case, a new or expanding town close to London is likely to be preferred. Keeble suggests that similar considerations apply to firms employing unusual numbers of more highly qualified research staff.

The type of firm that moves has several important consequences for the area into which it moves. As we have seen these are almost always firms which are growing. Howard found that employment in his sample of firms had grown by 60 per cent in the period from between six to eighteen months of their move, by a further 20 per cent in the following year, by 10 per cent in each of the two subsequent years, and by another 12.5 per cent in the next seven years. So in eleven and a half years total employment had more than doubled.[16] A G.L.C. survey bears this out for the expanding towns. It found that, in the twenty-two firms surveyed, employment had grown by 40 per cent since they moved.[17] Therefore areas which receive mobile industry will find that they have created a rapidly expanding source of new jobs, even after the inflow of new firms ceases or is reduced. The G.L.C. survey showed that this process had occurred in the expanding towns. It found that the industrial estates had a gross density of nineteen workers per acre after four years, increasing to fifty workers per acre after fifteen years. Obviously planning and housing programmes must recognize this situation before it occurs.

Dunning has drawn attention to another aspect of mobile industry which can create difficulties. In a book which considers what sort of industries the expanding town of Basingstoke ought to try to attract, he notes that many of the firms going to peripheral areas were branch factories and suggests that the town should be wary of these.[18] He writes that studies of the costs of alternative locations have frequently underlined the dangers to their industrial prosperity of a particular area becoming too dependent on employment in branch plants. If a recession develops it is often the branch plant which is first to curtail its output, particularly when it is simply duplicating the products manufactured by the parent company. This factor, in combination with the dependence of

---

[16] Howard, op. cit., page 21, para. 62.
[17] G. L. C. Town Development Division, *Research and Development Note No. 32, Employment in Expanding Towns. Report of the Industrial Land Use Survey, 1965.* (London: G.L.C., 1967).
[18] Dunning, op. cit., pages 106-107.

many mobile firms on export markets, may mean that some of the areas which receive mobile industry will be particularly hard hit in a recession.

One further characteristic of mobile employment is important. Howard discovered that manufacturing industry which moved gave employment to a lower proportion of males (62.2 per cent) than did manufacturing industry as a whole (68.0 per cent).[19] Partly because of the shortage of skilled labour (which forms a major inducement to move) expanding industries have been trying to automate. If this is not possible they have tried to substitute cheap unskilled and semi-skilled female labour for male labour. A report by the Organization for Economic Cooperation and Development has noted this trend. It is bound to be particularly serious for new and expanding towns because their growth is dependent on making an increasing number of jobs available for incoming male heads of households.[20]

Another problem is that much of the employment growth of firms, after they have moved to the new or expanded town, is likely to be in female jobs. It may even be the case that the town needs to attract more employment for males who have been in employment but are displaced by women. Of course such a trend is more likely to affect unskilled and semi-skilled workers than skilled ones, because of the continuing absolute scarcity of the latter. Yet it is the former rather than the latter who are likely to be those who most need to move to a new or expanded town for housing reasons. Some confirmation of this pattern can be gained from the survey which has already been referred to.[15] This showed that on average, employment had expanded by 40 per cent after firms had moved. But this was made up to a 200 per cent increase in female employment and only a 10 per cent increase in male employment. The G.L.C. commented on the factors which seemed to them to lie behind this situation. They felt that there were often too many towns chasing too few firms. They concluded: 'Some towns have a tendency to grasp at any firm that is willing to come to them. The result is that a bad balance often occurs between the employment diversity and the ratio of female and male job

---

[19] Howard, op.cit., page 33, para. 96.
[20] O.E.C.D. *Manpower Aspects of Automation and Technical Change* (Paris: O.E.C.D., 1966).

opportunities, often to the detriment of the firm, i.e. a lack of labour tends to push up wages or hold·back expansion through a general labour scarcity and to the detriment of the town where the housing programme is put out of balance by the excessive number of female rather than male employees'. They also referred to the spread of automation. This reduced the number of workers in large, capital-intensive plants and increased shift working by those that remained. Both these changes created economic and social problems for the towns. Because of the highly standardized production processes which had been evolved, industries such as electronics required large numbers of unskilled and semi-skilled, mainly female, workers.

In interviews G.L.C. officials enlarged on the picture which has been revealed by these studies. Most of the expanding towns are small. Because of this few of them (apart from Swindon and Basingstoke), could absorb a concern which employed many more than 500 people. Consequently the L.C.C. and the G.L.C. have concentrated on persuading small firms to move. These have the additional advantage that they are far more able than large firms to persuade the Board of Trade to give them an Industrial Development Certificate. Many of these firms move their entire operations and are very concerned about the level of amenities that their new locations offers. To persuade key workers and management to move, this has to be high. So far as the G.L.C. was concerned, the main problem is the shortage of skilled men, especially in engineering, who want to move. In 1971, at the time of these interviews, only about 25-30 per cent of the skilled jobs available in the expanding towns could be filled from those in housing need on the lists of the Industrial Selection Scheme.

In this section basic trends and patterns in the British economy and in mobile industry during Swindon's expansion have been reviewed. Against this background, it is now possible to understand the policy towards industry that was adopted and its outcome.

Industry in Swindon

Figure 4.2 summarizes Swindon's industrial progress from 1952 to 1965. The three indices that have been chosen are industrial floor space created, total employees, and overspill

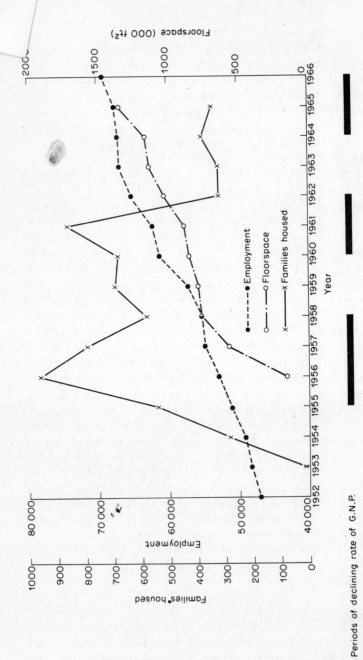

FIGURE 4.2 Overspill families housed, employment, and industrial floor space in Swindon. Source: *Swindon Borough Records.*

Periods of declining rate of G.N.P.

families housed. Before discussing the figures, some feature
the statistics used must be mentioned. No details are available
concerning the build-up of floor space on the Parsonage Farm
Estate. This was completed by about 1960. It accounted for
2 266 000 square feet of floor space, out of the total 3 856 000
square feet which had been built by the end of 1965. The
graph shows only the build-up of floor space on the estates
which remained in the ownership of the Corporation.
However, this may give a clearer picture of how economic
circumstances affected expansion, as the Parsonage Farm site
was dominated by one firm (Pressed Steel with 1 750 000
square feet) which built up its factory over a very short period
(1955-60). However the decision to build was taken at an
earlier period and was not affected by the shorter term
fluctuations in the economy in later years. Floor space figures
are not available before 1956, but it can be seen from the
graph that there was very little built before that time. The
figures of employment were obtained from the former
Ministry of Labour's records. They cover the whole of the
Swindon Employment Exchange area. This includes the
subregion, and therefore it is a better measure of the growth
caused by expansion than could be obtained from figures for
the Borough alone, remembering that many of the new
factories were outside its boundary. The Marlborough area
was not included in the Swindon figures before 1958; so an
estimate of the employment in this area for the previous years
has been made and added on to the Swindon figures to get a
comparable series of figures for the whole time span. The
statistics of the numbers of families housed include those
housed in relets, as the policy was to offer these to overspill
families when they preferred them. Also, as the rate of relets
rose, new housebuilding was reduced, so a graph which based
solely on new housing would seriously underestimate the
number of new families actually coming in as a result of
expansion.

The periods when the national growth rate was declining
have been inserted underneath the graph. The graphs of floor
space and employment show that in each of these periods of
stagnation the rates of increase of floor space and employment
in Swindon fell. Fewer new factories resulted in fewer new jobs
and a slow-down in the number of families coming into the
town. The graph shows that the most dramatic changes were

in this factor. The fluctuations in the variables do not occur at exactly the same times; as the growth rate fell there was usually a lag in the reaction of other factors. This was because it took time for businessmen to realize that growth was falling off and even longer for the impact of reduced investment programmes to be felt locally. However the progress of the national economy clearly affected the progress of town development.

One of the main problems was to co-ordinate the production of housing with the creation of new jobs, ensuring that there were neither too few houses for the newcomers to move into nor too many standing empty. Industrialists were asked to tell the Council how many houses they would need in the current year and give a tentative estimate for the next year. In practice many firms were not even sure what their requirements would be in six months' time. So the council officials had to develop their own assessment of future economic trends in order to supplement the firms' estimates. These estimates tended to be over-optimistic when the economy was growing, and over-pessimistic when it was stagnating. The correspondence files contain several letters from firms who suddenly announced plans for a rapid and unexpected expansion and expected houses to be available or, equally often, firms that suddenly cut back on their plans and left the Council with the possibility of a large number of empty houses. The graph shows that the officers had a fair degree of success in keeping houses in step with jobs. The one occasion when they were caught out was in 1960-61, when firms confidently expected to expand. A large number of houses were in contract when the balance of payments began to deteriorate and a credit squeeze was re-imposed. The graph shows the major cut in the housing programme for 1962 that was then necessary. This sudden and unexpected change forced the Council to incur heavy abortive costs for abandoned contracts.

A further feature which affected the Council's industrial policy was the run-down of the railway workshop. This began to occur in the sixties. Figure 4.2 shows its effects on the intake of overspill families more clearly. Although floor space had begun to increase again after 1961, the growth of employment over the next four years (after an initial spurt in 1962) was lower than in any comparable period since expansion began.

The graph also shows that the number of incoming overspill families fell to the lowest level since 1954 and stayed there for the rest of the period. About 4000 jobs were lost in the railway works in these years and most of the new jobs which came to the town at this time went to those who had been made redundant. The need to find jobs made the search for new industry, at a time of unsettled economic conditions, a difficult but urgent task, and it explains why town development played something of a minor role in the thinking of officials and councillors for this period.

We have already referred to the relative scarcity of mobile industry in postwar Britain and the large number of places competing for it. We have also seen how the fluctuations in the national economy aggravated this situation. How was policy in Swindon affected by these factors? It has already been stated that expansion was seen as a way of diversifying the town's industrial structure. In policy discussions before development began, it was assumed that the domination of engineering employment should be reduced, so that not more than about a third of the labour force was in this industry. Therefore, given the fact that the County had only agreed to let the town expand to 92 000, hardly any new engineering could be accepted in the town. The aim was to attract industries which the town lacked, for example, food, drink, and tobacco firms, offices, and other white collar employment.

It rapidly became clear that this policy was unrealistic. As we have seen a great deal of the mobile industry in the fifties and sixties was in the engineering sector which Swindon had hoped to exclude. Also the town had the reputation of having a highly skilled engineering workforce and as one of the main reasons why most employers moved was to get more labour it was not surprising that the town attracted more of the same, rather than radically different, employers.

In contrast, office employment had very little pressure on it to move from London until the sixties, as it was not until the very end of our period, 1965, that controls were imposed. As the Location of Offices Bureau reports show, office employers followed the early pattern of manufacturers, being unwilling to move very far away from London. Just as Swindon had found that few industrialists were prepared to relocate eighty miles from London in the fifties, so it found that few offices were prepared to go this distance in the fifties or sixties. But by the early seventies, offices were following the lead of manufacturers and increasing numbers were becoming interested in moving to the town.

Swindon soon abandoned the attempt to pursue a pre-planned policy for the attraction of employers to the town. In several interviews it was suggested that social and physical planning considerations had been sacrificed to the goal of attracting more jobs. One G.L.C. official felt that Swindon had been 'quite ruthless' in taking in new industry and had just 'spread it around all over the place'. They had not tried to pick and choose industries according to a plan. These criticisms are exaggerated; the firms are located on well laid-out estates and some firms, such as those which employed few males or which produced noxious waste, were not encouraged. It is nevertheless true that the town did accept most of the new industry it could get, without too much discrimination. One of the officers agreed that they had been opportunists, grabbing at almost everything that came their way. But he felt that if they were to succeed in town development, in the circumstances in which the town found itself, such an attitude was both essential and inevitable.[21]

We have already discussed, in general terms, some of the factors which determined this approach. The recurrent crises in the national economy caused severe fluctuations in the supply of mobile industry, which was not plentiful anyway. Under these circumstances the original plan for the town development scheme, which envisaged a smooth build-up of population and housing based on new jobs, was impossible to achieve. It was clearly necessary, if town development was to go ahead on the scale proposed, to adopt a shorter-term strategy, aimed at maximizing the benefits to be obtained from favourable economic conditions while they lasted. Of course Swindon could have chosen to abandon its target of a rapid build up of population and have been content to grow more slowly, picking and choosing the firms that seemed to be

---

[21] One interesting difference between expanding and new towns seems to have been the relative abundance of firms willing to move to them that the new towns experienced. This allowed the development corporations to be quite selective in their choice of firms; for example in Crawley approximately 1200 firms were interviewed, but only 80 were selected by the Corporation.

best for the town, as and when they became available. Many of the smaller expanding towns seem to have followed this strategy when it proved to be far more difficult to attract industry than they had expected. There are two reasons why this course was not adopted in Swindon. Firstly, the town had committed itself to large investments in the infrastructure, such as a new sewage works and a new town centre. In the early years these capital projects were a heavy rate burden, so there was an urgent need to attract more population in order to spread the burden. There was also a need to create more industrial rateable value for the same reason. Once expansion was started on the scale that had been agreed for Swindon, the penalties for reducing the rate of progress or the scale of the scheme were likely to be severe Furthermore the officials and councillors who were running town development were personally convinced that it would be beneficial for the town to expand as rapidly as possible. So they would have been reluctant to lower their sights. In some of the smaller schemes there may not have been this degree of commitment. More importantly, they did not require the massive capital investments that were needed at Swindon. Moreover the L.C.C. often gave additional financial help to these towns, thus shielding them from the effects on the rates caused by a slowing down of the programme. Swindon was the only town development scheme which did not receive this additional financial help from the L.C.C.

Swindon's opportunistic attitude towards the attraction of industry was reinforced by the belief among officers and councillors that the Board of Trade, when considering Industrial Development Certificate applications, took an unsympathetic and unjustifiably restrictive attitude to the town's needs. The Town Clerk preserved a bulky file which documented, with lengthy correspondence, the battles that he had with the Board.[22] After some initial confusion official replies always made it clear that, as we have already written, the expanding towns have a priority for Industrial Development Certificates that is below the development areas.

---

[22] On some occasions he attempted to get the Ministry of Housing to intervene on Swindon's behalf; he even addressed an impassioned plea to Dame Evelyn Sharp when she was the Permanent Secretary at that Ministry.

However, from Swindon's point of view this was equivalent to no priority at all. In an interview the Town Clerk said that, while the Board of Trade paid lip service to the needs of expanded towns, they actually came very far down its list of priorities. The Clerk certainly had a considerable list of firms which were willing to come to the town, which would have employed many thousands and diversified the industrial structure, but which did not come because they could not get Industrial Development Certificates. The Clerk said that these experiences reinforced his realization that they could not pick and choose the firms that they preferred because so many of these have eventually been refused Industrial Development Certificates. They simply had to seize any opportunity that occurred.

However, interviews with the G.L.C. officials who were helping the expanding towns to attract industry do not entirely corroborate this account of the Board's attitude to expanding towns. Nor do the academic studies of its policies which were referred to in the previous section. Was Swindon treated rather differently from the other expanding towns, and if so, why? The evidence suggests that this may well have been so. The reasons for it also help to explain some important features of the present day employment structure of the town.

According to G.L.C. officials, most of the expanding towns had little or no difficulty in getting most of the Industrial Development Certificates that they required. The reason that most of them were only able or willing to take relatively small firms. As we stated above, few could absorb enterprises which employed more than 500 men and the average size of incoming firms was far smaller than this. Furthermore, they all had agreements with the L.C.C./G.L.C. These tended to ensure that they used those authorities' officials to persuade London industry to move out. Even if the terms of their agreement with London allowed it, they were unlikely to have enough resources to look for mobile industry from elsewhere and to employ their own officers to do it.

Consequently the staple diet of most of the expanding towns was (and still is) small, London-based firms who are forced to move out. It was not difficult for such firms to prove to the Board of Trade that they could not survive a move to a development area. In these circumstances, the policy of giving second priority to new and expanded towns usually ensured that permission was granted for small firms to move to them. This helps to explain the pattern which was referred to in the previous section, of small firms moving short distances and larger enterprises moving to peripheral areas. The contrast between these small towns and the Swindon situation is apparent for the town had both the capacity and the willingness to absorb far larger firms than all the other early expanding towns and than all but one or two others even now. While most towns could not accommodate any firms with over 500 employees, Swindon had, in British Railways, Plesseys, and Pressed Steel, three firms which each employed over 5000. In the early days the Council expected that there would be a rapid flow of small firms from London and relied on the L.C.C. to provide the introductions to such firms. We have already shown, in Chapter 2, that only a fraction of the job requirements of the town actually came from this source, mainly because Swindon was too far away from London to fit into the pattern of short distance dispersal that was the distinctive pattern of such firms.[23] As the original policy was not achieving the results that Swindon hoped for, they began to search for industry themselves, not restricting their approaches to London firms. The L.C.C. did not object, if only because it had no legal town development agreement with Swindon. This meant that the only help it gave Swindon was a housing contribution for each one of its nominees housed and was therefore in no position to object to what Swindon was doing.

The other factor which persuaded the Borough to try to attract the larger firms was the example of Pressed Steel. In part this seems to have been the result of the sort of informal deal between the Board and large companies that Cameron and Clark refer to. The company had wanted to build a new plant at Oxford, to serve the Morris works at Cowley, but the Board was not anxious to see further expansion there. Pressed Steel agreed not to pursue their plans, so long as they could locate their plant within reach of Oxford. Swindon, which was not in the South East region but had a supply of the right sort

---

[23] This is in sharp contrast to the majority of the London-linked expanding towns. The G.L.C. Industrial Land Use Survey referred to earlier found that in these towns as a whole 73 per cent of the firms on the estates had come from London, 17 per cent were new firms or branches of firms located outside London and 10 per cent were local firms.

of workers, was an expanding town, was close by, and seemed the ideal compromise solution. The Board made some effort to resist this move but in the end it gave the company an Industrial Development Certificate. The Council was delighted that one firm should bring so much new employment into the town. They realized that the time, effort, and energy that had been expended on dozens of small firms could be put to far better use trying to attract larger firms as these would offer more employment, more quickly, and with less risk of company failure than the small firms. In fact it seemed that an expansion of the size proposed at Swindon could only be based on larger firms, so the Council soon abandoned the attempt to attract small firms. While they did not stop them coming to the new estates, one official felt that they had probably planned the estates with little or no concern for the requirements of such firms.

Unfortunately this policy conflicted with that of the Board of Trade. At first it was prepared to allow Industrial Development Certificates for most of the firms that wanted to go to the towns. Its attitude was so co-operative that the Town Clerk even wrote to thank the department. It is clear that the Board regarded this phase as a 'pump priming' operation, to allow the scheme to get off to a good start.[24] After about 1958 the Board became far more restrictive, reverting to their policy of trying to steer most of the larger firms that wanted to come to Swindon to the development areas. In 1960 the Town Clerk sent an anxious letter to the Ministry of Housing. He had heard that a Board of Trade official had told an industrialist that they were unlikely to allow any more really large firms to come to the town in future. The information was that the Board expected Swindon to revert to attracting the smaller firms that other expanding towns relied on. They also believed, rightly as we have seen, that most of the firms that had already come to the town would grow rapidly, thus allowing the town development programme to go ahead. Nevertheless, despite the fact that they were trying to make themselves a special case and an exception to a very firmly established national policy, Swindon continued to try to

---

[24] In much the same way, they more recently gave Milton Keynes top priority for Industrial Development Certificates for a temporary period.

attract the larger firms. They achieved success in attracting further industries and did get many of the Industrial Development Certificates that they required. But most of the really large employers that expressed an initial interest were not able to come to the town and when the railway workshops began to close down there was not enough new industry available to deal with this problem and keep town expansion going on a large scale. So, as we have noted before, the scheme came to a virtual halt. Nevertheless the initial population target was reached and surpassed, mainly as a result of the continuing expansion of Pressed Steel, Plessey, and the medium-sized firms that the Council had attracted.

We have seen that Swindon was a unique town in some respects. It was far larger than most of the other expanding towns, was not so tied to London, and so, in order to grow at a reasonable rate, it both needed and was able to attract larger firms. In this respect it was more like the new than the other expanding towns but here again there were significant differences. The new towns were closer to London and offered a rather more attractive environment than Swindon. As we have seen in the case of Crawley there was no shortage of firms that wished to go to London new towns, and even if some of them could not get Industrial Development Certificates there were plenty of others willing to take their place. Most of these towns were able to offer a more pleasant environment for the sort of white collar or science-based industries that Swindon hoped to attract. Thomas's recent study of the London new towns shows just how successful many of them have been in attracting middle-class residents.[25] Swindon's situation was illustrated by a letter from one of the world's largest chemical companies which had decided against locating its British headquarters in the town. Apart from the distance of the town from major airports in the London area, the managing director wrote, 'The second less important reason is in a much more difficult, because subjective, area. To put it in a nutshell it is the question of "image". You may remember that this was a point brought out in our discussions. People are the principal asset of a business. It is out considered opinion that news of a move to Swindon would cause an unacceptably large

---

[25] Thomas, R. *London's New Towns*. (London: P.E.P., 1969).

number of staff to leave us'. This letter was written in 1968, when the town was well-established as an area of growing opportunities and had lost much of its old railway image. Nevertheless some firms were still unwilling to come to the town because of this factor. Obviously fifteen years earlier the situation was even more in Swindon's disfavour. As, for many years at least, the town could not hope to attract the same sort of firms that went to the new towns and as it was also necessary to bring in relatively large employers of labour, it became clear that the town was, unlike most other new communities, in direct competition with the development areas for large employers of skilled and semi-skilled manual workers. In the light of this knowledge, the particularly strained relations between the Council and the Board of Trade is understandable.

An examination of the structure of industry in Swindon and the other expanding towns underlines some of the differences that we have referred to and demonstrates the similarities between the town and the development areas. The size factor has already been discussed, but the type of industry is also of interest. Cameron and Clark mention vehicle plants as one of the main types of factory that have gone to peripheral areas rather than overspill towns. The G.L.C. survey concluded that this industry was barely represented in the expanding towns, except at Swindon where Pressed Steel and Plessey employed 22.6 per cent of the economically active population in 1966 and dominated the town's labour market. Many of the expanding towns' firms are plants which moved in their entirety to the town, whereas many of the plants in the peripheral areas are branches of firms with headquarters elsewhere. Almost none of the new major employers of labour that have moved to Swindon since expansion began have moved their whole enterprise there. They have either moved a part of their activities from elsewhere, or started a factory in the town in order to carry out some wholly new process. The proportion of women that are employed in Swindon's newer factories also compares closely with the proportion in the development areas. The G.L.C. sampled the proportion of males to females employed in eight town development schemes and found that by far the highest proportion was on Swindon's Greenbridge estate, where there were 93 female employees to every 100 male workers.[26]

We have shown how the working of national trends and policies presented some obstacles to the expansion scheme. However certain aspects of the processes we have outlined provided the Council with a powerful lever which enabled it to circumvent, or at least greatly to weaken, the attempts of the County Council and the surrounding districts to limit the geographical area and the size of the development.

In Chapter 2 we showed that by the end of the fifties there was an urgent need for more factory land. This had to be found across the borough boundary, in the area of the Highworth Rural District Council. This was not envisaged in the original plan. The main reason for this misapprehension was the unrealistic assumption which was made in many places in the early fifties, that firms would settle in the expanding towns and immediately fill their sites to capacity. In fact, as we have seen in the previous section, most of the firms that moved were expanding their employment for many years after the move. To do this they wanted to purchase or rent sites on the new estates which were far larger than their immediate requirements would justify. So the planned densities were not achieved for a long time. The general lack of foresight is illustrated, in Swindon's case, by an exchange of letters in the mid-fifties between the Ministry and the Council. The Ministry accused the Council of leasing extravagantly large sites to industrialists and wasting valuable land.

When the Council realized that the land that they had set aside for industry would not be sufficient, given their commitment to a rate of population growth which outstripped the rate at which the existing industrial estates could generate jobs, the need for more industrial land became obvious. However, as the new estates filled up and the older estates continued to expand it was equally clear that the growth potential of the firms that had been attracted was such that more jobs would be created than were originally planned. This in turn meant that more houses had to be built than in the initial plan. As we have seen, most of these were private houses and they were sited just outside the Borough, so that the total population of the town proper was not much above the planned target. However the total population generated by

---

[26] The next highest was Witham where there were only 78 females to every 100 males.

town development, including those beyond the boundary, was
far more than originally intended. If it had not been for the
need to find many new jobs for redundant railwaymen in the
sixties, this effect would have been even greater than it was.

A further consequence of such a situation, given the fact
that most of the newcomers were young couples of child-
bearing age, is that the second-generation demand for new
jobs and houses will be far larger than originally predicted,
thus creating a further demand for houses and factories. This
in turn, will generate more jobs over successive years. This
pattern is inevitable so long as a policy of forced growth
continues and only ceases if industrial expansion and the
population inflow are allowed to tail off naturally, as has
happened in some new towns. It only began to be recognized
in Swindon at the time of the town's first major expansion over
the border in 1960. The County Council and the Rural
Districts then became uneasily aware that, unless it was
controlled, this 'leap-frogging' process could continue almost
indefinitely. However, the Borough Council, far from trying
to slow the process down, realized that as long as they could (in
the Town Clerk's words) 'keep the momentum going' even on a
small scale, they could reach, and even surpass, their original
population target by a process which it would be difficult for
any outside agency to control. Of course there may be physical
limits to the expansion of the town. It may also be limited by
the availability of enough industry with the right sort of jobs,
or it may even be stopped because the political will to grow is
lost. But unless this or some similar circumstance, such as a
central government ban on more firms going to the town,
occurs it seems that town development has initiated a dynamic
process of growth, which could continue even if the G.L.C.
abandoned its policy of supporting such development.

Conclusion

The difficulties we have analysed in this chapter were
probably the severest that Swindon had to face, because jobs
were so essential for expansion and because of the lack of
much local control over both the numbers and the type that
came to the town. The industrial pattern which emerged from
this situation differed markedly from the pattern in the other
expanding towns and, indeed, from Swindon's original plan.

Some of the consequences of this pattern may not be desirable in the long run.

Although the town is still dominated by engineering, and the diversification of industries has been less than initially hoped for, there has been some diversification of employers within this industry. There has also been a growth of other opportunities for, although engineering still dominates, other industries have come into the town as well. However two firms, Plessey and Pressed Steel, employ a very large number of the town's workforce. So if either of these companies fall on hard times the town would be very severely affected. A number of other local companies are also wholly dependent on the fortunes of these giants. Moreover both these firms depend on the market for cars for further expansion, and this has fluctuated sharply. The incidence of layoffs and short-time working in Swindon has increased since the motor industry took over from the railways as the dominant employer. This fact must be set against the higher wages that the industry has brought into the town. The manager of the local Labour Exchange referred in an interview to another aspect of this situation. While Swindon has some of the best apprenticeship and training facilities in the country for school leavers who wish to go into engineering, it is noticeably lacking in such opportunities in other areas of manufacturing industry, especially science-based ones. There are also few large employers of white collar or construction workers and, as a survey of local firms discovered, opportunities for promotion in the firms that do exist are very limited.[27]

Apart from the difficulty of finding enough jobs for unskilled male employees which are common to all new and expanding towns, perhaps the most serious legacy for the future that has been created by Swindon's policy concerns the balance between male and female employment. We have already seen that mobile industry tends to employ more

---

[27] Hudson, K. *An Awkward Size for a Town* (Newton Abbott: David and Charles, 1967) Chapter 6. This chapter describes the situation in the late sixties. However in the 1970s there is an increasing flow of office employment into the town and the Town Clerk has suggested that in future the town may become an office and service centre employing a high proportion of white collar workers. If this is so the problem referred to in the next paragraph may become acute.

females than non-mobile industry and that much of the employment growth in expanding towns is in female jobs anyway. The previous section referred to a G.L.C. report which suggested that some towns had grabbed at whatever industry they could get. As a result, a bad balance between male and female job opportunities had resulted. It is not surprising that Swindon was one of the three examples which the G.L.C. gave of towns where this inbalance had occurred. Thus in March 1966 there were 562 outstanding vacancies for female labour in the town. This acute shortage of female labour had developed several years previously and there were unfilled female jobs in the town, even during the worst phase of the economy in the sixties, when male unemployment rose to a far higher level than it had ever reached in the fifties. There were signs in the later years of expansion that this shortage was inhibiting the expansion plans of some firms. However, the real problem for town development was the increasing difficulty of finding enough male jobs to keep growth going.

The growing popularity of the town as a centre for wholesale and retail distribution was another problem. The Council began to receive many applications from firms who wanted to build warehouses because of the town's strategic location on the route of the South Wales motorway and within easy reach of the West Country, the South Coast, and the Midlands. The largest mover in this category by the end of the sixties was W. H. Smith, who moved their main distribution depot to Swindon in 1967. For an expanding town the disadvantage of such firms is that they do not provide a great deal of employment, particularly when they have been relocated in modern premises which enable them to make the best use of mechanization. Of course their presence is of financial benefit, because of the rates and rent they pay on their premises. However, because of the small amount of employment that they generate the Council had not encouraged them to come to the town in the fifties or early sixties. But, as the difficulty of attracting any new employment grew in the permanently unsettled economic conditions of recent years, even firms that made a small contribution to employment had to be accepted. There seems little doubt that, given the advantages of the town's location, this industry will expand in the town still further.

This distinctive pattern was a direct result of the attitude of Swindon's key policy makers to expansion. As we saw, their main motivation for embarking on town development was in order to improve the economic and physical state of the town. This was why expansion was a popular political move within the town, but it was unwilling to give up any of its independence and freedom of action in the process. Given these attitudes and the size of the expansion, quite unlike anything else that was being implemented in the fifties, Swindon inevitably became a special case. This was so because of the type and quality of mobile industry coming from London. Although it was ideal for the majority of town expansion schemes, it was insufficient to support an expansion of Swindon's magnitude. Others were content to remain within the rules set by national policy, and accept a limited rate of growth if necessary. But Swindon refused to accept the limitations that this would have placed on them and used the ability they did have for independent action to attract industry — be it big or small, from London or elsewhere — to the utmost.

The recurrent stop-go cycles in the British economy also had a profound effect on expansion and this, together with the factors mentioned above, created an atmosphere in which the policy makers and executives adopted an opportunistic strategy, seizing chances to press ahead with growth whenever they occurred. We have seen that this method of working was successful; it did bring industry into the town, did allow the original population target to be reached, and was skilfully manipulated in order to minimize the constraints imposed by those who were hostile to expansion. In conclusion, the town's original industrial goals were significantly modified during the course of expansion because of its relatively weak bargaining position in this sphere. The outcome was a compromise which, while it achieved much that was desired, was possibly going to be a source of some problems in the future.

Chapter Five

Estate Development

Land acquisition

The last two chapters showed how town development puts new demands on the local authority carrying it out. The influx of population requires a rapid build-up of jobs, houses, and social services. It is necessary therefore to eliminate, reduce, or circumvent obstacles to accomplishing these ends. However, the first step after concluding a town expansion agreement must be to obtain the land on which all these developments can take place. A wide range of obstacles had to be overcome during the process of land acquisition in Swindon and a similarly wide range of techniques were used to do this.

Land was required for expansion in two distinctive locations: in the town centre for shopping and commercial expansion, for the provision of amenities, and for a new road system; and at the periphery, for new houses and factories. Different, though overlapping, interests, problems, and attitudes were involved in each case. This makes it necessary to deal separately with the histories of the conflicts that were generated and the ways in which they were resolved. This section deals with the problems of peripheral expansion and the next section with the redevelopment of the town centre.

When a new town is proposed the Minister makes a draft designation order to which objection can be made. These objections are then the subject of a public inquiry at which with some restrictions, the 'pros' and 'cons' of the proposal can be debated. The Town Development Act does not have any similar procedure. If a council wishes to become a receiving authority all it has to do, apart from getting Ministry agreement, is to get planning permission from the planning authority and obtain the land to develop, either by agreement or by compulsory purchase. There will only be a discussion of the proposal at an inquiry if there are objections to a compulsory purchase order, or 'if the development involves a substantial departure from the statutory development plan and the Minister decides that there must be an inquiry.

There was no statutory development plan when expansion started in Swindon. However there was a draft plan, drawn up by the County Council, which was soon itself to be the subject of an inquiry. This plan envisaged development in an area to the east of the town, and as we have seen the County Council, urged on discreetly by the Ministry, agreed to give planning permission for the scheme. So there was no inquiry which dealt specifically with the planning proposals, despite the fact that some wanted the scheme to be considered at the landowners' development plan inquiry. However there were objections to the subsequent compulsory purchase order and for a time it looked as if the whole future of town development in Swindon was in doubt.

The development of Swindon's postwar housing programme in the Moredon area, to the north of the town centre, had used up virtually all the available land within the borough boundary. One substantial area of land remained untouched. This was the Walcot district, to the south east of the town (see Figure 2.2). In the 1930s there was some small-scale private development on the western fringe of this land, but only a small part of the area was suitable for building. The limiting factor was the absence of adequate sewers. As Moredon neared completion the Council turned to the development of the Penhill area to the north of Moredon, beyond the borough boundary in Highworth Rural District, as it was unable at that time to build the major new intercepting sewer that was required in order to develop Walcot. Highworth opposed this scheme and the Ministry of Town and Country Planning did not like it but, because there was no real alternative, was forced to agree. The area was finally brought within the Borough boundary by the Swindon Corporation Act 1951, the

Rural District having resigned itself in the meantime to the loss of the area.

In the course of the Penhill controversy the Borough had promised the Ministry that they would not try to develop further beyond the boundary before they had used up the land at Walcot. Plans were drawn up for the new sewer and by the time town development was being considered the work was about to start. After this was completed there was no impediment to the use of all the land in the area. The plan was for comprehensive development in five neighbourhood units. So the Council made two compulsory purchase orders, the Swindon (Walcot and Lawn) Compulsory Purchase Order 1952 and the Swindon (North of Marlborough Road) Compulsory Purchase Order 1952. These orders covered about half the available area. The smaller order covered 89 acres, to the north and south of the old mansion at The Lawn (which had been bought as an open space by the Council). This was intended to provide land for the growing demand for new private housing. The larger order, for 427 acres, took in the land of three farms immediately east of this area. It was to provide the land for some more private and all the public housing development for the next few years. In making these orders, Swindon was motivated by the need for more land for its own local housing needs, but also by the knowledge that negotiations over town development were likely to be successful and that some of the area would be used to house London overspill. However, the Council found itself in a dilemma which made it decide to claim that the orders could be entirely justified by the extent of unmet local housing needs. This lay it open to damaging attacks on its credibility at the public inquiry and was the cause of a major setback to town development before it had even begun.

When the 1952 compulsory purchase orders were made the Town Development Bill was still going through Parliament, so it could not be used to justify the orders. The only alternative was to make them under the 1936 Housing Act, for the needs of the local waiting list and the reception of overspill. The problem was that this act referred to providing housing to meet 'the needs of the district'. Could provision for people not initially in the district fall within this description? According to a legal judgement this phrase could be interpreted in a wide sense, and not just to mean 'the needs of the people in the district'. Therefore, as Swindon had been accepted as a receiving authority by the Ministry, the Council felt that it could go ahead and make an order under the 1936 Act. Counsel's opinion was taken and it confirmed this view.[1]

Swindon's case received a setback when the counsel conducting their case before the inquiry decided that he could not accept the construction put on the 1936 Act and present evidence of the need to accommodate London overspill. Probably this was because the evidence that Swindon was a receiving district was of little legal validity until the Town Development Bill became law. At this stage it might have been sensible to wait for the law to be passed, but the problem which came to be known as 'maintaining the momentum' made essential the early acquisition of more land. In developing Penhill and Moredon, Swindon had built up a large house-construction organization. This consisted of a direct labour force which prepared sites and roads, and a few big contractors who built the houses. The main limitation on expansion of the housing output was the acute scarcity of skilled building labour. Unless these two labour forces could go ahead with new work as soon as the Penhill estate was finished, in the autumn of 1953, the men would disperse. It might then take a very long time to assemble a new building organization. In between the uncertainties of the law and the problem of development, the Council chose to risk the former and go ahead with the orders.

In fact the Minister confirmed the smaller order, but the case for the larger order carried no conviction and it was rejected. The decision letter said, 'As regards the Swindon (Walcot and Lawn) Housing Compulsory Purchase Order, the Minister observes that at the public local inquiry into this Order it was argued on behalf of your Council that all the land included in this Order was needed for houses to be built for people now living in Swindon, and it was said that if any land

---

[1] It might be thought that Swindon should simply have asked the Ministry for their view but it has to be remembered that government departments will never interpret the law as this is up to the courts, although they may hint at their views. Also the Minister concerned here was also expected to act in a quasi-judicial role and decide whether to grant the orders so he could not be seen to act in a partisan way by openly advising one side before the inquiry began.

had been included to provide for houses for people from London that should be excluded from this Order. The Minister is not satisfied that given those conditions a case has been made for the acquisition of the land included in the Swindon (Walcot and Lawn) Housing Compulsory Purchase Order, 1952, and he has therefore decided not to confirm it'. The tension between the role that the Minister plays as an impartial arbiter and his role as the initiator of housing and planning policies often results in such oracular statements. In this case the Ministry wished expansion to go ahead but could not, acting in the role of arbiter, allow this order to be confirmed. The decision letter hinted at a way out, the key phrase being 'The Minister is not satisfied that *given those conditions,* a case has been made for the acquisition of the land . . .'. The Council realized that the Ministry was obliquely suggesting that a compulsory purchase order made under other powers, i.e. the Town Development Act (which was law by this time), would be considered. This was confirmed in informal discussions with the Ministry. Later on the Town Clerk learnt that the Ministry lawyers had agreed with Swindon's initial interpretation of the 1936 Act, and they would have upheld an application under this Act for town development purposes and even taken the case to the High Court if necessary.[2]

The crisis created by this decision was resolved by building on an area to the north of Penhill, known as the Valley. Originally this area, which was cut off from the rest of the new estate by a steep slope, was to be left as open space. As we saw in Chapter 3, the social consequences of this decision were bad, but it was a necessary compromise if building operations were to be maintained. This pattern of crisis and compromise, already evident in the decision to accept the reduction of the ultimate population target insisted on by the County Council,

---

[2] Objectors can appeal to the High Court concerning a Ministerial decision about a compulsory purchase order, but only if they can argue that the Minister has misinterpreted the law or associated rules and regulations. The fact that they felt that they could not tell the Council about this before the inquiry but had to leave them to make a wrong decision clearly illustrates the extent to which the Ministry would avoid intervening in a local controversy which they were being asked to judge at a later date.

was to be a common feature of town development. Meanwhile a new order was made under the Town Development Act and the Council took steps to ensure that they had a far stronger case than before. Apart from retaining a series of expert witnesses, they reduced the compulsory purchase order to about 250 acres. The order was confined to two farms and unlike the previous order it avoided cutting across other farm boundaries. This was only a part of the land that would be required for expansion, but the Council hoped that once they had a successful compulsory purchase order the rest could be gained by negotiation. As it turned out this assumption was correct.

The making of these compulsory purchase orders gave local opposition to expansion the best opportunity to intervene that it was to have during the whole process of town development. The main opposition to the orders came from the farming interests. These included not only the tenant farmers directly affected and the owners of the estate, the Goddard family, but the National Farmers' Union, the local Conservative Members of Parliament, and a powerful element on the County Council. The Ministry of Agriculture was also unhappy at the prospect of losing farming land. In the early fifties there was a great deal of public concern about this issue and several newspapers attacked the Swindon 'land grab'. Many of the county interests believed that the order was nothing more than another attempt by Swindon to increase its population sufficiently to become a county borough. In fact the Borough's major concern was with revitalizing its economic structure. There is no doubt however, that the Council hoped that expansion would enable them to sever their connections with the County Council.

On the other side, the Council was supported by the L.C.C. and Tottenham Borough Council, who both hoped to send people to Swindon. The Ministry was also enthusiastic but for the reasons already discussed neither they nor the Ministry of Agriculture could give direct public support to the contestants. Having accepted Swindon as an expanding town and having agreed to give financial help, all they could do further was to pressure the Ministry of Agriculture not to object to the order.

Each side attempted to mobilize support for its case. The

local N.F.U. contacted their national headquarters and a lobby of M.P.s was arranged. The well-known broadcaster and farmer A. G. Street made dire remarks on the radio about the scheme, and wrote in the *Farmer's Weekly* that 'Unless there is a determined and united protest 2500 acres of agricultural land in the neighbourhood of Swindon will be taken over for rehousing one of London's suburbs . . . Must we wait until hunger is knocking at the door before the nation puts its food supplies first?'.[3] An article in *The Times* gave publicity to the farmers' case, although at the insistence of the Town Clerk they later published a story giving Swindon's case. The *Daily Mail's* cartoonist, parodying a Cruickshank etching, showed the victorious march of an army of building implements over the defenceless fields under the banner 'On to Swindon'.

The *Daily Mail* also referred to the tragedy of two farmers and concluded that 'this is not a question of amenity but of mere survival'. The claims that were made became more and more lurid as the propaganda battle went on. A local farmer said that Swindon wanted to take 2785 acres and twenty farms to transfer 'I don't know how many people from Tottenham, industry and all. These people have made a slum in one part of the world, and now they want to come and make one in Swindon'. This statement was deeply resented in London. Even the lunatic fringe got in on the act. A spine-chilling letter to the Council said that, 'Great Angels, who were working in connection with other planets, became aware that a terrible cataclysm was hanging over the earth planet and they are now gathering to prevent it'. The letter concluded, 'In every country the terrorists will be found dead, and they will never return. The affairs of all nations will come under control, and everything will be rightly ordered, for the first time. The eviction of farmers will cease entirely'.

The Swindon conflict assumed national significance because it provided a focus for the disquiet among rural interests about the takeover of land for housing which had been steadily growing as the postwar housing and new towns programmes got under way. A group of backbench

---

[3] *The Farmer's Weekly,* 21 March 1952.

Conservative M.P.s tried to put pressure on the government to veto the Swindon operation, and one of them moved the adjournment of the House of Commons on the issue. Despite the fact that the Town Clerk preferred to maintain a dignified silence and negotiate and conciliate rather than campaign, some of the attack had to be countered. The local newspaper supported the scheme and was a valuable propaganda weapon but there was also a need to mobilize support, or at least prevent objections, from the main interest groups within the town. The Labour movement supported the Council, not surprisingly as it was Labour controlled, and the M.P. (also Labour) spoke for the town in the Commons, refusing to associate with the farmers' successful attempt to involve all the other Wiltshire M.P.s in their cause. Local business interests were another main source of possible opposition. The Town Clerk addressed meetings of the Chamber of Commerce and the Rotary Club, trying to persuade them that expansion would benefit them, and that the alternative was stagnation. From the report of the Rotary meeting in the local press it appears that he had a rather sceptical reception, but a later report of a meeting with the N.F.U. suggests that the farmers were given a fairly unsympathetic hearing.[4] Perhaps they acted as unwitting advocates for the Town Clerk's case. Anyway, there was no opposition to expansion from the business community and over the years their positive support for it seems to have grown. Even the prospective Conservative candidate, who might be expected to oppose a plan inspired by his political opponents, differed sharply from his party colleagues in the surrounding county and supported expansion, agreeing that it should not be made 'a political matter'.[5]

The second inquiry was an embarrassment for the Council because they had to justify the new order soon after the first had been rejected. It claimed that the situation had changed, town development was now a reality, and so the land was needed. The problem of how the local needs would be met which it had claimed would take up all the far larger area of

---

[4] See reports in the *Evening Advertiser*, 20 March 1952 and 11 April 1952.
[5] *Evening Advertiser*, 14 August 1954.

land it had wanted at the first enquiry, was passed over lightly. It argued that it now wanted only a small area of relatively poor farming land. Expert witnesses were called to counter the N.F.U.'s claim that the land was of good agricultural quality. Sir Frederick Osborn came along to give the Town and County Planning Association seal of approval to the scheme. The L.C.C. and Tottenham gave evidence of the pressing housing needs in their areas and the willingness of people on their housing lists to move to Swindon. Of course the Ministry could not come out in Swindon's favour at the inquiry, but letters were produced from them which approved the scheme and promised financial support. The Trades Council also gave evidence in favour of expansion. The County Council confirmed their agreement to the scheme, provided that Swindon stayed within its boundaries.

For the opposition, Sir Henry Wells, then Chairman of the Hemel Hempstead Development Corporation and a partner in one of the largest estate agents and surveyors in the country, attacked the choice of Swindon as an expansion project. His warning 'It is my belief that Swindon will ultimately regret expansion if the Minister approves it' was reinforced by the Chairman of his town's council.[6] It can only be a matter for speculation at this distance in time, whether the rather strange coalition of farmers and new town interests occurred because of new town antagonism to the Town Development Act, or was a purely professional and temporary alliance.

This order was the first one that had been made under the new Act and the Ministry of Housing was anxious to see that it was successful. No doubt there was a high level of political interest and support for this new measure. The Ministry of Agriculture provided the main opposition within government to the order, so an important part of the argument took place in Whitehall rather than at the inquiry. However the Minister of Housing had his way and so the opposition adopted a defensive strategy. This had been illustrated by the Parliamentary Secretary to the Ministry when he had spoken to Wiltshire farmers, at the time of the first inquiry. He told them that it was not possible to stop new houses; they could

---

[6] Inquiry Transcript, Evidence of Sir Henry Wells.

only try to direct new development so that it would do as little damage to agriculture as possible. He concluded 'We feel we are fighting a rear guard action'.[7] Eventually the second order was confirmed and the Ministry of Agriculture could only ensure that the land was taken over in an orderly way, and that large tracts were not left derelict to spoil the surrounding farming land.

After this battle, the rest of the 1000 acres of land within the Borough boundary needed for expansion were acquired by negotiation. The Goddard Estate and the Church Commissioners, who were major land owners in the area, accepted that the land would now be developed and were mainly concerned to minimize the hardship to their tenants. However, the Ministry of Agriculture was unhappy and the Ministry of Housing worked hard to ensure that it did not object to the takeover. Not until the County Development Plan, which designated the whole area for expansion, was settled at the end of 1954 were the objections finally overcome. The delicate nature of the situation was summed up in a letter from a Ministry of Housing civil servant to the Town Clerk. The Clerk wanted to press ahead with the acquisition of the remaining farms, justifying this action by the fact that the County Council had granted planning permission for the area.

The civil servant wrote, 'I do not think that the Department [of Agriculture] is in fact aware that you have a planning permission for this area. If they did know I have no doubt that we should be pressed to make an order revoking it. You can imagine that I am not at all anxious to stir up this sort of trouble'. However more housing land was now urgently needed as Pressed Steel had decided to come to the town. But the Ministry of Agriculture did not capitulate until April 1955, and finally agreed that the whole of the Walcot area could be released for development. By the middle of 1956 the Council possessed all the land required for the first phase of growth.

By 1959 there was increasing pressure for more private housing in Swindon, but little open land remained within the town boundaries. Swindon tried to persuade Local Government Boundary Commission that its boundaries should

---

[7] *Evening Advertiser*, 26 April 1952.

be altered in order to make more land available. Meanwhile private builders were buying up farm land in the area adjacent to Walcot, just over the border. The Council wanted to make a comprehensive plan for this area but the private operators were endangering this aim. The Council applied for planning permission for 400 acres of this land. It also asked the County Council to designate all the 'white land' between the border boundary and Ermin Street as an area of town development. The boundary issue was left to be settled later.

The 1959 Town and Country Planning Act had altered the basis of compensation, so that farmers got development value for their land rather than the lower agricultural value. This made them far more willing to sell for development. Concern about the loss of farming land in the area had subsided and the Ministry of Agriculture was either unwilling, or unable, to object strongly to its loss. Luckily for Swindon large parts of the area were owned by the Church Commissioners who, to ensure orderly development, were prepared to ignore the many letters that they were getting from speculators who wanted to buy their land and sell it to the Council. Other parts of the area had already been bought by negotiation. The pattern of land ownership was completed by two areas owned by local builders, and one each by Merton College, Oxford, and by a farmer. The assembly of all this land required a complex series of negotiations and bargains which stretched over the next seven years. The initial problem, however, was to persuade the County Council to designate the whole of the 1400 acres involved as an area suitable for town development. This involved a major departure from the development plan.

The County Council understandably felt that, if the whole area was designated as an area of town development, this committed them to a whole new phase of town development, in the course of which the original limit that they had placed on the growth of the town would be exceeded. Indeed, according to a counsel's opinion that they obtained, before the County could make the designation Swindon would have to declare that they were going to take more overspill from London. This was difficult because the Borough did not at that time want to go ahead with a new scheme. They only wanted to make sure, when they did go ahead, that the price that they paid for any land that they bought in the area would be set by the district valuer at a level which disregarded the element of value added to the land by the likelihood that it would in fact be used for such a purpose. Despite the fact that borough officials were keen to expand even further, no policy decision had been taken. Also the essential negotiations with ministeries, exporting authorities, and the rural district in whose area the land lay would take time. Meanwhile there was every sign that speculators, having realized that such negotiations were going on, would buy up as much land as they could. So the immediate objective was to safeguard land for possible future development, and to get planning permission for houses and factories on the northern part of the land.

The Ministry of Housing agreed with the County that the designation of the whole area for town development would raise broad issues of principle which might warrant a public inquiry. So Swindon obtained the immediate planning permission they required and the designation issue was shelved. Despite the fact that this permission involved a substantial departure from the Development Plan, and therefore had to be approved by the Minister, this was done without a public inquiry. In fact there were few objections because Swindon had managed, by a series of purchases and exchanges of land, to conciliate the major interests in the area. However the apparent ease with which this permission went through can also be traced to the influence of the civil servant dealing with the matter. He had a great interest in Swindon (stimulated by the Town Clerk) and played a major role in conciliating the Ministry of Agriculture and in mediating between the Borough and County Councils.

By late 1961 the Council controlled all the land at the northern end of the 1400 acres, so they controlled access to the whole site. They had also bought up enough land on the rest of the site to ensure that the other developers would have to co-operate with them. The County Council, faced by the pressure that Swindon's growth had put on the villages in the subregion, agreed that the housing should be located in the area to the east of Swindon rather than elsewhere. Furthermore, if this was to be done it should be as a part of a comprehensive plan. In these circumstances the Borough could afford to take their time about preparing proposals for the rest of the land. It was not until 1966 that they produced a scheme for this area (known as South Dorcan), which then became the first stage proper of the second phase of town development. Despite the fact that a part of the 400 acre site (which came to be known as North Dorcan) was originally required for public housing, the credit squeeze of 1961 forced Swindon to reduce the rate at which it went ahead with development. By the time that the brakes were taken off the demand for public housing could be met by the existing stock for reasons which have been discussed already. Ultimately the North Dorcan site was used for industry, private housing, and for the Corporation's houses for sale scheme.

Central area development

Reference has already been made to the rather dreary nature of Swindon's town centre. J. B. Priestley was not the only person who found it a depressing place to be in. Councillors and their officials were also aware that something needed to be done. The first postwar planning scheme for the town centre has been described in Chapter 1. It was clearly not a practical plan. According to Ginsburg, the plan had 'obvious *beaux arts* origin' and 'an attempt to graft early 20th century town planning on to an old town centre'.[8] It ignored the fact that a living town centre already existed and proposed to sacrifice everything to a grand series of exhibitions of civic pride. There is no evidence that anyone took this plan really seriously, except perhaps its originators, and when Wiltshire County Council came to submit their statutory development plan to the Ministry in 1953 they left out this scheme from the Town Map. It had no traffic value and would therefore be unlikely to get a road grant; also there was not likely to be money available for development of this nature in the foreseeable future.

Very few counties or boroughs had anything like an adequate planning staff at this time and so, in the absence of any realistic plan from the Borough, the County Council submitted a Swindon Town Map which was simply a statement of the *status quo*. This unsatisfactory situation continued when, in 1954, the County withdrew even this proposal

---

[8] Ginsburg, L. B. 'Swindon — A Break through in Central Area Re development', *Official Architecture and Planning*, November, 196? pages 705-11.

simply defining 126 acres as the Central Area on a Supplementary Town Map which it then submitted. It did not make any definite proposals for this area.

Meanwhile town development was underway. When the Council started expansion they had little or no awareness of the need to renew and enlarge the obsolete facilities in the town centre that it would create. Certainly calculations of the costs and benefits of this operation did not enter into the financial appraisal of expansion by the Borough Treasurer which played a large part in persuading the Council to agree to take overspill. However, by 1954 the officers realized that something needed to be done. The close study that they had made of the new towns provoked this realization. In addition, local estate agents and surveyors began to report an increased interest in shop lettings in the town centre. Also, early in 1954, a firm of developers became interested in a site in the centre of the main shopping streets. Unless it was developed in accordance with an overall plan, any future comprehensive development of the surrounding areas could be prejudiced. The problem was the lack of any plan which could provide a sound basis for development control.

As a result of these pressures there was a rapid realization of the urgent need to have a plan for the orderly redevelopment of the central area. Little help was available from the county planners as their meagre resources were fully stretched. Anyway the Ministry had always expected county districts such as Swindon to take the lead in planning their own centres. This responsibility was gratefully accepted by the town, ever eager to assert its independence of the County. However, the task proved to be more difficult than either the councillors or officials could have expected. At first progress was rapid. A document from the Town Clerk's office, dated April 1954, stated that central area redevelopment was an urgent priority. It was essential that the Council gained some of the benefit of the expansion of commerce caused by town development in order to pay for the new public buildings that the enlarged town would require. Noting the rapid growth of private enterprise plans to redevelop, it concluded that a detailed central area plan should be prepared immediately.

The principles of development were stated by the Borough Surveyor in an interim report in August 1954. The development plan had contained a new road from the Walcot expansion area to the edge of the town centre. The Surveyor's plan proposed to carry this new road on to the station. One of the town's main eyesores was the filled-in course of the Wiltshire and Berkshire canal which ran right through the town centre, cutting across the main shopping area. Half way along the new road there was to be a roundabout and a road leading off, built on the site of the old canal, going through the central shopping street. This Canal Road would be linked with new shops and would provide, together with the existing main street, a new shopping area, bringing traffic from the new estates right into the town centre. Ginsburg aptly characterizes this as the Haussman approach.[9] Its deficiencies are all too obvious with the benefit of hindsight but it was several years before these became apparent to the Council and its officers.

Having prepared an outline plan, the Surveyor went ahead with working out the details. The Council did not receive another interim report until early 1957. By this time the Ministry were pressing Swindon to accelerate their pro- gramme. One reason for this was the example of Bletchley, which had left matters for so long that it was eventually pre- empted by private enterprise and was unable to assemble enough land to control development. The Ministry said that it was necessary to recoup some of the public money that had been put into the unremunerative elements of the town development scheme, by rebuilding the town centre and gaining ground rents and enhanced rateable value, thus echoing the Town Clerk's original paper. There were two reasons why the detailed work which was done in this period took so long. These were lack of expertise and staff shortages. These two problems will be discussed again later, but problems were regularly created during expansion by the inability or unwillingness of Swindon to pay the level of salaries that would attract rather more of the small numbers of skilled planners and architects that were available. Some of these problems were solved by using consultants.[10] However

---

[9] Ginsburg, op.cit.

[10] Thus, in 1956, Frederick Gibbard was hired to design a new neighbourhood shopping centre at the Park Estate and to act as architectural and civic design consultant for the central area.

the paucity of staff planning resources can be judged by the fact that, even at the time when the final plan emerged in 1962, the whole planning section of the Surveyor's department only consisted of two qualified and three unqualified staff. Furthermore, according to Ginsburg, the town planning group in the capital works section of that department (actually doing the plan) were a 'very dedicated and enthusiastic . . . three men and a boy'.[11] Of course the Town Clerk and the Treasurer were also deeply involved in matters such as controlling finance and assessing the social aspects of the plan implementation, but their skills could be of little use in doing the actual physical planning.

The interim report retained the features of the outline of 1954 but worked them out in greater detail. However it was not certain that the plan would be a commercial success. The planners' skills were of little use here, so a firm of specialist surveyors was commissioned to prepare a feasibility report. This was the start of the golden period for property developers that Marriott has reviewed.[12] The abolition of building licences by the Conservative Government, in November 1954, had released the pent-up demand for commercial property that had accumulated over the years. Vast fortunes were made by speculators and developers over the next decade. The most publicized developments, such as Centre Point, were in the big cities but, as Marriott shows, there was some redevelopment of provincial centres in the last half of the fifties and this business grew quickly after 1960. According to Marriott, the main reason for the lack of provincial activity in the early years was the scarcity of land in town centres. This made Swindon a fairly rare opportunity for developers and one likely to be much in demand. A number of estate agents made a good living by searching the country for good sites, acting as advisors to local authorities, and putting them in touch with likely developers. One of the firms that were often involved in such deals was the London-based agents Goddard and Smith who, hearing of the situation in Swindon, had contacted the Council and offered to become the sole agents for the development. It was this firm that was commissioned to examine the financial feasibility of the Surveyor's plans.

---

[11] Ginsburg, op.cit.
[12] Marriott, O. *The Property Boom* (London: Hamish Hamilton, 1967).

The agent's report revealed a conflict which was to become a common feature in town centre redevelopment. In 1962, by which time there was a flood of such schemes, the Royal Institute of British Architects and the Royal Institute of Chartered Surveyors became alarmed at what was being done. They issued a memorandum on 'Methods of Tendering for the Redevelopment of Central Areas' which, among other things, highlighted this conflict.[13] It was that 'the same developer rarely puts up the highest bid and the best scheme . . . The local authority is usually compelled to choose the most attractive financial offer or the best scheme . . . The local authority, particularly if its experience in this field is limited, is often tempted to choose what appears to be the most attractive financial offer, although by doing so it may be accepting an indifferent (if superficially attractive) scheme, and may be sacrificing the long term interests of the town for a shortlived financial gain'.[14] Swindon had to face this choice when the consultants presented their report in 1957. The officers of the Council wanted to start the new shopping development on the north-east side of the main shopping street (where there was a compulsory purchase order pending), and to link this with the new road to the station and a new bus station sited on this road. This would ensure orderly development and would site the major transport interchanges in the same area. A problem with this scheme was that part of the frontage of the new Canal Road opposite this site, which would have to be redeveloped as the next stage, was occupied by a school which might take some years to move. However, in the long term this would go. The resulting development would be a better planning solution than Goddard and Smith's plan, based on short-term financial considerations, which was to develop the other side of the main shopping street. The conflict was precisely that outlined in the R.I.B.A./R.I.C.S. memorandum, and a debate ensued at a special meeting of the councillors between the consultant and the officers. The Town Clerk stated the official view when he said 'I will be prepared to sacrifice something economically in order to make the town attractive'.

---

[13] *Methods of Tendering for Central Areas* (London: R.I.B.A./R.I.C.S January 1962).
[14] Ibid. page 2.

However, the conflict was not only one of planning versus economics. The method of disposal of whatever site was adopted to the developers was equally important. The R.I.B.A./R.I.C.S. memorandum strongly urged local authorities not to allow developers to tender competitively for a scheme, as they were not likely to submit an offer that was best both in terms of design and finance. Local authorities had to choose, within limits, between what was best for their town in terms of amenity and what was best financially. They should either specify the basic layout and architectural form, and then get the highest financial offer on that basis, or *vice versa*. A limited competition among selected developers on this basis, rather than a competition without restrictions was more likely to be successful. It was also important to ensure that as the rents of the shops and offices rose, the local authority shared a proportion of the increasing income with the developers. Some authorities had leased their town centres to developers for 99 or even 150 years on a fixed ground rent without any agreement of this sort. Consequently, the developer gained by far the greater benefit from the scheme, and the ratepayers got less rather than more of the benefit as the years went by. The councillors and officials in Swindon faced all these problems without the benefit of such eminent advice. Goddard and Smith suggested that bids be solicited from their select list of developers on the basis, later condemned by the professional bodies, of asking for design and financial proposals. Furthermore they suggested that they should hold a private auction between the selected developers. They enthusiastically told the Council that they had just auctioned the ground rent of part of a town centre for twice the reserve value, fixed on the basis of the district valuer's estimate of its worth. They concluded 'It was quite obvious in the Hall, however, both from the bidding and from the general boisterous attitude of the rival developers towards one another that the competition so created was alone certainly responsible for the later stages of the bidding'.

The dangers of this approach are neatly illustrated by Marriott in a chapter entitled, 'White Elephantiasis' in the case of Doncaster. 'Doncaster, on the advice of Gibberd [who was Swindon's consultant but not involved in their negotiations] and Goddard and Smith, one of the more thrusting among firms of estate agents, chose a crude method

of selecting a developer for their land. They auctioned it.
There are variations on this system but the variation picked by
Doncaster was to commission Gibberd to draw up an
extremely loose plan of the shopping centre and then allow
Goddard and Smith to invite developers to gather in an
auction room and bid for the privilege of developing the land.
This process of invitation was seldom discriminating. With
Doncaster the winner was a company which had little
experience of town centre development . . . the dangers of
such competition — over development and shoddy architecture
— are intense in an industry of limited knowledge'.[15]

The result of the almost inevitable overbidding that
this method produced on the part of the very inexperienced
developer that bought the site was that the shops were
too expensive for the amount of trade in the city so that,
by 1967, only about one in six of the ships were let and
Doncaster was only receiving a fraction of the rent it expected
to get.[16]

In summary, the confrontation between the Town Clerk
and the consultants was a conflict between a conception of
what was in the town's longer-term interest and what would be
in its short-term financial interest. The Council preferred its
officers' advice to the estate agent's and, in the light of the
experiences quoted above, this was probably the right choice.
The history of this division illustrates the benefits that
Swindon gained from having officers with a high degree of
competence and with the confidence of their Council. They
were able to persuade the Council to ignore expert advice,
which would probably have been impossible in other towns
without these advantages. After this episode the Town Clerk
and the Treasurer took effective control of the
implementation of redevelopment and, with the aid of the
plan and Gibberd's architectural advice, began to contact and
interview possible developers.

By 1958 the first stage of the planner's work was complete.

---

[15] Marriott op.cit. pages 289-91.

[16] A few pages later Marriott refers to the case of Preston where a ten-
storey office block stood empty for two years: 'It was an unhappy case of
the local authority owning a site . . . and letting it off at auction to the
highest bidder, who turned out to have been excessively sanguine. In this
instance Goddard and Smith organized the auction'.

The scheme was incorporated in a draft plan and twenty-year programme which was sent to the County Council for their comments and for eventual transmission to the Ministry as part of the Statutory Development Plan, which had still not been approved. Meanwhile there had already been several years of town development without any effective guide to action for those wishing to build in the town centre. Given the inordinate time it took the Ministry to approve development of plans and the immediate pressure for action, it was necessary to go ahead with piecemeal redevelopment, trying to ensure that the overall plan was not compromised. In 1956 the Council had decided that it would make its own start in the area to the north-east of the main shopping street, by making a compulsory purchase order. The immediate reason for action in this area (which, as we have seen, was a good place to start on general planning grounds) was that the Council was under pressure from a private developer who wanted to do a scheme there. As happened so often in the history of town development, the national economic situation made the Ministry unwilling to give loan sanction for this 'non essential development'. This situation also affected the expanding town of Bletchley. Together they sent a deputation to the Minister later that year, and this had the effect of changing his attitude, thus allowing Swindon to go ahead.

When the application for planning permission that accompanied this order was published the Council had to make outline plans clear for the first time. Public reaction, especially from the town's traders, could greatly affect the success of the new plan. The local paper heralded it as 'the final awakening from a ten year dream'.[17] The traders' reactions were more cautious and tinged with a certain cynicism that marked much public reaction to town development in its early years. According to the paper the most common reaction was that 'it might not be a bad thing', but the proposal to pedestrianize the main shopping street was disliked. It is probably lucky that this proposal did not come before an inquiry until 1962, when the success of pedestrianization had received some publicity and had been put into practice in a part of Swindon's central area.

---

[17] *Wiltshire Herald*, 11 November 1956.

After a number of setbacks, including the rejection of a compulsory purchase order on technical grounds, the process of land assembly which enabled the first part of redevelopment to go ahead was completed with the granting of the Swindon (Central Area) Compulsory Purchase Order in January 1959. In the absence of a statutory plan, orders under the planning acts were difficult to obtain, so Swindon made use of powers under the Town Development Act. These enabled it to argue that the development was required immediately, without waiting for a statutory plan, because of needs generated by town development. The scheme which formed the basis of this first stage of development involved building shops and offices to the north-east of the intersection of the new Canal Road with the main shopping street. In the first instance the northern side of the road was to be built on. This was to be followed as soon as the school on the other side of the new road could be removed by redevelopment of this side as well (and this was the subject of a whole series of negotiations with the County Education Officer and the Ministry of Education).

About sixty developers responded to the initial approaches of the Town Clerk and the Treasurer, but few of them were prepared to take the whole of this area while the school remained to break up the shopping frontage. In 1958 however, agreement was reached with the Oddenino Property Company. This company had followed a pattern which was similar to many of those that mushroomed in the fifties. It was originally a hotel chain, but was bought up by Instone Bloomfield in 1955. He sold off most of its hotel business, using the company as a 'shell' in order to get a Stock Market quotation and attract investment. Such companies were unlikely to appeal to investors (or local authorities looking for developers) on their own, largely untried, merits, so the next step was to get sound financial and technical backing. Bloomfield did this by getting the Pearl Insurance Company to guarantee his financial soundness, the well-known estate agents Marcus Leaver and Co. to be his main letting agents and negotiators, and, in Swindon's case, the firm of Shingler and Risdon to be his architects. Many people have wondered what the developer actually contributed to this mixture in order to justify the enormous profits that some of them gained. Beyond the ability to get the various experts and institutions working together, it is difficult to answer this question. As we shall see, this fact gradually became apparent to the officials and Council in Swindon.

The architects prepared a detailed scheme on the basis of the local authority brief, and this was approved by Frederick Gibberd. The Corporation was to purchase all the land required, most of this was done by 1959 either by compulsory purchase or negotiation, then they would lease it for ninety-nine years to Oddenino's for an agreed ground rent. When the lease came up for renewal at twenty-one year intervals the enhanced rents were to be shared between the town and the company on a predetermined ratio. By this means the rate-payers would gain some of the benefit of the increase of property values in the town centre.

The first shops in the new development were expected to open in 1960 or 1961, but one final delay in the long and complex process occurred. Towards the end of the fifties planners began to rethink the relationship between the pedestrian and the motor car. This reached the general public with the publication of the Buchanan Report in 1963 of course, but before this some planners had concluded that the two users should be segregated whenever possible, particularly in shopping centres. A number of towns pioneered this new approach, for example Coventry, Exeter, and Stevenage. However Swindon still planned to put an eighty-foot wide road through the middle of its shopping centre. This plan, with a road which would be wider than Regent Street in London, began to look dubious to some of the officers, particularly the Town Clerk and Treasurer who had seen and read about these new centres. However it is one thing for officials to present a united front to councillors in opposition to outside experts' advice, as had happened with Goddard and Smith, but much more difficult to oppose a brother officer's recommendations, especially on an issue where that officer is supposed to have the expert knowledge which his critics lack. The Surveyor was convinced that a road was the correct solution, so it looked as if his plan would go ahead, despite the fact that this would have left the town with a centre cut in half by a major barrier, and completely unable to cope with the pedestrian/vehicular conflict. It required the influence of a higher authority to alter the plan. When the Ministry approved the final compulsory purchase order in 1959, they expressed the wish that traffic should be discouraged from entering the area on the new road. In subsequent discussions the Ministry's technical experts went one step further, insisting that the new road be abandoned altogether and be replaced with a pedestrian precinct. By this time Oddenino's were anxious to start development but the Ministry now made it clear that they would not willingly approve the scheme unless the road was scrapped. The County Planning Officer was also keen to make this change, so somewhat reluctantly, but with at least the tacit approval of some of their officers, Swindon agreed.

Oddenino's were then able to go ahead and build the first stage fairly quickly. It was ready by 1962 and the other side of the precinct was rebuilt in the following few years.[18] Although this was done under Town Development Act powers, the rest of the central area plan had to rely for its acceptance on the successful designation of a comprehensive development area. Because this proposal was not contained in the 1953 development plan, there were three time-consuming processes to be gone through. The first was the approval of the 1953 plan. This involved a public inquiry and took until 1959 finally to clear the Ministry. The second was the submission of a combined Supplementary Town Map and Comprehensive Development Area, and the third was the making of compulsory purchase orders. As we have seen, the Town Map was ready by 1958, but after the scrapping of the Canal Road it had to be rewritten and did not have its public inquiry until 1962. This plan had many of the same features as the 1958 plan, but had an altered road network which, besides omitting the Canal Road, saved the historic Railway Village from destruction. Among other proposals, it designated for compulsory purchase sections of an area of twelve and a half acres to the west of the main shopping street. This was to be the site of the second phase of the pedestrianized shopping centre. Some of the area was already owned by the Borough, or was being bought by negotiation, but it was necessary to designate the rest so that a compulsory purchase order could be issued under planning act powers in order to complete the land assembly for the new centre. This, in turn, involved yet

---

[18] In all, this first phase of central area renewal contains 200 000 square feet of space (replacing the 25 000 square feet there before) consisting of 28 shops, 3 supermarkets, offices, and a hotel.

another public inquiry and the issue was not finally resolved in the Council's favour until 1968.

Before that date however, there had been a great deal of rethinking about how the second stage should be carried out. Initially it was intended to go into partnership with a developer on the same basis as before. A report from the Treasurer in 1962 discussed the terms of such an arrangement, but at the end of the document he suggested an alternative. The return to the town would be far greater if the Council supplied the developer's long-term finance after the development was finished, thus gaining the interest that he would pay on this finance, as well as the normal ground rent and a proportion of the rack rents. The developer would only have to find bridging finance during development. To do this, Swindon would have to get loan sanction to borrow the money over sixty years. The great benefit would come in the last thirty-nine years of the ninety-nine year lease, when the developer would carry on paying for a loan which Swindon would have liquidated. It was estimated that, if the Council lent £3m., these payments would amount to £225 000 per annum. This approach, which the Ministry christened the 'Swindon dodge', was a novel ideal and, in the words of a civil servant, required 'brooding over'. The question was whether local authorities should involve themselves in risk-taking ventures which were usually left to private enterprise. With a Conservative government in power, it was clear that this was a sensitive issue. Swindon argued that the risks were minimal, given the successful and continuing expansion of the town. Furthermore, as this had happened as a result of local enterprise and initiative it was only fair that they should reap the benefit. There were doubts about the legality of Swindon's proposal, but the Council pointed to the existence of little-used powers in the 1947 Town and Country Planning Act and powers contained in a local act which would enable them to go ahead. The argument that the required loan would encourage inflation was countered by the assertion that the equivalent amount of private borrowing would not be necessary if Swindon did the financing. Eventually the Minister agreed to the scheme, but then there was an election and Labour was returned to power. Surprisingly this seemed to renew the controversy. The Treasury said that the new Government thought that this type of expenditure should come from private enterprise: 'While politically the Labour Party might well be in favour of local authority ownership there was a proper distinction between owning and carrying out a scheme'. After some pressure, however, the previous government's permission was renewed, probably as a result of a decision which was taken at ministerial level.

This part of the history of the central area development illustrates one of the ways in which town development involved the local authority in new and unfamiliar roles but, as so often happened, discussions were overtaken by events. The 1963 Local Government Act gave local authorities the power to capitalize interest. With this new freedom the need to have outside finance during the unremunerative building phase disappeared. Reference was made above to the co-ordinative role of the developer, and it now seemed that the Council could itself carry out this role, hiring the necessary experts in much the same way as a commercial developer. In this manner the town would maximize the profits from redevelopment. Towards the end of 1965 the Minister personally approved this proposal, and so the second stage of central area development went ahead under Swindon's own auspices.

One of the main reasons for wanting to accelerate the pace of redevelopment which was quoted in the Town Clerk's original policy paper in 1954 was the need to provide new public buildings in the town centre. There was no large public hall, the library was housed in Nissen huts, the Arts Centre was in an inadequate building, and there was no theatre. Furthermore, there was a need for new police headquarters and a new court. The 1958 plan located all these functions in a new civic centre, but it was not until the sixties that a start could be made on this plan. Not surprisingly the court and the police headquarters proved easiest to finance; these were not the Council's responsibility anyway, but the volume of complaints within the town at the lack of an adequate cultural and recreational centre grew as the years went by. By 1964 town development was beginning to produce a profit and, as had always been intended, it was now possible to use this to finance amenities. In that year the first compulsory purchase order for the new civic hall was issued, and the architects Casson and Condor were commissioned to prepare plans. The detailed negotiations which then ensued are outside the scope of this book, but it is amusing to note that the complexity and difficulties that inevitably attend central area developments resulted in the new theatre, which was one of the lowest priorities in 1965, being built first, and the civic hall, the first priority, being left till last.

In retrospect the protracted history and difficulties of central area redevelopment in the town can partly be blamed on the inadequacy of the then current planning legislation, especially the 1947 Town and Country Planning Act. The cumbrous process of development plans, town maps, and comprehensive development areas was made even more long-winded by the fact that each stage had to be gone through separately, in this case mainly because of staffing shortages which made it impossible to submit a complete plan in 1953 and the many changes in a plan which was rapidly outdated by new ideas in town planning and by the growth in the town caused by expansion. Even if the plan had been ready in 1953 it is unlikely, given the amount of time the Ministry took to approve it, that any action would have occurred much before the early sixties anyway. By this time the pressure from private enterprise would have made it impossible for the Council to gain as full a share in the rising rental values in their centre as they did, but for the fact that they were able to make a start on redevelopment using the powers of the Town Development Act, thus circumventing the need to obtain the powers under the planning acts. This short-term expedient was reinforced by the extensive use of power of a local act which enabled Swindon to get loan sanction on property bought by agreement for the purposes of town centre renewal. While this start on development was going on, the longer process of replanning and gaining consent for the whole of the central area could also be pursued. It was not until almost ten years after the start of town expansion that Swindon could finally be said to have a firm statutory plan for its central area.

Conclusion

In this chapter we have seen how opposition at local and national level affected the process of land acquisition and central area development in Swindon. We have seen how, in both cases, what resulted were long and complex processes of conflict and resolution, in which bargains were struck or advantages gained over these who were in a position to offer effective opposition to Swindon's proposals. In this process professional planning and estate development skills also played an important role, but these were rarely decisive in themselves. What ensured their success was their adoption by those who had the power to decide. For example, the success of Swindon's technical argument about the value of the agricultural land they wished to purchase depended, in the last analysis, on its acceptance by the Ministry of Housing and that Ministry's ability, within the government, to press its policy of town development in the face of opposition from the Ministry of Agriculture. Similarly the arguments between the planners on pedestrianization were eventually resolved by ministerial action.

Because planning decisions, such as those analysed in this chapter, often involve a complex series of activities in which the numerous interests that are involved have many opportunities to intervene, they are apt to take a long time to reach fruition. This is an aspect of major planning proposals which is often criticized. It is a particularly serious problem in the case of town development, where the rapid increase of population puts an accelerating strain on obsolescent central area functions and, more generally, demands rapid and large-scale land acquisition. This in turn puts a premium on the degree of skill with which the development authority is able to overcome the constraints. The better they are at doing this the less delay that is likely. Also it is important that the financial benefit which comes from development or redevelopment is available to the authority to offset the cost of expansion. So, in both these cases, professional and political skills are required. Finally, land acquisition and redevelopment is a good example of the issues arising in town development which set the authority new organizational and financial problems demanding new solutions. It is these problems which form the topic of the next chapter.

Chapter Six

Organization and Finance

Financing expansion

In previous chapters we have looked at the basic ingredients of town development, the growth of population and social services, jobs, and land acquisition. There were two general problems which these new operations created, and to which answers had to be found. The first concerned the financing of physical, social, and industrial growth. The second concerned the organization required to carry out growth. Furthermore these two problems were interconnected; the new management disciplines that effective financing required had important effects on the organizational form that expansion took. However the sources of the problems which arise in the processes of financing and organizing expansion differed. The organization of expansion was largely determined by internal decisions and conflicts. In contrast the familiar range of external participants in town development, the Ministries, the L.C.C., the County Council, and the Rural Districts, had an important influence on the financial aspects of expansion. Control of finance is one of the main levers of power in government, so it is not surprising that a study of the financing of expansion is illustrative of the attitudes of most of the major participants in the scheme and reveals a crucial set of problems whose outcome often determines the success or failure of town development proposals.

The financial aspect of town development has often been a severe constraint, especially for the smaller towns which started with very few resources. The prospect of a rising rate burden has deterred many local councils for, despite the fact that growth creates rateable value, there is a gap between the time when heavy capital expenditure is incurred and the time when this becomes supported by increased revenue from rates and rents. In 1952 towns like Swindon were at a great disadvantage in comparison with the new towns. They were constrained by the rules of local government finance. These required that the loan charges on any new capital expenditure be serviced immediately from revenue. In contrast, new towns were allowed to capitalize the interest on such expenditure for a limited number of years, by which time revenue from the investment was available to meet the annual debt charges.[1]

In the early days of expansion the Minister of Housing and Local Government was empowered to make a contribution for each town development house which was equivalent to the statutory obligation that every local authority then had to give a fixed rate subsidy for each council house.[2] The Minister could also meet the cost of acquiring land for development, preparing sites for housing, sewage, water supply, and drainage. In fact central government grants were restricted to water supply, sewage, and drainage. Despite heavy pressure from exporting and receiving authorities, the Ministry refused to exercise its full powers under this section of the Act. Initially it was not even clear what percentage of the capital cost of these items which were eligible for grant would be covered by the government. However in 1956 the Minister announced that 50 per cent of the cost of new capital investment in these services which was attributable to town development would be provided by the government. This formula was to cause great confusion, but remained constant throughout Swindon's expansion.

---

[1] Eventually the government agreed, after much pressure from the local authorities, that they should have a similar power and the Local Government (Financial Provisions) Act 1963 allowed them in special circumstances such as those caused by town development to capitalize interest charges for up to five years. This came too late to help finance much of Swindon's expansion however.

[2] Town Development Act 1952, Section 2(2).

The expanding towns tried to persuade the Minister to make grants for amenity provision. They used the example of development corporations who were allowed to make a *per capita* amenity grant to the relevant local authorities. Swindon asked for money for common rooms, play areas, and other schemes which would always be unremunerative. They also wanted help with the redevelopment of the town centre and to develop a civic centre. The Ministry took the view that the town centre would eventually pay for itself, and even generate enough revenue to pay for other improvements such as the civic centre. So, perhaps understandably, they were unwilling to give a subsidy. However, the lack of the power to capitalize interest (until 1963) delayed redevelopment, and when it did occur a lot of the benefit accrued to private interests, rather than the ratepayers.

There can be less justification for the refusal to grant aid as far as the other amenities were concerned. This decision was dictated by financial stringency. In such a climate it was commonly held that social expenditure was an unnecessary frill, a short-sighted view. Eventually this policy was reconsidered, and when the Town Development Act was revised in 1968 grants were made available for amenities. However Swindon had suffered from the previous policy. Because the Council had to conserve its resources, original estates had to wait for many years before they got facilities which would today be regarded as essential and which were enjoyed by the new towns.

Expansion involved other major investments in the infrastructure. Expenditure on roads was the most important of these. We saw how the Ministry of Education at first seemed to overlook the special needs of expanding towns, but the Ministry of Transport was even less inclined to help. From 1939 to 1954 there was no national programme for road building. Highway authorities were forced to delay much needed repairs and improvements for years because of the national economic situation, so there was a massive backlog of urgent schemes when the roads programme was restarted in 1954/5. Even then little could be done, as only £5m. was available.[3] Schemes were only selected for grant aid if they would improve safety and reduce congestion. These narrowly-

[3] See Griffith, op.cit. Chapter 3.

defined aims were allowed to remain until, and even after, the Buchanan Report of 1963 criticized the lack of connection between road construction and urban planning.[4] Neither the new nor the expanding towns qualified for grant aid under these rules and, although the Ministry gave some help to the new towns, it was not prepared to help the expanding towns as well. Only when these towns' roads became overcongested, because of the increased burden created by town development, could they be considered for grants. The ridiculous nature of this procedure became obvious when these towns tried to get grants to help meet the cost of the new roads required to service the industrial and residential estates. In Swindon's case this is illustrated by the example of Queen's Drive, the major spine road linking the Walcot area with the town centre. Despite the fact that without this road some 20 000 people would be without access to the town centre, the Ministry's rules did not allow them to give a grant until the need was actually present. Presumably this would have required the Council to build the estates and then apply for a grant. Of course this was totally impracticable, so the Council built the first carriageway of the road at the ratepayers' expense. Only when this was seen to be insufficient did the Ministry give a grant for the second carriageway to be built. To add insult to injury, they refused to give a retrospective grant for the first carriageway. They argued that this single width was not up to the standard which allowed it, when built, to be designated as a major road, which could then qualify for a grant.

Swindon also suffered from the reluctance of the major roads authority in the area, the County Council, to contribute towards the cost of the required road improvements. Given the situation, this attitude was understandable. There was little money available and Swindon might easily have swallowed it all up. This would have led to allegations of favouritism from other parts of the County, as in the case of school buildings. The Ministry of Transport was slow to agree that the expanding towns had special needs which would not neatly fit into the set of rules governing the allocation of grants. In 1965 it was finally agreed to set aside a special quota for the towns. It also proposed to try and ensure that at a time when the road

---

[4] *Traffic in Towns*, (Harmondsworth: Penguin in association with H.M.S.O., 1964).

programme was cut, the expanding town programme would not be disrupted.

Under the Town Development Act, county councils could make contributions to town development authorities in their areas. This was only a permissive power, but a number of counties, notably West Suffolk and Worcestershire, did give help. In most cases the receiving authorities were small and could not have gone ahead with expansion without some help. The county councils favoured development, because it would help to revitalize towns which might otherwise become a heavy burden. It also enabled the counties to exert some control over what went on. Hampshire County Council agreed to, and participated in, the expansions of Basingstoke and Andover in exchange for the L.C.C. abandoning its ambitions to build a new town at Hook.[5] In Swindon's case the situation was entirely different. The County disliked expansion, and the Borough was determined to avoid putting itself under the control of the County. In these circumstances, no help was available beyond that which the County was bound to give by its responsibility for certain services, and, as the Town Clerk made clear, none was requested.

The L.C.C. was, however, prepared to help receiving authorities by contributing some of the costs that the Minister could have borne under section 2(2) of the Act, but refused to do. Many of the smaller towns could not have succeeded without this help but Swindon did not ask for assistance. This was, of course, because the councillors and officials who were running expansion wanted to avoid any possibility of the L.C.C. gaining control over development. If this occurred, it would leave the way open for local politicians to claim that the elected representatives of the town had surrendered their responsibilities to outsiders. Anyway when it was clear that Swindon could manage on its own resources, the L.C.C. was fairly reluctant to help unless the town insisted far more strictly that the new population and employment only came from London. This would have slowed down the pace of expansion and was not acceptable to the Borough.

Therefore, for most of the period that we are considering,

---

[5] Seeley, I. *Planned Expansion of County Towns* (London: George Godwin, 1968) page 25.

the only financial assistance for expansion, apart from the Ministry grant, was a statutory contribution from the exporting authorities towards the cost of every family housed through the Industrial Selection Scheme. In 1952 this amounted to £8 per annum for ten years. The Exchequer also paid the standard subsidy on every house built, which amounted to £26.14.0d per annum for sixty years. The collection of the special grant involved cumbersome and impractical administrative arrangements. The Borough had to make separate legal agreements with each exporting authority in the Greater London area, and then recover the money from them annually. Each agreement was subject to time-consuming negotiations. The collection of the grant also took time; some councils even refused to accept responsibility for the people that had moved from their areas. When the Conservative government recast housing subsidies in 1956 a far more satisfactory procedure was adopted. The Ministry paid a basic subsidy of £24 and a special contribution of £8 over ten years, and half of this latter sum was then recovered by the Ministry from the exporting authorities. This removed the necessity of endless negotiations and annual collections from the exporting authorities. In 1961, after much pressure from the towns, the special contribution was increased to £15 per annum for fifteen years for every town development house. This plus the basic subsidy of £24 for sixty years compared with the lower general needs subsidy of £10 per annum for sixty years for most local authorities (areas carrying out slum clearance received £22.1.0d for sixty years however). These changes were part of the Conservatives' policy of switching the country's housing effort away from general needs building towards slum clearance. In 1961 the basic subsidy for town development was changed to £28 over sixty years.

These housing subsidies were useful but they were of less strategic importance than the Ministry's capital works block grants. These were paid in the early stages of expansion at a time when the deficit on development was at its peak. At first the Ministry agreed that capital expenditure of £528 000 on sewage, drainage, and water supply was eligible for grant. Fifty per cent of this sum was therefore paid by the Ministry. But it was soon clear that the initial estimates of the cost of development were too low. In fact over £1.2m. of works were needed, of which it was agreed that £675 000 were incurred wholly and necessarily because of expansion. In 1958 the grant was increased to £337 500. But Swindon still felt that there were some further works which ranked for grant, and in 1959 a further £82 500 was made available. Another grant of £73 625 followed in 1963, but the Borough were still not satisfied and pressed a further claim.

It had become obvious that the whole procedure for claiming town development grants was unsatisfactory in the peculiar circumstances of Swindon's expansion. Most expanding towns had a definite population target and therefore there was a definite amount of capital works to be done. It was not difficult to pay the grant in stages as the population in the town increased towards the target, but Swindon did not admit that there was any fixed end point to expansion and therefore there was no definite point at which the Ministry could conclude that the works for expansion had been completed and that their financial liability was at an end. Furthermore, the town did not restrict itself to receiving population from London through the I.S.S. Most other towns took a proportion of their workers from elsewhere, but this did not usually exceed the 10 per cent allowance for key workers that the Ministry accepted was necessary if the new factories were to get going, and for which they were prepared to pay the statutory housing allowance.

These difficulties occurred because there were two elements to Swindon's expansion. Many migrants came to Swindon under the Town Development Act through the I.S.S. Most of these people came from London but there were also key workers from elsewhere. However there was also a second flow of migrants consisting of workers recruited by firms who had been unable to get the skills they required from London. Swindon was prepared to house this second group but they were not eligible for the special subsidy. The Treasury became increasingly concerned about the open-ended financial commitment which the town seemed to create for them, and the Ministry of Housing ruled that only the first sort of growth was eligible for grant aid.

So the problem of distinguishing between expenditure caused by sponsored and private migration was added to the problem of separating out capital expenditure on needs generated by natural growth from that caused by town expansion. No set of rules could be applied to this situation

and so the Ministry relied on the *ad hoc* assessments of their
engineering inspectorate. Faced with an increasingly complex
problem, bureaucratic inertia set in. Swindon's last
application for a grant, lodged in 1963, remained unanswered
by the Ministry until 1967. By this time town development was
producing a steadily growing contribution to the Borough
revenue and there seems to have been a declining note of
urgency in the periodic letters from the Council to the
Ministry, asking what had happened to their application.[6]
Anyway the grants that were received made only a small
contribution to the cost of expansion. For many years the
scheme generated a heavy financial burden. The management
of the finances of expansion was a difficult task which altered
many of the ways in which the local authority operated and
demanded new skills. We shall discuss these changes in the
next section, so the rest of this section outlines the financial
policies that were adopted.

Swindon had been a financially prudent authority. It had
managed to finance much of its essential capital expenditure
from surplus revenue so that the total loan debt of the
authority when it started expansion was only just over £4m., a
fairly low figure for a borough of its size. In addition, the
housing revenue account and the general rate fund had com-
fortable working balances. The Independent group on the
Council was concerned with maintaining this tradition of
financial conservatism, so they made the need to avoid wasteful local authority expenditure a central part of their appeal to
the voters. The Labour group shared this cautious attitude and
it is interesting to note that the former leader of this group
became the Chairman of the County Council's Finance
Committee, despite the fact that his party did not control that
council. Therefore it is not surprising that the possibility of
town development causing an unacceptably high level of rates
was the main worry when the Council was deciding whether or
not to go ahead with the scheme. The decisive evidence which
settled its doubts was contained in a financial appraisal
carried out by the Treasurer.

---

[6] Eventually the Treasury put a ceiling on the grant per head housed
available for town development purposes.

Many of the expanding towns were concerned with the same issue, but most of them relied on guess work to predict what the financial outcome of their schemes would be. The Swindon Treasurer seems to have been the first to attempt a more informed forecast. He compared the likely rate level in ten years' time on the basis of two different sets of assumptions. The first was that the town continued to grow naturally. The second was that it carried out forced growth by adopting the town development scheme. The ten-year period was chosen because, initially, the special town development housing subsidy was only to be paid for that period, on the assumption that the expanding towns would have created enough additional rateable value to meet the costs of development by that time. The Treasurer concluded that it would actually be advantageous for the town to expand as the likely rate in ten years' time would only be 13/1 with town development, but it would be 13/11 without it. There were three principal reasons for this rather surprising result. The value of the Ministry's grants would offset some of the major capital costs caused by development, but if town development did not go ahead some of these costs would still have had to be incurred as the population rose. For example the town badly needed a new central sewer and sewage works. Of course it would cost more to build a works for the expanded population than it would for the existing population plus natural growth, but the increase in costs for town development, given the fact that this work needed to be done anyway, was relatively small. So the advantage of a 50 per cent Ministry grant for that portion required for the expansion population, which would be based on *average* rather than marginal costs, was obvious. The second favourable factor was that a number of services already had spare capacity which could be utilized with very little additional expenditure for the extra population. In this case the falling marginal costs resulted in a lower level of average costs for the whole population, and so a reduction in the rates that the individual had to pay for these services. (In the very important area of housing this did not apply because, for a number of reasons we will refer to below, marginal costs were higher than average costs). Finally the rates burden would be reduced by the creation of new rateable value, especially from the factories and commercial developments. The Treasurer calculated that one-third of the rateable value of the town was non-domestic and made the assumption that one-quarter of all future value created would be of this type. On this basis the penny rate product in ten years would be £2430, compared with a product of £1950 without forced growth, and the town development scheme would be viable.

In the years that immediately followed the decision to go ahead with town development the main financial difficulty was that a great deal of capital expenditure was necessary before the benefits were felt in terms of increased revenue. The net loan debt rose rapidly. For example, it doubled from £4m. in 1952/3 to £8m. in 1955/6, and in 1956 the Treasurer calculated that expenditure had been rising at an annual rate of 10 per cent in the previous three years, whereas rateable value had only risen at a rate of 8 per cent. This was an inevitable result of the gap between the investment required and its recoupment in increased revenues. However, because the town had been prudent and accumulated reserves it was possible, in the short term, to prevent the burden falling on the ratepayers. The total rate rose in these years from 23s 6d to 26s 5d, but this was almost entirely due to an increase in the amount that the County Council precepted; the increase was not caused by Swindon's expansion. The County Treasurer had concluded that general increases in the cost of county services, and not town development, would have any effect on county requirements.

By the end of 1955, however, difficulties had arisen and it is possible that some of the councillors were beginning to have second thoughts about the advisability of continuing with expansion. In a letter to the Chairman of the Finance Committee, the Treasurer argued that to stop at that stage would be disastrous. If this happened the Council would be left with a great deal of debt for abortive work, and they would forego the chance to increase their revenue so that this debt could be serviced. The major reason for this crisis can be seen from Figure 4.1 (page 133). In 1955 there was a credit squeeze. The Bank Rate rose from 3 per cent at the beginning of that year to 7 per cent by the end of 1957. This increased the cost of servicing Swindon's rapidly growing debt. It had also become clear that the range of redevelopments that were made necessary by town development was wider than had been expected. The urgent need to start the redevelopment of the central area, and the need to finance the construction of the

major link road from the expansion area to the town centre,
are both good examples of needs which were not originally
forseen by the Treasurer. In a letter at this time the Treasurer
recalled that they had originally hoped that while some
services would need to be improved, others would have
sufficient reserves to meet immediate needs, and that these two
factors would cancel one another out. He concluded
'Unfortunately experience shows otherwise'. The steeply rising
cost of staff was also a problem. The establishment of both the
Borough Surveyor's and also the Architect's departments
doubled between 1952 and 1955. There were also sizeable
increases in the Town Clerk's and the Treasurer's department.
Furthermore, new skills and more highly trained personnel
were required to carry out operations that were far removed
from the normal, rather humdrum, business of a medium-
sized local authority. So it was necessary to raise the level of
salaries in order to attract the right people.

In his letter to the Chairman of the Finance Committee, the
Treasurer suggested that the only way to resolve the crisis was
to tighten up the process of financial management. Some of
the maturing debt could be refinanced, further revenue
balances could be used to stabilize the rates, land must be held
for as little time as possible before being sold to industry or
private residential developers, and all capital budgets must be
carefully scrutinized. At the same time there had to be an
increase in the efficiency of all his own department's financial
services, with more effective accounting systems and a more
professional management of the rapidly accumulating loan
debt. Also, new skills were required to carry out tasks such as
the scrutiny of contractors' accounts. This re-organization of
the Treasurer's department marked the start of major changes
in the operation of the local authority which will be described
in the next section.

The Treasurer's advice was followed. It had important
consequences for the future style and pattern of development
in the town. The most obvious result was that any capital
expenditure that was not absolutely essential to development
was deferred, so very few of the amenities planned for the new
areas could be provided when they were first required. As we
have seen, this created hardship. A more subtle effect of the
financial policy was that the need to minimize the Council's
holdings of unremunerative land made it difficult to plan and

develop large areas comprehensively. So a piecemeal approach to the matters of land acquisition and development became the normal method of progress. Of course this fitted in rather well with the political strategy adopted by the Borough in the face of the hostility to expansion on the part of the surrounding areas, as it avoided the confrontation that the implementation of a comprehensive plan, covering a large part of their territory, might have provoked. However, some benefits were lost, such as a wholly rational system of roads and service allocation in the expansion area. Luckily, in the middle of this crisis period Pressed Steel made its decision to come to Swindon. Although the town did not benefit from the rates it generated (the factory was in Highworth Rural District Council), the Council had bought the freehold of the remainder of the Parsonage Farm site that the new factory was built on. This was sold off to a number of other firms, and the handsome capital gain which resulted helped to ease the Borough's financial difficulties. At the same time, a number of firms settled on the Council's own estate at Cheney Manor and this began to show a profit in 1957/8, rather sooner than had been expected.

Apart from the measures already referred to, the Treasurer recommended that all charges made by the Corporation should be reviewed. The Council therefore took a decision to raise council house rents and to introduce a differential rent system. We have already mentioned that the marginal cost of council housing, in an era of rising interest rates, exceeds the average cost of a council's existing stock. This is because the annual charges which have to be met on each house reflect the cost of the house when it was built, i.e. its historic cost. Therefore as inflation raises the cost of building new houses, the charges on each new house will be higher than those on the older stock. Also, in times of rising interest rates, more will have to be paid on the money borrowed to finance these new houses (and possibly on the older houses as well if their loans are due for refinancing). Swindon was not only adding rapidly to its stock of housing, but doing this at a time of sharply rising interest rates.

As a result, the revenue from rents, Exchequer subsidies, and the ratepayers' statutory contribution became insufficient to meet the cost of servicing the housing loan debt and paying for the housing administration.[7] The average rent required to meet these costs rose from 24s 9d in 1952/3 to 36s 6d for houses which got the additional town development subsidy, and 43s 8d for the other houses in 1956/7. As the increased costs were mainly a consequence of town development, it would have been possible to raise the rents of the newcomers' houses quite sharply and keep the others near their existing level. But, as we have seen, the Council decided that it would be socially divisive to reserve the new houses for Londoners, so it decided to make its entire stock available in order to house them on the basis of preference and need. In these circumstances, a two-tier system of rents would have meant that Londoners and Swindonians would be living in identical houses but paying different rents, solely because of their geographical origin. This would also have been highly divisive and was rejected. However, a pledge had been given that expansion would not cause a heavy increase in the rate, so rents had to be raised by a considerable amount.

Naturally such a policy was alien to a Labour council whose philosophy was opposed to high rents. The increase probably raised more political opposition than any other single issue during the course of expansion. It was largely because of the skill and foresight of the Treasurer that the changes made in 1956 created a rent system which did not require revision until 1963. This avoided the regular rows over rent increases that were a feature of many expanding towns (for example Bletchley) who were forced by rising costs, to make frequent increases. The officers persuaded the Councillors to introduce a differential rent system, with a rebate scheme for those who could not pay the maximum rents. The range of rents was raised to a maximum 47s 6d (for a modern three-bedroom house), and a minimum 34s 2d (for a one-bedroom flat). The level of rents was related to the size of the property and the level of amenities, not to any multiple of gross rateable value. All tenants were able to claim an income related rebate of up to 10s per week. It was calculated that initially two-thirds of the tenants would qualify for some rebate. The maximum rents were fixed, on this assumption, at levels which ensured

---

[7] A further strain was caused by the need to import skilled labour to meet the demands of the housing programme. The Treasurer estimated that this added £100 to the cost of each new house.

that the deficit on the housing revenue account would be met. Town development tenants paid the minimum rent for six months, giving them time to establish themselves in their new jobs and homes before having to meet the full rent that their incomes then determined. The political and economic advantage of this scheme was that as incomes rose more and more tenants paid the maximum rent. Thus the rent revenue rose as the cost of housing services was rising, without the need for general rent increases. A separate scheme was adopted for old people; their accommodation was subsidized by the general rate fund. The maximum rebate of 10s seems very small by modern standards but in 1955, when only a minority of local authorities had introduced such schemes, it was regarded as a fairly generous measure. This policy decision solved the crisis over housing finance and virtually removed the question of council house rents from the political agenda until 1962, when worsening economic conditions forced a further rent review. The next economic crisis, in 1966, again led to a review of rents, but the implementation of this increase was delayed by the operation of the Government's prices and incomes legislation. Over the years a number of amendments were made to the rebate system so that, by the time of this last review, tenants who received a gross weekly income of less than £10 per week paid a minimum rent which was 13s 6d less than the maximum rent, and tenants earning over £14 paid the maximum rent.

Throughout the whole period of town development the Council kept the level of subsidy from the general rate fund to the housing revenue account at £25 000 per annum. This was the amount that the Council had had to contribute in the last year before the 1956 Housing Subsidies Act removed the obligation on local housing authorities to make any contributions at all. Given inflation and the rise in rateable values, it meant that the ratepayers actually bore a declining proportion of the cost of council housing during the course of the expansion.

The period from 1955 to 1957 marks the time when town expansion faced, and overcame, its greatest problems in Swindon. By the sixties capital investment was beginning to produce a growing return. It will be recalled that the Treasurer had forecast that town development would be a financial success if one-quarter of all the rateable value that it created was non-domestic. By 1967 just over one-half of the total rateable value was non-domestic whereas, when town development began, the proportion had only been one-third. So, although it was not possible to be precise about the costs and benefits of the scheme, the financial benefits forecasted by the Treasurer when expansion began were more than fulfilled.[8]

These benefits would have been even greater if so much of the industrial and private residential rateable value created by expansion had not been located in Highworth. By 1964 the rateable value per head in the rural district was £46.5 (compared with Swindon's £35.8), making it one of the richest rural districts in the country. Fifty-seven per cent of this value was contained in the parish of Stratton St Margaret, adjoining the Borough, where Pressed Steel, the Greenbridge industrial estate, and most of the new private enterprise residential development was located. In addition, there was a higher industrial rateable value in the Rural District than in the Borough, and this was an extremely sore point with the Borough.

Organization

In 1952 Swindon Corporation had, according to the Town Clerk, the sort of organization and staffing resources appropriate for a medium-sized non-county borough. This statement is not entirely accurate because the Council had managed to retain, under schemes of delegation from the County, some powers in planning, education, and health. In addition the Council had decided to retain their own architect's department, unlike very few other authorities of Swindon's size and status. However while these additional strengths meant that the town was better prepared than many to cope with the organizational requirements of town development, the Clerk's suggestion that Swindon differed very little from a traditional local authority is true. The authority was arranged in a number of hierarchical depart-

---

[8] The rate level in Swindon during expansion stayed fairly constant, just above the average level of county boroughs. Swindon was also helped by the rerating of industry which occurred during the fifties.

ments, each jealously preserving their traditional areas of competence. The Town Clerk had the informal authority that went with his status as the senior chief officer, but the usual understanding in local government, that he was *primus inter pares,* limited his control of other departments to that which was a consequence of his role as a co-ordinator, and from the disposition of councillors to prefer his advice to that of other officers.[9] The internal working of departments also followed traditional practice. The chief officers or their deputies made most of the decisions and there was very little delegation. Communications between departments only occurred at the top so it took a long time to initiate action, especially when more than one department was involved.

The Council itself was organized into a large number of semi-autonomous service committees, with a proliferation of subcommittees. This was necessary because the officers were given little delegation, so councillors spent a great deal of time conducting routine business instead of deciding policy. Some idea of the lack of delegation may be gained from the fact that the Treasurer was not allowed to issue notices to quit to council tenants on his own authority until 1963, and as late as 1967 quite junior appointments had to be approved by committee, even when the applicant was merely filling a vacant post on the establishment.

The impact of town development on the key departments was reflected in the increases in the size of their establishments between 1953 and 1964 (see Table 6.1).

Between March 1952 and December 1964 the total establishment of the Council (excluding teachers and workmen) rose from 283 to 790.

Town development not only required more staff to carry it out, but it also called for skills that had no place in the normal routine of local government.

Previous chapters have indicated what these skills were. The chapter on social development showed how the Council appointed neighbourhood workers and a Social Development Officer, attached to the Town Clerk's department. Before

---

[9] The difficulties that this could create were referred to briefly in Chapter 5 in the case of pedestrianization of the central area shopping development.

Table 6.1

Establishment of key departments 1953-64

Date	Town Clerk	Borough Surveyor	Borough Treasurer	Borough Architect
August 1953	36	76	73	23
August 1955	43	81	99	43
April 1957	44	87	103	48
April 1961	46	87	107	50
December 1964	82	98	108	60

Source: *Swindon Borough Council Records.*

expansion the Clerk's department was staffed by a very small number of senior officers with legal qualifications, and the remaining career officers had qualifications in municipal administration. The development of the industrial estates called for people who had trained in estate management, and the vastly increased size and complexity of the financial operations of the Council required people who were able to deal with the problems that arose. By the early sixties, when the work of the Council had greatly expanded, a computer was installed and staff able to manage and programme the machine were added to the Treasurer's department. More modern methods of management were required, so a work study section was added to the Clerk's department.

Apart from increasing the size of the establishment and expanding the range and number of skills required, development also posed problems for the old organizational structure of the Council and its departments. The hierarchical structure was unable to cope with the new need for speed and flexibility in decision making. Also the sheer increase in the number of decisions that had to be made meant that the chief officers and their deputies were grossly overworked. The committee system was subject to similar constraints. Gradually these problems were overcome but it is clear that the staffing and organizational consequences of expansion were not foreseen by the councillors or the officers, and the problems which arose from the need to make changes created a source of conflict throughout the period of expansion which was more serious than any other which we have outlined. The Town Clerk stated, in an interview, that he felt that expansion had come closest to total breakdown over the question of staffing and organization.

In their book *Local Government and Strategic Choice,* Friend and Jessop describe a typical local authority structure, similar to that which existed in Swindon before expansion.[10] In this model decisions are taken by individual committees and departments with little reference to one another. Within departments most of the decisions, however trivial, are taken at the top. Friend and Jessop argue that, with the increasing complexity of local government, a new organization is needed. This should ensure that the top decision-makers, be they councillors or officials, concentrate on making the key, or strategic, decisions. They must not be so burdened by routine that important matters are left unexamined or unevaluated before decisions are made. The new structure should also attempt to ensure that interrelated parts of the decision-making structure are connected so that problems of departmentalization are minimized.

In one of their final chapters, Friend and Jessop develop an organizational structure for a fictitious council which, they believe, will fulfill their aim of producing a system able to make the strategic choices that are required. They suggest the establishment of a central board of management, consisting of senior members of the ruling party, with a chief executive reporting to it. A set of departments would be responsible for controlling the various services of the council. They group these functions into financial, manpower, developmental, and legal services. Within these broad groupings separate departments might continue to exist. Friend and Jessop make no detailed recommendations about this for, as they say, 'Our particular interest is the relationship of the various common service functions to the processes of strategic choice and, provided these functions can be fulfilled in a way which can allow the necessary linkages to develop with other parts of the decision making system, the problems of incorporating them in a formal departmental structure need not concern us.'[11]

They envisage a small nucleus of senior officers, between three and six in number, each bearing special responsibility

---

[10] Friend J. K. and Jessop, W. N. *Local Government and Strategic Choice* (London: Tavistock, 1969).
[11] Ibid. page 255.

for a group of service functions. The key to the processes of the allocation and forward planning of resources will be financial, manpower, and capital budgets. The four main committees would allocate the budgets, but the chairman of each of the committees would be a member of the other three, and they would all be on the central board. The chairman of the various service committees, responsible for running services, might all be on the board as well. The allocation of resources to these committees would be firmly in the hands of the four main committees. However, special problems would be dealt with by setting up *ad hoc* policy groups, as the central board would concentrate on forward planning and overall scrutiny of the council's actions. The service committees would scrutinize the running of their departments, but they would not have the same degree of control over them as they would have in a traditional set up. Friend and Jessop admit, however, that it might be difficult to persuade lay councillors that they still have an important role to play.

The main committees and the policy groups would be served by interdepartmental groups of officers, and much of the detailed planning work would also be carried out by interdepartmental groups. The first officer, or chief executive, would be the principal advisor to the board. He would not be associated with any purely departmental function but would be required to maintain links with, and oversee the work of, all of them. The central board and the first officer would be concerned with the problems of strategic control.

Friend and Jessop opt for a 'power concentration' model for their council. This vests most of the power in the hands of a relatively small number of officials and senior councillors, in the belief that only such a system can cope with the complex problems that local government faces. They hope that the need for democracy can be satisfied by the involvement of most of the councillors in the service committees and the need to delegate responsibility to officers can be met by changing the relationship of these committees to the departments so that their detailed control of affairs is replaced by a scrutineering role.[12] We have outlined this model in some detail because it

---

[12] Variants of this model have actually been applied in a number of local authorities in recent years, with rather mixed results.

provides a useful example to compare with what occurred in Swindon as development proceeded. Expansion faced the Council with the problem of strategic choice sooner than many authorities. The resulting changes, all in the direction of increasing power concentration, bear a marked resemblance to many of Friend and Jessop's recommendations.

The management of the central relationship between houses, people, and jobs required an organization which would take speedy decisions, and which was flexible enough to alter these decisions quickly. In the fifties few local authorities planned ahead much beyond the next financial year. The housing programme, for example, would probably be settled with sufficient time to obtain the necessary consents and put the work out to tender. Once the programme was agreed by all concerned, it would go ahead unless some totally unforseen circumstance affected it. But far more uncertainty occurred in Swindon because town development housing was tied to job availability and, as we have seen, this could alter very quickly. Also a large house-building machine had to be assembled and, as this took time, it was important to try to forecast future demand for at least three years ahead. The abrupt series of changes in the size of the housing programme for the years 1960-62 illustrates some of the problems.

In March 1962 Pressed Steel confidently expected that there would be a boom in the car industry, so they told the Council that they would need to expand their workforce. The officers reviewed the housing programme and stated, 'At a conservative estimate there will need to be 1000 new dwellings per annum over the next two or three years'. At this time Swindon had one large contractor working for them, as local builders had not been able to meet the strict deadlines that the Council had set, and this contractor was asked to produce the bulk of these houses. But then the car industry went into a recession, Pressed Steel cancelled their expansion plans, and by October 1960 the building machine was going all out to produce houses for which there was no longer any demand. So the run-up to a programme of 1000 was thrown into reverse. Naturally this took some time; it was thought that the 1961/2 programme could not be reduced much at such a late date but the 1961/2 programme was cut to 500. However, by the middle of 1961 demand was beginning to revive and by the next May it was clear that more houses would be needed. The planned programme of 500 for 1962/3 was therefore thought to be inadequate. Once again the machine was thrown into reverse. But the officers reported that time did not allow much to be done about this figure, so the 1963/4 programme was increased. Half way through 1963 it again became clear that industry was in a recession and the Council was left with far more dwellings than it really needed. These were absorbed by taking the opportunity to demolish some prefabs and rehouse the occupants but, yet again, the programme for future years was drastically cut.

The point of this example is to show the skill that was required to avoid on the one hand a surplus of houses, and on the other hand angry protests from industrialists that there were not enough houses for their workers. Officers had to develop their own methods of assessing future demand and forecasting the economic developments on which this demand was based. The Council's machinery for land acquisition, planning, site preparation, and road construction had to be capable of speed and flexibility. There had to be a high degree of co-ordination between departments. The officials had to have a far more positive approach than most local authorities have had to the attraction of new industry, and had to develop techniques of persuasion and bargaining that are not a normal part of the training of a local government officer. When she opened one of the new shopping centres in Swindon, Dame Evelyn Sharp aptly referred to the 'business of town expansion'. The Council did indeed develop an organization that was far more akin to a business than an ordinary local authority, although this did create the conflict between the methods adopted and the ideals of a democratically elected body that Friend and Jessop recognize.

We shall have more to say in the next chapter about the Town Clerk's role, but it must be obvious from previous chapters that he was more responsible than any other single person for the policy of town development, and his department was the centre from which the scheme was run. The Clerk, Treasurer, Surveyor, and their deputies were the main officers responsible to the Council for expansion as, between them, they controlled all the most important aspects of development. As new needs and duties arose they tended to be attached to one or other of their departments, so power was increasingly concentrated in the hands of these three, the 'triumvirate' as they were often called. Apart from overseeing and co-ordinating the whole scheme, the Clerk conducted negotiations with industry, the ministries, and other bodies, notably of course the County Council. The Social Development Section was a part of his department and he played a large personal role in developing policy in this area. These duties, in another authority, might well have carried out by the education, or health and welfare departments. Establishment and organization and methods of work were also his responsibility. The Treasurer controlled all the financial aspects of expansion, but he also had responsibility for housing. Swindon did not have a separate Housing Department until 1967. At the start of expansion responsibility for planning was transferred from the Architect to the Surveyor, who was also responsible for roads, sewers, water supply, and public works generally.

With so many of the necessary powers shared between these three officers, development was co-ordinated in an informal way by regular contacts between them. As the Town Clerk recalled, 'We virtually lived in one anothers' pockets'. This process helped by the fact that both the Clerk and the Treasurer held their offices throughout the period of expansion, and there were only two Surveyors during almost the entire period we are reviewing.[13]

As the volume of work grew it became clear that good contacts between the three departments were necessary at all levels. Because many of the problems required common policies and action, *ad hoc* interdepartmental groups of officers were set up to deal with them. At first such groups did not have executive power and had to report back to their respective chief officers, but this was slow and created too many conflicts and duplication of work. So by the mid-sixties a series of groups to deal with specific large-scale projects were set up. These had full responsibility for formulating and

---

[13] D. Murray John O.B.E., B.A. was the Clerk throughout the period of expansion. The Treasurer, E. Eckersley F.I.M.T.A., F.S.A.A., also served throughout. There were two Borough Surveyors, J. Ackroyd B.Sc. (Eng.), A.M.I.C.E., M.I.Mun.E., A.M.P.T.I., A.M.I.W.E. serving until 1958 and L. R. Robertson M.Sc. (Eng.), A.C.G.I., A.M.I.C.E., M.I.Mun.E. from that date up to 1965.

executing action within previously agreed boundaries. Of course the extensive delegation of power to subordinates that these changes necessitated meant that the authority had to recruit people capable of taking these responsibilities, so the level of qualifications required and the salaries demanded rose. We shall come back to this matter below. A similar need to have delegated power applied to the chief officers themselves. The volume of business, and the speed with which much of it had to be carried out, no longer made it possible for part-time unpaid councillors. to take all the important decisions. Therefore there was a steady increase in the freedom of operation of the three chief officers.

So far as the Council itself was concerned, the same pattern of concentration and delegation occurred. As in many other councils, the Finance, Law, and General Purposes Committee was the senior committee of the Council. The most senior and influential members of the town's main political groups sat on it. All the chairmen of the other committees were on it and many of the vice-chairmen (who in Swindon were opposition members). This committee was completely responsible for the planning and execution of town development. The other committees merely managed parts of the scheme, after they had been completed and handed over by the Finance Committee. These other committees could, and did, press for more resources for their particular services, but decisions about the allocation of resources were firmly kept in the hands of the senior committee.

However, power was even more concentrated within the Finance Committee. Most development matters were dealt with by a small sub-committee which only consisted of the Mayor ·and the chairman and the vice-chairman of the main committees involved in the expansion. In fact these were the most senior councillors from both the Labour and Independent Groups. In an interview, the Leader of the Labour Group for much of the period of expansion made it clear that town development was the most important and interesting council work, so senior members of the Council paid increasing attention to it, leaving what he described as the 'hum-drum, bread and butter work' of running the rest of the town to the others.[14] Membership of the Development Sub-Committee marked a councillor out as one of the small central group of powerful men on the Council. Its membership changed little during the whole period of expansion, and its claim to rank as the most important decision-making body can be gauged from Bown's remarks, and from the fact that the Leader of the Council (and the majority party) was always chairman of the Finance Committee and, until the work of both offices became too much, Chairman of the Development Sub-committee. The leader of the Opposition[15] was the Vice-chairman of both committees until Bown gave up the chairmanship of the sub-committee, when the two men changed roles. Bown and Lewis held these posts for most of the period of expansion. It says much for the close co-operation of the two parties that they could swop offices in this way.

Two other Finance sub-committees dealt with social development and manpower requirements. Once again the concentration of power may be seen from the fact that Mr Bown and Mr Lewis were chairman and vice-chairman respectively of the Establishment Sub-committee throughout expansion. Although most of the power to take decisions concerning expansion was delegated to these sub-committees, the need to seek almost daily authority for action, which in itself led to increased delegation to the three chief officers, also resulted in Bown and Lewis, as Chairman and Vice-chairman of the Finance Committee and the various sub-committees, having many powers delegated to them. So a very small group of officers and councillors effectively ran town development. The committees increasingly assumed the role of scrutineer that Friend and Jessop suggest they should have, and the officers and leaders bore the real responsibility for the evolution of policy.

Friend and Jessop propose that the activities of their Council should be organized round financial, manpower, and capital budgeting. They propose four main committees for this purpose. In Swindon, apart from the day-to-day short-range decisions which were increasingly taken by officers at various levels in the three central departments, the annual financial and capital budgeting procedure provided the main means by which the town development programme was reviewed and

---

[14] Councillor A. J. Bown, M.B.E.
[15] Alderman H. G. Lewis for most of the period reviewed here.

planned. The Finance Committee performed the roles which Friend and Jessop allot to their four committees, and the detailed preparation of the estimates for their approval was very largely a product of discussions between the key councillors and officers to whom we have referred. Manpower planning is referred to below.

These developments occurred as a result of the demands that town development placed on an organization that, at the outset, was incapable of coping with them. Nowadays the need for such changes in local government is fairly generally accepted. The Maud Report on the staffing and organization of local government and books such as that by Friend and Jessop have helped to popularize the view that local authorities must move towards new forms of organization which concentrate the power to make key decisions in few hands.[16] However no such conventional wisdom existed in the fifties, and the changes that occurred in Swindon ran counter to the view that responsibility should be shared equally by all the elected representatives, and to the tradition of chief officers of equal status, heading independent departments with sole responsibility for the service that they administered. As delegation increased and power became concentrated in fewer hands, some resentment and dissatisfaction was expressed at both the political and the official levels. The changes that occurred were not foreseen at the start of development and it was some time before what was happening became apparent. This served to increase feelings that these changes were unnecessary, and postponed the time when a thorough re-organization along new lines was introduced. Not until 1971 did the Council accept a new, corporate system of organization, with fewer committees and departments and a Chief Executive performing a similar role to that which Friend and Jessop outline.

There are few references in the Council minutes to the conflicts that occurred, but the local newspaper's reports of council meetings are more revealing. In 1954, soon after the setting up of the Development Sub-committee and the delegation of more power to the Chairman and Vice-

[16] See also, *The New Local Authorities: Management and Structure, (The Bains Report) (London: H.M.S.O., 1972).*

chairman, the two Conservatives on the Council (supported by a prominent Independent ex-Mayor) objected to these two men approving the tender for Plessey's new factory, which was being built for them by the Council. In his speech of opposition the ex-Mayor referred to the tendency of the power of the Council to concentrate in a few hands.[17] Later on that year, a proposal to waive standing orders so that the Chairman and Vice-chairman could approve tenders was opposed by two Independents.[18] In reply, the Chairman said that this was essential to save time and suggested that the standing orders might be outdated. In 1955 a Labour councillor wrote to the Town Clerk asking if the full Council could meet more often in committee (this would exclude the press) to discuss expansion, as he felt that non-members of the Finance Committee 'don't get all the information that they are entitled to'. A prominent member of the Independent group pressed for more information on town development to be made generally available, adding 'It is only too commonly said that none in the town knows where we are going'.

Committees also resented the control that was kept over their activities. For example, the Parks Committee tried in vain to persuade the Finance Committee to allocate more money to them. However the biggest political row occurred in 1961, when the long-serving chairman of the Housing Committee resigned. His reason for this was that he felt that the Finance Committee had pre-empted his committee's work. The Social Development Officer resigned in sympathy, saying that he doubted whether the Housing Committee any longer had effective control over the housing programme. Despite these protests, the concentration of power continued and at no time did a sufficiently concerted group of people arise on the Council to reverse the process. This was probably because all were agreed that town development was worthwhile, and no one could produce arguments to counter the claim that the changes were necessary to carry it out.

The feeling of exclusion that these objections reflect was also present at the official level. The initial re-allocation of functions between the Architect and the Surveyor created

---

[17] *Evening Advertiser*, 3 July 1954.
[18] *Wiltshire Herald*, 5 November 1954.

some controversy as the Architect felt that Swindon should be like the new towns, where the architects had the major responsibility for planning. He felt that the Surveyor's job was to provide services to fit in with this plan and that these should not dominate the town. This was an example of the old demarcation dispute between engineers and architects but it was also an argument about power. Likewise the Borough Education Officer felt that the activities of the Social Development Officer infringed on his duty to make provision for educational and recreational facilities for young people and adults. There were two reasons why the Education Department was almost entirely excluded from the social aspects of development. Firstly, it was partly controlled by the County and the Town Clerk wanted to minimize their involvement in town development. Secondly, the department was very much a separate empire, with its own strong committee, so it would have been much less amenable to the close co-operation that existed between the Clerk's, Treasurer's, and Surveyor's departments. In an interview, the Town Clerk admitted that the other chief officers sometimes felt excluded from what was the most interesting and important aspect of the Council's activities. He claimed, however, that they were always brought in and consulted about anything that affected their departments. This is undoubtedly true but, by concentrating many of the powers and duties in the three leading departments, in some cases by taking them from others and in others by setting up parallel responsibilities, it became less necessary to involve other departments in important decisions.

As we have seen, town development required more and better trained officers to carry it out. As the decisions multiplied and delegation became essential, it was particularly necessary to have well qualified and experienced staff at the third and fourth levels in the departments. Unfortunately, at the start of development no-one really understood that this would be necessary. The Council had always prided itself on its economy in the use of staff. It had also refused to break national agreements relating the pay of senior officers to the size of the authority, although many others had done so in order to attract more of the short supply of skilled staff. Initially it was thought that town development would require some enlargement of the staff, but that this would be relatively small and that the then current level of salaries would be adequate to attract the people required. Although it became clear that this was not the case, the Establishment Sub-committee refused to recognize that their policy needed to be changed. In an interview the Chairman of this committee, Mr Lewis, (who was of course also one of the leading people running town development), revealed why. He thought that they had 'done a reasonable job' on staffing but added that 'they always had to be careful to stop empire-building by officers'.

By 1955 the Town Clerk was pressing the Sub-committee for more senior staff in order to carry out the complex negotiations that were required. It was impossible to find these at salaries set according to the nationally agreed rates. The Surveyor, the Architect, and the Treasurer echoed these comments, and the Treasurer pointed to the low quality of many of their new recruits and the need to spend more money on attracting and training people to take the new responsibilities that were occurring. One of the problems was most sharply illuminated by the Chief Officers' claim that they should be getting more money because of the additional burdens created by developments. They were paid on a scale related to the size of the town and the type of authority, but they argued that these national scales wholly failed to take account of the fact that, by carrying out town development, they were having to do far more than their counterparts in other local authorities. They referred to the special new towns scales which paid more, recognizing the exceptional nature of the task that was involved in these new towns. The Sub-committee was unwilling to accept any of these arguments and merely said that all these questions should be deferred to the next review of staffing in 1956. This technique was used with increasing frequency over the following years and it created a great deal of frustration among the staff. It seems difficult to escape the conclusion that the committee simply used it as a device to escape the evil day when they might be forced to face up to reality by raising salaries and staffing levels.

Eventually, the chief officers' salaries were raised by the expedient of placing them on scales relating to a larger population than Swindon actually contained, but it was not until 1958 that the committee conceded this. There were also some regradings but the technical departments in particular still found it impossible to attract enough staff. Posts were advertised on inadequate salary scales and, when no replies were received or when those that came in were unsuitable, the job might then be re-advertised at a higher rate. Or, alternatively, somebody would be promoted from within the organization. This merely recreated the problem at a lower level. Another way out was to delete the senior appointment from the establishment and appoint two more junior staff. This increased the strain on the senior staff in the departments. Whichever course the committee adopted, posts remained unfilled for months, and the difficulty of keeping the town development programme going increased. One of the reasons why shops and other amenities were late on some of the estates was that there were not enough staff to design them. The use of consultants also increased and, as the auditors pointed out on several occasions, this was a waste of money when the work could have been done by the Council's own staff if they had been available.

The wholesale deferment of decisions by the committee — in 1958 they even deferred the usual biennial review of salaries — had the effect of increasing the rate at which frustrated staff left for better-paid jobs elsewhere, having gained their training in Swindon. By 1962 the staff were making formal complaints to the Council that there were more and more unfilled posts because of this factor, and that they must be realistic and recognize that increased salaries were required to retain experienced staff and get staff of the right calibre. In a letter to the Chairman and Vice-chairman of the Sub-committee in 1961, the Town Clerk warned that 'The position is getting so serious that the work of the Council is being prejudiced', and the Architect repeated that he now only had one qualified man in his housing section, paid at a lower level than many inexperienced architects in other authorities, 'dealing with nearly £1m. worth of building contracts by working overtime most nights'.

Of course changes were made but they were difficult to achieve. The eventual designation of the Principal Assistant Solicitor as Assistant Town Clerk in 1963, ten years after the clerk first suggested it, is an extreme but illuminating example of the reluctance of the Council to face up to the manpower demands of expansion. The committee stuck tenaciously to the line they expressed in a staff review in 1962 that, while they agreed that some people were being paid less than they deserved, 'we have not been impressed by the frequent argument that upgrading was justified because if the present occupant of a post resigned it would be necessary to re-advertise it at a higher rate'. They also repeated their concern not to bid up the price of staff by competing with other authorities. However to some extent this was bound to happen in a situation where the skills required were in short supply. The committee's restrictive attitude also affected their willingness to delegate responsibility over staffing matters. In an interview the Labour Leader pointed out that they felt able to delegate extensively to officers because they had confidence in them. However, in the vital matter of staffing they obviously felt that the senior officers were too closely involved themselves to be able to take extensive responsibility for it. Accordingly, the sub-committee agenda was overloaded with routine and detailed decisions; this was one of the reasons why so many matters were deferred, and why the committee never seems to have tried to formulate a set of considered manpower policies. It was also true that the officers were not in a strong enough position to formulate policies to put before the councillors.

This situation continued throughout the whole period that we are dealing with but it is worth referring to events that occurred after this time because they brought about changes. A separate Water Department had been set up in the early sixties and the officers concerned had worked out the establishment needed to staff it. They cannot have been surprised when the Establishment Sub-committee arbitrarily deleted some of the posts and changed the gradings of others. By the middle of 1966 the minutes contain a resolution from the Water Committee 'that the Finance, Law and General Purposes Committee again be informed of the serious effect that the continual shortage of technical staff is having on the programme', and in his report on the Council's accounts the following year the District Auditor referred adversely to inefficiences and consequent loss of revenue in the Water Department. This was a very serious matter which caused the Ministry of Housing and Local Government to intervene and might have involved the surcharge of those responsible. In an outspoken report to the Council, the Clerk blamed the problems on the intolerable delay in meeting the Department's requirements. He went on to refer more generally to all the difficulties which have been mentioned above and suggested that the committee agenda was too long and that the Chairman and Vice-chairman were overburdened. When one remembers that these two men were also their group leaders, and ran the Finance Committee and the Development Sub-committee, the conclusion must be that power had become so concentrated that it was creating inefficiency and disrupting expansion. The Clerk recommended that:

1. Proposals from a Chief Officer supported by his Establishment Officer should more readily be accepted.

2. The Establishment Officer should be free to deal with routine matters.

3. The Establishment Sub-committee should be more ready to accept the advice of Chief Officers.

4. The Chairman and Vice-chairman should have more power to make final decisions about urgent cases.

5. Chief Officers should be able to appoint staff on their own responsibility to a much higher level. Above this, with the exception of Chief Officers and their deputies, staff should be appointed by the Chairman and Vice-chairman.

This crisis gave the Clerk the opportunity that had been previously lacking to present the Council with the reforms that he felt were necessary. Most of his recommendations were agreed and implemented.

Conclusion

One of the dominant characteristics of Swindon's history was the desire of the town to remain independent, avoiding outside control and maintaining freedom of action to pursue locally determined goals. In the chapters on industry, land, and social development we have seen how this attitude affected the town's approach to expansion and we noted the problems, as well as the benefits, that this created. Therefore it is not surprising that the town also refused to take advantage of the possibility of extra financial help from the L.C.C. because of the additional control that would have occurred. The difficult relationship between the County and the Borough were also a part of history, so the lack of financial help from the former was predictable. The Town Clerk regarded it as 'quite futile' to approach the County for assistance. However, it must be doubted anyway whether the Borough would have accepted County finance which, if the example of other such assisted schemes is a good index, would have involved some measure of control over the scheme as well. The lack of money for 'non essential expenditure' was one of the major costs incurred by the refusal to seek financial aid. We have also seen throughout this part of the book that the disjunction between local and national priorities was a source of conflict. This factor appeared again in this chapter, being highlighted by the disputes with the Ministry of Housing over finance and the Ministry of Transport over roads.

To summarize, this examination of the financial aspects of expansion has shown how the combination of minimal outside help and uncertain economic conditions created great difficulties, especially in the early days of expansion. Many of the towns that had hoped, when it first became law, to use the Town Development Act to improve their situation, subsequently failed to make the Act work, and either abandoned the attempt or achieved very little for a number of years. Swindon was able to overcome these problems for three main reasons. The first was the size of the pre-expansion town which meant that it had sufficient resources to tide it over the difficult period in the middle and late fifties. The second was the skills of some of its key officers. We have seen how the Treasurer persuaded the Council to adopt a differential rent scheme and the importance of his mutual financial appraisal. The third element which played a part was simply luck. If Pressed Steel had not decided to seek a new factory site in 1955 and come to the town, thus giving a boost to employment when it was most needed, the history of town development in Swindon might have been a very different and shorter one.

One useful byproduct of Swindon's independence was that it contained, within its establishment in 1952, most of the departmental skills required to make a rapid start on expansion. However, the impact of growth soon required changes in the Council's organization; this created a major internal conflict, the only one of any length and seriousness during expansion. In other operations the willingness to adapt to change and innovate, which is essential when any new large-scale policy is being implemented, was evident in Swindon. The reluctance to act in the case of staffing meant that, in some aspects, the scheme came close to breakdown. Furthermore, many of the deficiencies that occurred, such as indifferent design layout and a lack of facilities, derived from the chronic shortage of staff as well as from the financial constraints.

Part Three

Town Development: Politics and Policy

Chapter Seven

The Politics of Development

Politics and the management of conflict

In the Introduction town development was described as a political process. Each of the participants in the process have a contribution to make, to expansion. As we have seen throughout this study, conflict occurs when the goals of the various participants are contradictory. For example, in Swindon's case the rural interests wished to preserve their own way of life. They were not responsible for the town's economic and physical problems, so there was no common basis for agreement between the town and the country, at least in the early days of development. On the other hand some participants partially shared common goals but only within limits which, when exceeded, resulted in conflict. For example, the Board of Trade agreed that town development should take place and was willing to bend its rules in order to help in the early days. However they saw this as a 'pump priming' operation only, much to Swindon's irritation. The principal participant in, and supporters of, expansion were, however, the officers, councillors, and residents of Swindon. The newcomers and the town had complementary goals, the town needed the growth and prosperity created by expansion and the newcomers needed the housing that it provided.

The politics of planning largely consists of attempts by participants in any scheme to achieve their goals by the exercise of power. This power consists of their ability to withhold their contribution to the scheme, or to determine the terms on which this contribution is made. These contributions take varied forms, for example money, planning or other consents, loan sanctions, votes etc. The middle section of this book was concerned with the most critical factors in the development process. It analysed the situation in which Swindon was faced with a series of participants whose goals to some extent conflicted with its own. It described how these problems were overcome and how both Swindon's own goals and the outcome of the town development scheme were consequently affected.

In this chapter we draw on previous chapters and, with some additional material, analyse the politics of development in Swindon. This involves a study of the tactics and strategy used to manage the conflicts that arose in the attempt to achieve the goals whose generation we studied in Part I. The chapter shows, within a framework determined by social, economic and historical factors, the overriding importance of political processes in determining the course and outcome of planning actions. The comparison with the expanding town of Achford in the second section of this chapter serves to underline this conclusion.

In an interview, a senior G.L.C. official pointed out that behind every successful scheme there were two or three outstanding personalities. These were people with foresight and drive who could mobilize the forces necessary to initiate and implement expansion. He mentioned a scheme where this role was performed by the chairmen of the three major committees. These men decided on their own behalf that their town needed development, and they even started to negotiate with the G.L.C. before putting the idea before the Council. In Swindon the Town Clerk, more than any other person, performed this role. When the scheme was first debated by the Council in 1952, one of the leading Independent councillors described the Clerk as the 'prime mover' in the scheme. In an interview, the leader of the Independents said of the Clerk, 'If he never did another stroke of work he would have done a marvellous job . . . It was his brain that was behind the preliminary working out of all these ideas for expansion'. Outsiders were equally complimentary. A ministry official who had been responsible for town development for a number of years referred to the confidence that he had had in the Town Clerk, and similar sentiments were forthcoming from the G.L.C. referred to above.

The Town Clerk was aided by a small group of officers, of which the Treasurer and the Surveyor were the most important members. Personal motives are hard to uncover, members of the group often referred to their sense of pride and achievement at the changes that town development has made to the town. Expansion therefore gave a number of first-class officials opportunities for interesting and creative work. They might not have found· this in other authorities, and some, who could have gone on to more prestigious posts in the bigger cities, chose to stay in Swindon because of this personal fulfillment.

The Town Clerk, a solicitor who came to Swindon in 1937 and was appointed Clerk in 1939, at the unusually early age of twenty-nine, served his apprenticeship in local government in the North of England in the aftermath of the Depression. This made him acutely conscious of the social problems and misery caused by mass unemployment, and all the more determined to avoid that possibility occurring in Swindon. After the postwar failure of the town to attract industry, he searched round for some means to achieve this aim. In a letter to a brother Clerk in 1954 he said, in reference to the Town Development Act, 'I have been on the look-out for this for some years'. He persuaded the Ministry to agree to Swindon's expansion, although it had not thought initially that such a large town would be a candidate for town development.

Another motive which undoubtedly influenced the Clerk was his wish, and that of the Council, to be rid of the control that the County Council had over their affairs. As we have seen, the conflicts that this uneasy relationship caused had been a feature of the town's history for many years. The Council had first petitioned for county borough status in 1914, but this application had been shelved by the outbreak of the First World War. The next opportunity came in 1945, when a new Boundary Commission was set up. It recommended that Swindon, and nine other non-county boroughs, be given county borough status, but no changes were made. Town development offered Swindon the opportunity to demonstrate its ability to conduct its own affairs, and also increase its population to the level required to be considered for county borough status. (This was raised from 75 000 to 100 000 in the Local Government Act 1958.) However, history repeated itself and this aim was never realized. When the Labour Government set up their Royal Commission on Local Government in 1966 the Boundary Commission was dissolved, just when Swindon's case was about to be examined.

Apart from his foresight, the Town Clerk's mastery of the political arts of persuasion and manoeuvre played a key role in examining the success of expansion. This is made clear by an examination of his relationship with his Council and with the various other interest groups that we have referred to. On several occasions the Clerk referred to the singleness of mind with which they pursued town development, and his own approach was conditioned by this attitude. Above everything else, he was determined to ensure that no obstacle intervened to prevent the Council 'maintaining the momentum, maintaining the continuity, never letting things dry up'. He felt that, especially with the strong opposition from county interests to town development, if the scheme faltered it might never recover.

He also realized that this ceaseless drive forward had the advantage of outflanking much of the opposition. Whilst they talked, the town had already gone ahead and done the things that they were objecting to. This technique also had the advantage of committing unwilling partners to make their necessary contributions to the scheme, because Swindon's actions produced a *fait accompli* which they had no other option but to accept. An example of this was the way in which the town's actions committed the County Council to a large programme of capital expenditure on new schools in the area.

Internally, the Clerk took good care to prevent town development policy from becoming a controversial matter in the Council. In an interview, in which he confessed to revealing his 'inmost thoughts', he said that he always preferred to build up a strong case for new policy before presenting it to the Council and the town. He might even carry on quite extensive informal negotiations with outside bodies before a plan went to committee. However he was always careful to keep the leaders of the two main parties in touch with what was going on; in this way he avoided any possible political repercussions. As we have seen, the party leaders held much of the political power regarding expansion matters anyway, so the Clerk had a considerable degree of freedom of action which other officials, for example in the County, did not have. This made his ability to out-manoeuvre them even greater.

The Clerk tried to ensure that he had a convincing answer to any possible objection when policy reports came to committee. His aim was to be in the position where only one scheme, his scheme, seemed to be the right course of action. As the councillors came to have a high degree of respect for his and his two colleagues' ability, the ready acceptance of his reports was almost a foregone conclusion. He was firmly convinced that progress was only guaranteed by the activities of enlightened minorities, and the success that they could have was always under threat from the majority. A common criticism of town development in Swindon was the lack of publicity and information provided about it. Although secrecy was sometimes essential, it was carried to extreme in Swindon by both the Clerk and his brother officers, most of whom seemed to share his ideology. The Clerk felt that if committees were given too many options to choose from they might just have become talking shops. Also, it was better not to overstress the importance of some decisions as this tended to produce an over-cautious attitude, and the whole momentum of expansion could have been lost. Therefore the Clerk always tried to introduce changes step by step, almost imperceptibly, gradually building up an irreversible commitment. He felt that if the consensus was lost expansion would become a matter of political controversy and might incur serious opposition, so he would always back down if there was major objection to any proposal and, in his own words 'reculer pour mieux sauter'. A similar low-key approach determined the level of publicity and discussion about the scheme among the general public. This ability to maintain the Council's confidence in him, while exercising considerable freedom of action, was the basis of the Clerk's ability to persuade, or manoeuvre, outsiders into making the decisions that he required. The civil servant referred to above was responsible for carrying out a vital part of negotiations which led to 1400 acres of white land east of the town being released for town development without a public inquiry. This was quite exceptional help from the Civil Service; it only happened because the Clerk had cultivated a very good working relationship with him over a number of years, and had engaged his interest in the town. When interviewed, the civil servant recalled that Swindon had first-class officers with the confidence of their Council. He referred to the Town Clerk as 'the colonel of his regiment'. It was always possible to be frank with him, because he was not the sort of man who would reveal confidence to his Council. For his part, the Town Clerk always tried to avoid putting political pressure on the Ministries. He realized that, in the long run, the cultivation of good relationships with the civil servants responsible for town development policy was likely to be far more effective. But this did not stop him using the other method when he judged it to be the right one.

The Clerk took great care to avoid the possibility of objections to town development from the people of the town. The L.C.C. was needed as a source of population, but he realized that if they became too involved accusations of big brother treatment could provide a focus for popular opposition to expansion in a rather independently-minded town. An amused ex-L.C.C. official recalled that the Clerk even managed to avoid signing a legally binding town development agreement with the L.C.C.: 'He was masterly, sometimes he simply did not answer letters for months'. The Clerk himself said that in his relationship with the L.C.C. he had always been guided by an old eastern proverb, 'If the dog go hunting with the lion, let him beware least he himself be eaten'. Apart from ensuring that L.C.C. involvement did not create opposition, the Clerk and the Council 'sold' development to the town in two ways. Firstly, it was presented as the only way in which the town could get more and better employment. Secondly, a promise was made that expansion would result in more, not less, houses being made available for local needs. All this was part of a deliberate, and successful, strategy to avoid possible objections. Another was the policy of social integration, which the Clerk was personally responsible for persuading the Council to accept.

Of course the Clerk and his fellow officers were not always successful, as the last chapter showed. However, the records only show one important occasion when he seems to have allowed his enthusiasm to go beyond the point to which political support was given. In 1957 the Clerk wanted to press ahead with a second stage of expansion. The Chairman of the Development Sub-committee replied by saying that he would require far more information before he could recommend the proposal to his committee. After they had considered the Clerk's report, the committee instructed him to press for far better financial terms from the L.C.C. and the Ministry than he had thus far managed to negotiate. Eventually the plan became a victim of the next economic crisis.

Although he appears to have played a far less innovative role, the Treasurer was second only to the Clerk in the importance of his contribution to expansion. It was his financial appraisal that moved the main obstacle to the councillors' acceptance of town development. Later on his highly efficient financial management carried the scheme through its worst crises. An attitude of caution governed his approach to expansion, which formed the ideal counterpart to the Clerk's expansionist outlook. Although they often differed, the close co-operation between these officers and their departments was a crucial to the success of town development.

Throughout the period the Council was controlled by the Labour Party by small majorities. For much of the time there was a small Conservative group, never more than three, and one completely independent member. But the main opposition party was the Independent Group. Some of these councillors were Conservatives in national and county politics, but many of them were Liberals. The Labour councillors organized themselves in the usual way, discussing policies in group meetings before the Council met and then voting as the majority decided, although individuals could, and did, step out of line occasionally. For reasons that will become apparent, strict party discipline was rarely necessary, despite the small majority that the Labour party usually had. The Independents met as a group to discuss policies, but were free to vote as they wished. In fact, for most of the time they tended to vote as a block. Therefore the voting behaviour of the two sides was rather similar, despite the formal differences in group organization.

Most of the Labour councillors were working class. For many years a majority of them were railwaymen, or retired railwaymen, working in the workshops or on the trains. The Independents had some working class councillors and many of them also worked for the railways, but their members tended to be more middle class. Some of them were office workers at the railway works, others were local tradesmen and professionals. Election manifestos suggest that the major national political conflicts of the fifties and sixties had little or no effect on the local political situation in Swindon. The Independents' desire to keep national issues out of local government seems to have been tacitly accepted by the Labour side. Thus in 1955 the Labour manifesto simply recommended its candidates to the electorate by stating that 'you want the very best in local services that you can get and that means that you want a Labour Council'. The document avoids controversy, making no reference to local issues, and no attack on, or even a mention of, the Independents. In their manifesto the Independents referred to their wish to keep politics out of local government. They emphasized the need for strict control over Council expenditure, but made no attempt to suggest that the ruling Labour Party was being extravagent.

Evidently there was a consensus on most issues between the two major groups. This is underlined by the fact, already referred to, that power was shared, rather than contested, between the two groups. Nowhere was there closer agreement than on the matter of expansion, which both sides were determined to avoid becoming a politically controversial matter. This meant that on the rare occasions when there were disagreements, one side or the other would back down in order to preserve the consensus. There seemed to be strong support for this in the town. When a prospective Conservative parliamentary candidate attacked the lack of publicity about expansion, the local paper replied sharply, 'Expansion is not a political matter and we deplore the intrusion of politics into it'.[1] The candidate hurriedly explained that he wholeheartedly agreed. Nothing had been further from his mind than to attack a policy which was so obviously a wise one.

The reasons for this accord relate to the factors outlined in Chapter 1. The politicians shared a common economic situation; most of them were dependent, either directly or indirectly, on the continuing prosperity of the railway works. There were close and longstanding relations between the two sides. As the Independent leader said, 'We had grown up together and practically all of us were native Wiltshiremen, if

---

[1] *Evening Advertiser*, 14 August 1954

not Swindonians'. He went on to say that they all remembered when the works was on a three-day week before the last war, and how many of the shops in town were empty. It was the commonly felt need to avoid this fate again that made all of them keen to see expansion succeed. There was also a common belief about how local government should be run. This was summed up by this same councillor, in a talk he gave to a local society soon after expansion started, when he said that they did not go in for 'grandiose schemes' in Swindon but preferred to be governed by 'plain English common sense'. He added that they believed in prudence, and committees rarely spent all the money that they had budgeted for. The Labour leader summed up his relations with his Independent counterpart by saying that they used to have a joke about how they only stopped speaking to one another once a year — on polling day.

Hardly surprisingly, Council meetings tended to be uncontroversial occasions. Even when major decisions such as the annual rate fixing were taken, it was rare to find any opposition; even the decision to introduce the differential rent scheme, which might have been expected to raise some heat, at least on the Labour side, was passed in full Council without debate.[2] It is interesting to note that both sides, not merely Labour, had been opposed to means-tested rents until the officers persuaded them that it was necessary. This situation of political stability, and the close co-operation and confidence between the two sides that it created, was the ideal environment for town development to take place in. Sudden electoral changes that might upset the policy were unlikely furthermore, so officials would make recommendations without having to spend too much time and energy on tailoring them to avoid controversy. The councillors trusted their staff, and were prepared to give them considerable freedom of action.

In a relatively small town, such as Swindon, councillors are quite close to their constituents. This helped to ensure that town development was accepted. The Labour Leader remembered that many of the councillors who worked on the railways were approached by their fellow workmen at the start of expansion, and questioned about what was happening. Subsequently, the scheme was discussed throughout the works

---

[2] *Evening Advertiser,* 8 March 1954.

which generally shared the Labour Party's conclusion about the necessity of the policy. The minutes of the Trades Council display a similarly close relationship between the Labour councillors and the trade unions. On several occasions the possibility of adverse reactions was averted by the many councillors who were on the Trades Council and could give it an explanation of what was happening. For example the minutes show that a move to oppose the differential rent scheme was defeated. This occurred after the Chairman of the Housing Committee (who also happened to be a well-known and highly respected trade unionist) had explained that rising interest rates, the product of the Conservative government's policies, made this the only course open to the Council. He also showed how the proposal was much more equitable than a flat-rate rise for all would have been.[3] The working class background of many of the Council also helped when problems arose with the newcomers. One of the community workers recalled, with admiration, the way in which the Labour leader spoke to a group of discontented people on one of the estates. He was sure that the fact that there was no social barrier between the speaker and his audience contributed to the success of the occasion. The Independents had similar links with important sections of the middle class in the town. To summarize, the council members, by their consensus, made it possible for expansion to take place in a stable environment. Because they had the confidence of significant sections of the electorate, they were able to ensure that no strong body of opinion arose to challenge what was taking place.

On several occasions reference has been made to criticisms of the lack of publicity surrounding expansion. The Council did make its intentions known, albeit often in the form of a rather cryptic Council minute. Nevertheless it is true that none of those running expansion would have been strong supporters of the increased public participation in decision-making that Skeffington suggested, and which occurred to some extent in the surrounding rural areas.[4] In a talk in 1971 the Clerk summarized his views regarding the work of enlightened

---

[3] *Evening Advertiser*, 2 February 1956
[4] *People and Planning. Report of the Committee on Public Participation in Planning* (Skeffington Report) (London: H.M.S.O., 1969).

minorities. Interviews with the other leading politicians and officers suggest that they would have endorsed these views.

'Why do I hesitate about public participation? I find three elements in my reaction:

(a) I was brought up in the heyday of county boroughs and served in several in the north. Our view then was, and I am sure it was not a mistaken one, that the members of the Council did in fact in their opinions and decisions represent public opinion and they acted in a consitutional sense as representatives and not as delegates. We were indeed suspicious of vested interests and pressure groups.

(b) I have always been deeply conscious of the numerous obstacles in local government to effective and speedy action. We have to go through sub-committees, committees, and the Council. We may have to persuade a county council, we generally have to convince the Ministry, and there is always the District Auditor lurking in the background. I like to achieve results and I have frequently said that it is a miracle that in local government we ever achieve anything. Now another obstacle to action has been erected — public participation.

(c) I have never forgotten the historical fact, as I think it is, that progress is only achieved by enlightened minorities. The public referendum is the last ditch of the reactionary. I fear that the submission of proposals to the public at large cannot but mean not only delay but a significant watering down of the progressive elements that they may contain'.[5]

The history of other town development schemes where contentious issues were aired at public meetings[6] do tend to lend support to the view that *if* the successful implementation of a scheme is the major goal, the Swindon situation, where a small group of powerful men take charge, with the tacit acceptance if not the active participation of the community, is ideal. Whether democracy is served by such an arrangement is

---

[5] Talk on 'Some of Swindon's Recent Planning and Development Problems' at the University of Sheffield, Department of Town and Regional Planning, 12 November 1971.
[6] In the case of Barnstaple the whole scheme was even put to a referendum. It was defeated.

another matter. The most articulate and persistent criticism of development came from middle class intellectuals who are always likely to object to a lack of openness in local affairs. One of the leaders of this strain of opinion in Swindon was Philip Noel-Baker, the town's Labour M.P. from 1955 to 1968. In 1964 he suggested to Kenneth Hudson that the latter should write a book on the town. The resulting volume summarized many of the feelings of this group of critics.[7] It suggested that, despite the undoubted achievements of expansion, the town has few of the more cultured and civilized aspects that one would expect to find in a place where the middle class had a greater say in what went on. A chapter called 'A Benevolent Councillocracy' contends that the concentration of working-class railway employees on the Council is partly to blame for this state of affairs. According to Hudson, 'None of this adds up to accusations of incompetence or blindness, but rather to a certain narrowness of experience which could on occasion work to the town's disadvantage, especially when major projects were under consideration. It would also mean that the Council and the committees were not always in a position to offer the permanent officials the kind of informed constructive criticism which is needed if the democratic system of government is to be fully effective'. Hudson reported that the Labour M.P. found himself 'in the not altogether enviable position' of being returned to Parliament with gratifying majorities, but missing the middle class support that other Labour M.P.s had. He attributed this to the fact that 'Labour politics have a solid trade union base, with practically no intellectual content'.[8]

It is easy to see why criticisms voiced in this way had little popular support in a predominantly working class town. Apart from the condescending tone in which they were expressed, they ignored the fact that it was precisely because councillors had personal experience of the problems caused by a one-industry town that they became such strong supporters of expansion. Towns where the middle class were politically predominant tended to be far less enthusiastic about overspill. Hudson also referred to the lack of cultural, artistic, and

---

[7] Hudson, K. *An Awkward Size for a Town* (Newton Abbott: David and Charles, 1967).
[8] Ibid., pages 46 and 53.

aesthetic qualities. But there was very little evidence that the majority of the population would have seen this as a serious omission from the expansion programme.

On the other hand there was undoubtedly some popular support for the feeling that town government was the preserve of a few long-serving councillors. This feeling is reflected in letters to the local paper in the early years of development. It was suggested that expansion was simply a means by which officials could increase their salaries, and that only three groups, the officers, the local paper, and the Labour Party, wanted it.[9] Others regarded what was happening as the height of folly, 'the bubble is getting bigger and bigger and may some day burst'.[10] But as expansion went on and the bubble did not burst, and as the positive benefits such as new jobs and new facilities occurred, such criticism in the local correspondence columns died away.

The almost total lack of political controversy surrounding expansion, and the very low percentage who usually voted in local elections, could be explained by apathy. However, this may be a rather misleading way in which to characterize the reaction of the local population to town development. There was probably little incentive for anyone other than the party stalwarts to vote in the absence of any well-developed criticism of what was happening, which could gain popular support (unlike that mentioned above), and as long as the benefits that were promised were seen to be occurring. Voting must have seemed particularly unnecessary as most of the candidates supported expansion, and differed very little from each other on other issues.

Only two groups who opposed expansion can be traced, apart from the local traders who, as we saw, soon forgot their doubts. The first was the local ratepayers' association, so often an influential body in other towns. It came out in opposition to the scheme in 1954, but failed to gain any popular support. The second was the small group of Conservative councillors who, in the early fifties, attempted to break the monopoly of the Independents over the non-Labour vote. There were never more than three of them, and they were hampered by the fact that many of the Independents were also members of the

---

[9] *Evening Advertiser*, 21 August 1954.
[10] *Evening Advertiser*, 12 April 1956.

Conservative Association and disapproved of what they were doing. Beyond token attempts to prevent civic involvement in commercial matters, such as the development of the industrial estates, they made no impact. The Conservatives who emerged as an active force in local politics in the middle sixties, and rapidly eclipsed the Independents to take control of the Council in 1969, were very different from their forerunners. Many of them were white collar workers in firms that had come to the town during the previous fifteen years. Some of them had even been a part of the official overspill scheme. Apart from their personal realization that expansion was good for Swindon, this feeling was so strongly grounded in local politics by that time that it would not have been electorally profitable to try and change the policy. Interestingly, the new Conservative Council soon found themselves in all the same conflicts with their party colleagues on the County Council that the Labour Council faced. So the tradition of close co-operation between the two sides on the Town Council, at least on expansion matters, continued much as before.

We have often referred to the attitude of the County Council towards expansion, and seen how the various conflicts that occurred between the town and the county affected the scheme. The then County Clerk was probably expressing a commonly felt view at County Hall when he bluntly told the Town Clerk, in 1954, that he personally thought that the whole scheme was misconceived. But there were also sound political reasons why the County should have been opposed to town development. Wiltshire is a very rural county, and even the few large towns that it does contain are market towns dependent on the business that agriculture creates. Swindon is the sole exception to this pattern. Swindon felt that the County had no experience of urban problems. However, as a later County Clerk pointed out in an interview, this is hardly true. On the other hand none of the other towns had Swindon's problems. Consequently they did not need to use the Town Development Act to import new industry, nor did they expand over their boundaries.

The possibility that Swindon would encroach on the surrounding rural areas was at the heart of the opposition to the town's growth. After the first few years, the rural district councils did not oppose new industry and private housing being developed in their areas. However they did not want to lose their political independence and face the prospect of increased rates if parts of their areas were included within the borough boundary. In a county dominated by rural interests, their views had more impact on the County Council than Swindon's claims. It is hardly surprising that for many years the town's activities were viewed with a distinct air of disapproval from County Hall.

The strength of the rural opposition to Swindon was demonstrated on a number of occasions, notably at a public inquiry in 1968. The town tried unsuccessfully to incorporate 1400 acres to the east of the Borough, containing the Greenbridge industrial estate and the Dorcan area. A series of startling figures illustrated the argument over rates. In 1953, when town development started, Highworth Rural District Council had a rateable value per head of population of £5 5s 0d and Swindon the higher figure of £6 4s 1d. By 1968 the order was reversed; Highworth had £53 16s 2d per head and Swindon £40 7s 0d per head. This made the rural district one of the richest in the country. The main reason for this was the heavy concentration of industrial rateable value in the parishes surrounding Swindon as a result of development initiated by the Borough. In 1968 Highworth, with a population almost two-thirds smaller than Swindon, had an industrial rateable value of £721 733, compared with only £546 414 in the town. The Borough wanted to benefit from their enterprise. However, the Rural District wanted to avoid the loss of this rateable value, which would have increased the rate levy required from the rest of their area. People in the transferred area would also have had to pay higher rates as a part of Swindon.

Of course the rural areas and the County were Conservative (or Independent) controlled and Swindon was a Labour town, but party political differences seem to have been far less important than these financial questions and a certain feeling of rural independence, even in areas where precious little rural life actually remained. This is shown by a remarkable article in the local paper about the parish of Stratton St Margaret.[11] This area, immediately adjacent to Swindon, was a suburb of the town from the thirties onwards. After the development of Pressed Steel and the Greenbridge/Dorcan

---

[11] *Evening Advertiser*, 30 May 1952.

area it contained very little agricultural land. Many of its inhabitants had lived in Swindon at some time. In later years many of them were overspill families who had subsequently moved out to buy their own homes. The article was written in 1952 and predated most of this latter development but even then the Parish Council was 100 per cent Labour and had been for some years. Yet they were whole-heartedly opposed to a takeover by Swindon. As the article stated, 'It regards itself as in the nature of a bastion of rural life resisting the tentacles of an expanding urban octopus'.

It is this attitude, coming up from the grass roots in the county districts, which coloured the County Council's attitude to expansion. But, this apart, the politics and organization of the County Council in the fifties sharply contrasted with that of the Borough. In an interview the County Clerk referred to some of these differences. The County Council had a number of very powerful personalities among its membership. Several of the County M.P.s and the larger landowners were usually served on it, and they devoted a considerable amount of time to its affairs. In Swindon most members had jobs which severely limited the amount of council work they could do. To illustrate the point, the Clerk referred to the fact that the County Council met in the daytime and never had any difficulty in getting members to attend them, whereas Swindon Council had evening meetings. In this situation the County members tended to play a far larger role in deciding policy than their counterparts in the town, and the officials had far less delegated to them. This division of power was reinforced by the fact that affairs moved at a far more leisurely pace in the county than in the town, where development made rapid decision-making essential.

Thus the style of government of the two bodies differed radically. The County Council left little discretion on major policy issues to its officers, maintained strong links with the grassroots interests in its (largely) rural districts, and tended to subject all decisions of importance to lengthy scrutiny by its powerful councillors. These in turn paid much attention to opinion in the county as a whole. The Town Council had, as we have seen, at least the tacit support of the majority of the town, and most of the decision making power was in the hands of a few officials and councillors.

As a result of these differences Swindon was perpetually

exasperated by the length of time it took the County to reach a decision which affected expansion, and by the difficulty of arriving at firm conclusions from discussions about policy held at the official level. The slow pace of the county administration also failed to match up to the urgencies of expansion. The length of time it took the County to agree to expansion in the first place is an example of this first sort of problem. The difficulties over getting schools built in time is an example of the second. On the other hand, the County were annoyed by the way in which Swindon went ahead with plans which committed them to expenditure, without an adequate time for consultation. Of course this was a deliberate strategy on Swindon's part. They wanted to prevent obstruction to town development by moving so quickly that the other necessary contributors to the scheme were committed before they had a chance to protest effectively. Summing up the differences between the County and the Borough, the County Clerk suggested that the town had been more willing to take risks than the county. It had also been led by a dedicated group of people who had 'been prepared to make town development their life'. He thought that the Borough members had been guided by the officers in a way that would have been impossible in the County.

The Borough were able to circumvent most of the obstacles that really determined county and rural district opposition could have put in their way for a number of reasons. Firstly, they had managed to gain considerable delegated powers in health, education, and planning, and were large enough not to need financial help or technical assistance from the County in order to carry out expansion. Secondly, the County does not seem to have had officers who were willing or able to play a particularly interventionist role in areas, such as development planning, where they could have exerted some control. Thirdly, the speed and determination with which the Borough pursued expansion could not be countered by the rather leisurely pace at which the County reacted.

Since the discussions began, in the mid-sixties, about a further expansion of Swindon, the County has played a far more active role than hitherto. The reasons that the County Clerk gave for this change illustrate some of the points that have already been made. Since local government reform the question of secession by Swindon to become a county borough has disappeared and the County now realizes that Swindon will continue to grow, as a part of the new county. Therefore co-operation seems sensible, if only to exercise more effective control over the nature of this growth than in the past. This change in attitudes, from strong opposition to some sort of acceptance, has been reinforced by the considerable changes in the composition and thinking of County members and officers that have occurred in the past decade. With these changes has come increased delegation to officers; this means that they are able to negotiate more easily with the Borough. The County has also modernized its internal organization. The growing importance of regional planning has given the County planners new responsibilities and a new outlook. As a result they now show interest in, and concern with, what is going on in the County districts. The new duty of the County, under the 1968 Town and County Planning Act, to prepare a structure plan has added to its growing involvement in work from which the town had successfully excluded it for many years.

We have already referred to the Town Clerk's reason for minimizing the involvement of the L.C.C./G.L.C. in expansion. Their financial contributions were limited to the housing subsidy, and were not a very significant element in the financing of town development. The most important contribution that the L.C.C./G.L.C. made to Swindon was the simple fact that they, more than any other authority, were committed to dispersing their population to expanding towns and were therefore a solid base on which Swindon could mount its scheme. The Abercrombie Report of 1944, which formed the basis for development planning in London for twenty-five years after the war, had recommended large-scale dispersal of population from London to a ring of new and expanded towns in the Home Counties and beyond.[12] The statutory County of London Development Plan followed up this suggestion by proposing to disperse 250 000 people to these towns. However the new towns had disappointed the L.C.C. They drew much of their intake from outer London, and many of these people were not in serious housing need. In a review of policy in 1958 the L.C.C. discovered that, of the

---

[12] See Foley, D. C. *Controlling London's Growth* (Berkeley and Los Angeles: University of California Press, 1963), especially Chapter 2, for a full discussion of this phase of post war planning in London.

195 000 that had moved to the London new towns, less than one-third had come from the L.C.C. area. Furthermore, the new towns were unlikely to take more than another 40 000 from Inner London before reaching their target population.

Because of the limited contribution coming from the new towns the L.C.C. was an enthusiastic supporter of the Town Development Act. It subsequently put more effort than any other large city into making it work. Initially it hoped to move 65 000 people to expanded towns.[13] However government restrictions and the unwillingness of many small towns to contemplate town expansion made progress slow. By the end of 1955 the L.C.C. had only managed to link up with three towns, Swindon, Bletchley, and Daventry, although it was negotiating with thirteen others. Swindon had promised to take 10 000 people from the L.C.C., more than the other two together. By 1958 the review mentioned above pointed out that Swindon had already taken 618 families. This was more than the L.C.C. had managed to place in any one of the new towns, despite the fact that the Swindon development had only been underway for two years.

The similarities between the political background to town development in Swindon and in London are interesting. The L.C.C. like Swindon, was controlled by Labour throughout this period, and both were firmly committed to the overspill policy. As in Swindon, a small number of L.C.C. councillors and officials took a special interest in this policy, and this explains the energy with which it was pursued. The key figures were Mrs (now Dame) Evelyn Denington, for many years Chairman of the New and Expanding Towns Committee and also of the Housing Committee and the Clerk (now Sir) William Hart who, like Swindon's Clerk, had taken personal charge of town development policy. These two people recognized that Swindon, unlike many other towns, had the determination and the skills required to make town development work. Swindon, for its part, recognized similar qualities in the L.C.C. who were, in its view, by far the most progressive and efficient exporting authority with whom it had dealt. It was, as the Town Clerk observed (quoting Peter Self) a 'marriage of convenience'.

---

[13] They also hoped to be allowed to designate a new town specifically for their overspill population; the ill-fated Hook study was a result of this aim.

However Swindon's independence from the L.C.C. — 'Of all the towns we saw the least of Swindon', one official remarked — reduced the contribution that the town made to the relief of inner London's housing needs. The clearest expression of the L.C.C.'s disappointment came in an exchange of letters in 1963. The Town Clerk was sounding out Sir William Hart's reaction to a second-stage expansion, with rather more financial participation from the L.C.C. Hart replied that his Council would be glad to see further growth at Swindon. However the current situation did not encourage it to persuade more London industry to go to the town, as it did not get a commensurate movement of population. Figures he produced showed that, despite the fact that over 2250 L.C.C. families had moved to Swindon, only about 1500 of these went through the I.S.S., and were therefore in housing need. Also, the proportions of those in need dropped from a very high initial percentage. He wrote that the L.C.C. were annoyed because it had, by law, to make a housing contribution for all those who moved to Swindon. But what benefit was there in paying for people who were not in great housing need to move out? He felt that Swindon should insist that firms recruit their labour through the I.S.S. and abandon their policy which was to press firms to do this but, if they were unsuccessful, then allow them to recruit at will in London and finally elsewhere.

Of course this freedom was one of the advantages that Swindon had gained by refusing to be closely tied to the L.C.C. The Council wanted to increase the size of the town, and if sufficient men with the right skills were not available in London it was not prepared to slow down the pace of expansion or turn away firms altogether by a rigid insistence on London I.S.S. recruits only. In his reply to the L.C.C., the Town Clerk referred to a further consequence of this independent approach. Very few of the firms came from London for, as we have seen, if Swindon had relied on firms moving from the metropolis, the size and pace of expansion would have been far less. So, despite its limited impact on London's housing problems, the scheme cost the metropolis relatively little because the L.C.C. did not have to invest a large amount of money and staff resources in it and because little of London's industry moved to the town. The Town Clerk summarized the situation aptly when he concluded, 'Neither of us may find in the relationship all we desire but it is clear that both of us have found substantial advantages in our relationship'.

Of all the participants discussed in this section, it is most difficult to analyse the reaction of the Ministry of Housing and Local Government to the development of Swindon. There are a number of reasons for this. Town development was only a small part of that Ministry's work, and most Ministers had little to do with it after the first few years. Conversations with civil servants tend to confirm this; the policy was uncontroversial and therefore tended to be left to the officials to run. Arguments about Industrial Development Certificates and boundaries seem to be the only issues that might conceivably have involved the politicians. Furthermore, town development matters were usually the responsibility of an Assistant Secretary at the Ministry, and these officials typically spent rather a short time in this role before being assigned to some other area of work. Consequently it was impossible to find civil servants who were able to speak with authority and long experience about what went on. Finally the tradition of secrecy which obscures the actions of the Civil Service, much to the irritation of the researcher, makes it far more difficult to examine the workings of central than of local government. What follows is based on an interview with one of the men who ran the Ministry's town development section for a number of years in the late fifties and helped the town considerably. Evidence has also been gathered from correspondence, the experiences of informed observers, and, in one case, the recollections of a former Minister.

The new towns programme has been one of the jewels of English planning policy. It has attracted attention from all over the world. The Ministry always contained a group of enthusiastic civil servants dedicated to ensuring that the programme was a success. No doubt the fact that the development corporations are nominated bodies, and the whole programme rather closely controlled by central government, made this close association inevitable. The expanding towns, in contrast, are mainly the responsibility of the respective local authorities. Furthermore they have not produced the same innovations and achievements in the fields of architecture and planning which have brought international repute to the new towns and plaudits to the Ministry. Accordingly, civil servants have tended to regard them as rather routine affairs and rarely become really involved in what went on in them.[14] A former Labour Minister of Housing recalled that when he was in office and wanted to go to Swindon, reaction was lukewarm. He got the impression that the Ministry had never forgiven Swindon for making a success of its scheme. This is undoubtedly an exaggeration but it illustrates the point.

Of course the civil servants did their duty. However if an expanding town wanted to get the additional help, as for example when Swindon needed control over the land to the east of the Borough, it had to try to engage the interest of the civil servant in charge of town development policy at the Ministry. The correspondence files reveal that the Town Clerk often managed to do this, although he recalled that sometimes this was impossible. Then the relationship reverted to one of 'aloofness and distance', and he knew that he could not expect to achieve much. The technique was interesting: if at all possible the new Assistant Secretary was invited down to the town and shown its many achievements. If this was not possible, letters and even personal visits from the Town Clerk would ensue. The civil servant referred to above was impressed both by the size of Swindon's achievements, and by the expertize of its Clerk and other leading officials. The records show that many of those who moved on to high positions in the Ministry went through the Clerk's education process, and remember the town with some attachment. This good relationship with the civil service often enabled the Clerk to apply pressure to sympathetic ears, and even take the officials to task without causing offence. One letter, for example, started with a single paragraph, 'Prepare for a veritable *cri de coeur!*' and another referred to 'one of my shocked amazement letters'. The civil servant who was interviewed said he regarded the Clerk as the 'colonel of his regiment' with the strong implication that, in the town development business, he was used to dealing with corporals.

Despite the effectiveness of the Town Clerk's approach to

---

[14] In an article reviewing town development, Mrs Denington refers to the Ministry's attitude as follows: 'It is noteworthy that a Government publication in 1955 *Town and Country Planning in Britain* did not even mention the expanding towns or the Town Development Act'. Denington, E. 'Town Expansion. An Exercise in Mutual Aid'. Reprint of *Housing Review*, vol. 16, no. 6, Nov–Dec 1967.

the Civil Service, there were limits to what could be achieved. Apart from the underlying attitude to town development mentioned above, the Ministry had to act as a broker between all the interests affected by the town's development. From Swindon's view point this was a constraint. The Ministry was the main intermediary between the expanding towns and the other Ministries, and transmitted many of the protests and requests for action that they made to these Ministries. Whether the Ministry of Housing put their own influence and weight behind these requests partly depended on the commitment of the individual civil servant involved to the town in question; here was where the Town Clerk's attempts to enlist their support was of significance. But it also depended on the priority that central government as a whole gave to town development. A review of some of the issues that arose in Swindon, and their outcome, bears out the view that town development was regarded as a minor issue.

Swindon often asked to be allowed to make representations directly to the Treasury about improving the scale of government grants for town development. This was refused, and the fact that the grants were not substantially improved for fifteen years suggests that the Treasury did not attach much importance to the policy. In contrast, relations with the Ministry of Agriculture did change over the years. In the early fifties agricultural production was a matter of great political importance, and public opinion was very much concerned about a possible loss of good farming land. The hand of the Ministry of Agriculture was strengthened by this factor, and it vigorously opposed some of the proposed new town sites. This meant, as we saw, that the Ministry of Housing had to perform a delicate conciliatory role to ensure that the proposal was not vetoed. After its initial policy of more or less wholesale opposition to urban growth associated with overspill programmes, the Ministry recognized that this was a national policy and used its influence to minimize the damage to agriculture. This being the case, once Swindon started to grow the Ministry accepted the principle. When the second major takeover of land occurred at the end of the fifties, it proved relatively easy for the Ministry of Housing to get its approval on Swindon's behalf. As the civil servant concerned said, 'The Ministry did not say no, and this meant that we knew they would eventually say yes'.

As we have seen, the conflict between the needs of the expanding towns and the development areas involved the Board of Trade. Here there was little sign that the towns managed to alter the basis of government policy over the years, or that the Ministry of Housing did more than convey the content of this policy to successive protesting authorities. Expanding towns had second priority to the needs of the areas of high unemployment, and one can understand the political and social reasons why this should be so. This policy was only relaxed when the general economic situation made it possible for the Board to apply less pressure to mobile industry to move to the peripheral areas. Apart from this, there is evidence from Swindon's history that the Ministry of Housing was prepared to intercede on behalf of individual expanding towns, but this only occurred when these towns were so short of industry that they were facing the possibility of becoming areas of high unemployment. In this situation, the Ministry could suggest to the Board that any action it took would be completely justifiable within the terms of the Board's overall mandate, which was to prevent and reduce the incidence of such areas. The Ministry helped Swindon in this way in the early sixties, when the railway redundancies occurring at a time of national economic depression threatened to create large-scale unemployment in the town.

The low priority attached to the town development programme also seems to have been reflected in the lack of pressure which the Ministry of Housing was able or willing to place on the Ministry of Transport. It was not until the early sixties, when the government greatly increased the resources available for roads, that the Ministry made a special allocation for overspill areas. There is no evidence from Swindon of any pressure being put on the Ministry of Education by the Ministry of Housing concerning school provision, but this may have occurred especially in the early days when there was a set of rules which prevented new schools being built ahead of the new population who would use them. But as soon as the initial lack of understanding was overcome, the Ministry's statutory duty to provide schools ensured that funds were available.

The Ministry of Housing had to mediate between the County Council and Swindon on several occasions, most notably at the start of development when the County sought its guidance about the expansion. By its reaction, the Ministry showed its desire to avoid appearing to show favours to either side or, in the official terminology, failing to strike a proper balance between the opposing interests. So, while indicating its approval of the scheme to the County, it suggested a compromise population figure, less than Swindon wanted but enough to get expansion away to a good start. At the same time, the Ministry privately advised the town to avoid making objections to the County Development Plan. The Ministry headed off a direct conflict between town and county on the issue by suggesting that Swindon could reserve the right to ask for a higher population figure at a later date. In 1959 the Ministry again intervened to persuade the County to redesignate the area to the east of the Borough for town development. The history of Swindon's successive attempts to gain boundary extensions and the opposition to these from the rural districts and the County suggests that the attempt that was made by the Ministry to strike a balance between the County and Swindon in 1952 has been its basic approach to this problem ever since.

Swindon and Ashford—the politics of expansion in two towns

Ashford is a small town in Kent that was, like Swindon, dominated by railway workshop employment. It is the major rail junction in East Kent and has good communications with London. As in Swindon, there was a need to diversify employment· as the railway declined. Town development seemed to be a good opportunity for the town to do this. Yet the first expansion plan was rejected by the local Council in Devember 1955, and it took four more years before a scheme, to expand from 25 000 to 55 000 in fifteen years, was concluded with the L.C.C. In a recent article, Brown, Vile, and Whitemore have analysed the nature of the local political system in Ashford which resulted in this series of events.[15] However, a comparison of events that were crucial to the sequence of decisions about expansion in Ashford, with the analysis which has already been presented for Swindon,

---

[15] Brown, T., Vile, M. J. C., and Whitemore, M. F. 'Community Studies and Decision Taking'. *British Journal of Political Science,* vol. 1 no. 2, pages 133-53.

reinforces the view that the outcome of town development schemes are largely determined by their political content.

Unlike Swindon, the first impetus for expansion came from outside Ashford. The Abercrombie Report mentioned it as the only town in Kent suitable for major expansion, and the Ministry and the County Council accepted this view and planned for it. The L.C.C. soon became keen to see the town expand as well. Brown *et al.* pointed out that, while the decision on whether to proceed was up to the Ashford Urban District Council, given this outside enthusiasm the actual terms of an agreement would be the product of negotiations with higher authorities, within limits set by them. For example, industrial growth had to go hand in hand with overspill population, otherwise Industrial Development Certificates would not be forthcoming. We saw that in Swindon it was the early realization of this that led to the acceptance of town development. Furthermore in Ashford, which unlike Swindon required financial help from the L.C.C., the siting and nature of the estates was also a matter for negotiation with the L.C.C. Brown *et al.* conclude 'Such matters were not merely a matter of detail to be settled once general agreement on expansion had been achieved. They were matters which were in part to determine the attitude of the community and of sections of it to expansion as a whole'.

The question of whether to accept expansion, and the various issues which were related to this, became 'the dominant and most divisive factor in local politics during the 1950s'. This is in sharp contrast to the situation in Swindon, where expansion was never politically controversial. The article lists a number of reasons why this opposition arose. Despite the fact that everyone in Ashford wanted industrial diversification, for many years there was a refusal to accept that this could only be achieved by overspill arrangements with London. Swindon had tried to avoid this but had realized that it was impossible by the late forties; in Ashford this realization took ten years longer to achieve. Furthermore Ashford had a strong middle class who objected to the possibility of new council estates in the middle of their residential areas. They also objected to the possibility of a temporary rise in rates, and to the spectacle of L.C.C. officials investigating a park site for possible use as housing. In Swindon the financial review allayed doubts about the rates.

Also the strategy of keeping the L.C.C. firmly out of affairs meant that no-one could say that the Council was being dictated to by Londoners.

The importance of maintaining as much independence as possible is illustrated in the case of Ashford by the attitude of the town's Chamber of Trade. From the end of 1954 they began expressing apprehension at the possibility of 'block development by the London County Council'. They asked for more information from the Urban District Council but, in comparison with Swindon where the Town Clerk came to meetings of local traders and addressed them, the Ashford Council refused to send the Chairman of their Planning Committee. The Chamber of Commerce found their alternative suggestion of a deputation unacceptable. This influential body was managed by the Council far more successfully in Swindon. It is also possible that the opposition of the Wiltshire National Farmers' Union to expansion helped to increase the solidarity of the town. The importance that the Ashford Chamber of Trade attached to local control is illustrated by a resolution they sent to the Council in 1954 which stated that it was not against development 'if the initiative was in Ashford's hands', but that the investigation of sites by the L.C.C. showed that it was 'just interested in getting people off their hands as quickly as possible'.

The Ashford Ratepayers Association also opposed expansion, and unlike Swindon it seems to have been an important body in the town. This importance was probably increased by the fact that the Council could give no reply to its demand for a statement of the costs, and consequent rate rises, created by development. As we have seen, the Swindon Treasurer's conclusion that rates would be lower with forced rather than natural growth was of great political significance. It probably undermined any case that the Ratepayers Association could have made against the scheme.

The other major factor which explains the rejection of Ashford's expansion in December 1955 relates to political changes on its Council in the early fifties. As in Swindon, the postwar Ashford Council consisted of Independents, drawn from the local business community, and Labour. However Labour did not gain an overall majority until 1957, in contrast with Swindon where they had control through the fifties. But the most important factor was that the extinction of the

Independents by Conservatives, which occurred in Swindon in the late sixties, happened in Ashford in the early fifties. By 1956 there were no Independent councillors left. As in Swindon, the Ashford Independents had been pro-expansion but the Conservatives were not. In Swindon, by the time the Conservatives gained power expansion was a success and generally accepted, but if the political change had occurred at the start of expansion there is every possibility that the subsequent course of events in the two towns would have been similar. Some confirmation of this may be seen in the fact that the tiny Conservative group on the Swindon Council in the fifties tended to oppose expansion for the same reasons, relating to cost and risk, that were expressed in Ashford. The Conservatives of the sixties were wholly different, many of them had first come to the town through expansion and others had prospered from it.

Brown *et al.* explain the wish of the Ashford Conservatives to replace the Independents in terms of their need to build a machine to oppose Labour in a Parliamentary constituency that was held by the Conservatives. Of course the situation in Swindon was wholly different as the seat was solidly Labour, so the same incentive to oppose Labour did not exist. Hudson even suggests that there was a need for really good Conservative and Liberal candidates to enliven local politics, something that only happened in the late sixties.[16] The article on Ashford also refers to the importance of experienced councillors in determining the outcome of the expansion issue. Only one of the new Conservatives in 1955, who had been a maverick Independent opposing expansion, had more than three years' experience on the Urban District Council. His opposition influenced the other inexperienced Conservatives just as, in Swindon, the support of a few senior councillors exerted influence in the other direction.

The split between the parties in Ashford on the expansion issue, allied with the fact that, until 1957, the Conservatives had a one-vote majority, led to the defeat of the proposed scheme. However, in 1957 a Labour Council took over. It lasted for three years, a long enough period of political stability to allow an agreement to be signed. An analysis of voting figures shows that this outcome was partly determined

---

[16] Hudson, op.cit., page 57.

by a swing in voting that reflected current national trends in the popularity of the parties. By contrast, in Swindon the lack of a replication of the national two-party system at the local level made changes in their national strength of no importance in determining the outcome of the expansion issue.

To summarize, despite great similarities between the Swindon and Ashford situations there were important political differences which affected the outcome of the expansion issue in the two towns. Partly because it was a large town with more resources, and partly because it was a solidly Labour town in national politics, Swindon was far more insulated from the external influences that effected Ashford. Swindon did not need L.C.C. help and could therefore accept expansion on its own terms to a far greater extent than Ashford was able to. Swindon was not a worthwhile place for the Conservatives to try to capture, and so the local political system did not reflect national trends. Finally, the management of the politics of expansion by the leading politicians and officials in Swindon seems to have been far more successful than in Ashford, where there was no chance of the emergence of the consensus which, in Swindon, made decisive action possible.

Conclusion

In this chapter we have reviewed the politics of the expansion scheme. We have seen how external political constraints on the progress of expansion were minimized by a series of factors. Some of these factors related to social and political phenomena which pre-dated town development, such as the lack of national party politics in the town. Others were the deliberate creation of the small group of people who ran the scheme. For example, the decision to exclude the L.C.C. was an action taken to avert the possibility of a successful attack on the scheme. The promise of additional local housing and the policy of social integration were other examples of this approach. We saw how, in the contrasting case of Ashford, the lack of some of these pre-existing conditions and policy choices generated opposition to the scheme.

We also saw how the Clerk in particular had a great flair for managing the politics of expansion, both in his relationship with Council committees and also in his relations with the various external bodies that had some measure of control over expansion in Swindon. We saw how the techniques used ranged from outwitting and outmanoeuvring the County Council to subtle and friendly persuasion with the Ministry. However, none of the Clerk's successes would have been possible without the support of leading councillors of both parties. They shared the officials' commitment to town expansion and were able to gain its acceptance, at first with suspicion but later with growing strength, by most of the community. The existence of a fairly high level of commitment and trust made possible the extensive delegation and concentration of powers from the Council as a whole to the leading Councillors, and from these councillors to the lay officers. Without this, it is difficult to see how expansion could have succeeded, given the external obstacles that it had to overcome. To underline this conclusion, we noticed in the last chapter that in the one area where this delegation did not occur, staffing, the scheme came closest to breakdown.

These conclusions relate specifically to the Swindon experience. But what can this study of conflict and its resolution add to our understanding of the nature of successful physical planning exercises in particular, and generally to the conditions under which innovative social policies are adopted and implemented by local government? Planners will probably find it odd that little or no mention has been made of the actual details of the physical plan. Yet it is the discussion of such attributes as the pattern of roads, the size and layout of housing areas, and the location of industrial estates that most conventional appraisals of planning schemes concentrate on. From such experiences conclusions are often drawn about the likely success or failure of plans or, if they have already been implemented, about the reasons for their failure or success. Of course it is true that if a plan does not reach a certain level of technical competence it is likely to create problems. These may be of sufficient magnitude for the general public to conclude that the plan has been a failure. The discussion of the technical aspects of plans is also important for the technicians, in order that they may refine and improve their skills and understanding of the problems that they face.[17] But there is, or should be, a wider and more interesting approach to the evaluation of plans. As we have hinted, the technical aspects of planning in Swindon left something to be desired and the scheme was subjected to several savage attacks in the technical press. Yet most of the people who actually lived and worked in the town would, if challenged, undoubtedly regard what happened as far more beneficial for Swindon than harmful. In this sense the scheme has been a success. Of course planners might argue that this test of success is not what they are primarily concerned with when they criticize plans. However, it is possibly the lack of such a perspective by them that is responsible for the widespread feeling that planning, far from being a beneficial product of our times, represent an incompetent and even malevolent intervention in ordinary people's lives.

Our explanation of why and how a successful piece of planning was carried out in Swindon has concentrated on describing and explaining the complex interplay of the political, organizational, social, and economic elements that determined the outcome. This method provides an interesting and fruitful approach to the understanding of planning because it generates a far stronger and more important set of criticisms of the defects in any plan than any aesthetic or purely technical criticism. Planners are gradually recognizing the importance of these 'extraneous' elements, because of the effect they can have on their ability to produce successful plans. The 1968 Town and Country Planning Act and the subsequent Development Plan Manual mark a stage in this acceptance.[18] But a great deal more needs to be done before the discipline and practice of planning is reconstituted along more effective and publicly acceptable lines. Changes in the content of planning education and the skills of the planners are a part of what is required, but a major problem is likely to be the frank acceptance by everyone concerned that planning is a political process as well as a social, economic, and physical one. Of course tacit acceptance of this fact, by the most effective planners, is common but the traditions of the discipline and the self image of the planner as a disinterested and value-free professional is an obstacle to the evolution of

---

[17] A plan can also be a device around which the political commitment and administrative organization required for action is mobilized. On the other hand it can also provoke dissension and delay and this might well have occurred if Swindon had produced a master plan.

[18] *Development Plans. A Manual on Form and Content.* (London: H.M.S.O., 1970).

new organizational forms and techniques of planning. It is no coincidence that the emergence of the politically motivated advocate planner and the planner/politician has first occurred in America, where the traditional divide between technical skills and politics is less evident, and entrenched political attitudes are weaker. The time has come when similar developments are necessary in Britain.

Turning now towards a consideration of factors underlying successful innovation in local government, the recent reform of local government and the reports which preceeded it all laid emphasis on the need for innovation and change in the service, in order to meet and deal with the wide range of new problems that it faces.[19] Re-organization of local authority boundaries and internal structures, and the acquisition of new skills, are all a part of what, it is felt, is required to make local government equal to the tasks that lie ahead. We have seen how important all these matters are, but there were other factors which, in Swindon's case at least, were important. Most local electorates and their councils seem to be rather conservative bodies. The need for innovation can exist but it may not be recognized and accepted unless powerful figures within the structure of local politics (including officials) have the ability and foresight to realize the need, and the willingness to do something about it. This recognition may come from officers or councillors, but whichever it is they need the active support of the others so a fairly high degree of mutual confidence is required, something that is not always present in government.

Of course this means that much depends on having the right people, in the right place, at the right time, and this is usually more a matter of chance rather than design. Once a successful policy is under way this problem may become a little easier because, as the knowledge of what is happening spreads, people who are in favour of the policy will probably want to

---

[19] See especially, *The Report of the Committee on the Management of Local Government* (Maud Report) (London: H.M.S.O., 1967); *The Report of the Committee on the Staffing of Local Government* (Mallaby Report) (London: H.M.S.O., 1967); *The Royal Commission on Local Government in England,* (Redcliffe-Maude Report) (London: H.M.S.O., 1969); and *The New Local Authorities: Management and Structure* (Bains Report) (London: H.M.S.O., 1972).

associate themselves with it, either as councillors or as officers. This certainly happened in Swindon; many officers were either attracted to service with the authority, or stayed there when they might have moved on to larger towns, because of the special interest that they had in town development and the opportunities it offered them for satisfying work.

Despite the fact that if one political party remains in power for too long, policy can and often does stagnate and the conservatism referred to above sets in, once an authority decides to innovate there are strong arguments in favour of the need for political stability and long-term support for the new departure. This is particularly so with a policy like town development where, after an initial acceptance of the scheme on the basis of the benefits it creates, there often follows a period in which the burdens it creates seem to outweigh the benefits. In some cases in Swindon, for example amenity provision, this period extended into the sixties — ten years or more after the development began. If there had been a sudden switch of political sentiment in these years, and the scheme had been abandoned abruptly, the town would have faced the possibility of a far worse future than it would have had if the scheme had not been adopted at all.

The reason for this long-term support was that the innovation of town development was not something that was simply produced by a few powerful leaders, like a white rabbit out of a conjurer's hat, having no relevance to the everyday problems that the local electorate faced; it could be shown to be of vital importance to all the major sections of public opinion in the town. Furthermore there were political leaders who were close enough to these groups to explain the need for expansion to them, and who were sufficiently in their confidence for these explanations to be accepted by them.

Apart from the possibility of the withdrawal of support for an innovation by the electorate and the political parties, it is also likely to be subject to criticism and attack from external bodies, especially if they feel that they are adversely affected by it. In Swindon we saw that the surrounding authorities and the County Council often reacted in this way. In this situation the maintenance of the support of the local electorate may be useful, but it may not be sufficient to preserve the policy from emasculation or failure — expecially when it is, to an extent, dependent on the co-operation of these bodies. What is then required is a person, or persons, with the ability to formulate and execute strategies designed to remove or minimize the constraints created by the opposing forces. We saw how, in Swindon, the Town Clerk was expert at doing just this. Of course these 'operators' need not necessarily be the same people who initially launched the new policy. Sometimes, for example, the idea might come from a group of councillors and be effectively implemented by officials, but it seems likely that in very many cases the initiators and the operators will be one and the same person, or persons.

A high degree of continuity in the identities of the key decision-makers is also important. Routine policies, which form a part of the duties of every local authority, largely define themselves to incoming administrators and politicians. But there is no such long-established certainty about what is required where an innovation is concerned. A rapid turn-over of personnel may result in the original aim of a policy being lost or abandoned. Also the tools and strategies required to operate the policy, which are rarely codified and accessible to newcomers, may disappear with the people who fashioned and used them. Of course there is a danger that these people will come to regard the policy as their own personal possession, and fail to ensure that the others are trained in the required skills and thus able to replace them when they have finally to leave the scene. Another problem is that these people may fail to recognize the changing environment in which their policy operates, ignore or resist the need for further changes, and become rooted in a narrow-minded parochialism. Traditional theories suggest that the democratic basis of local government allows channels for new demands and needs to present themselves to the decision maker. The Swindon example shows that this is a rather unlikely possibility. While the support and understanding of the electorate is a necessary factor in successful innovation, the actual content of the policy is not created and articulated by the general public. Obviously there are profound implications for our understanding and evaluation of local democracy here, but it is not part of the purpose of this book to discuss them. However this limit to the efficacy of democracy is an important problem which local government reformers have had to consider recently. It also has implications for our consideration of the necessary conditions for successful innovation. Unless the decision makers are able to react to changing circumstances, and accept that they may not have the final understanding of the problem that they are dealing with, today's innovation is likely to become tomorrow's conservatism. Again, the quality of the people concerned is important; having been open minded and receptive to new ideas when a policy is first launched, they must remain so throughout its duration, even to the extent of admitting that they have totally failed to recognize the full implications of their course of action sometimes, and revising their approach accordingly. It takes a considerable degree of intellectual honesty to admit that someone younger or less experienced than oneself may be right. The Town Clerk of Swindon showed these qualities in a letter to a civil servant who had successfully questioned the Clerk's claim that there would have been enough mobile industry for the town's needs if it had not been for the operations of the Board of Trade. The Clerk wrote to say that he accepted the argument and had concluded that in local government they were often 'far too parochial'.

Chapter Eight

The Policy of Development – an Evaluation

Swindon—a success or a failure?

In this chapter we examine the major costs and benefits of the Swindon scheme and consider the overall significance of town development policy, both in the past and in future.

The Government's South East Study, published in 1964, was in no doubt about the value of the Swindon expansion. 'Swindon is the outstanding example of a successful town development scheme', it reported, and the Town Council often quotes this glowing reference in answer to its critics.[1] Of course the Study was mainly basing its judgement on the statistics of expansion. As we have seen, a large number of jobs and people came to the town and for many years Swindon was the only scheme which, by virtue of its size, appeared to justify the Town Development Act.

However, mere size is not a sufficient basis for the sweeping conclusion of the South East Study. The success of the Swindon scheme varied according to the point of view of the observer. For example, someone who was in secure employment in the town and who disliked the rapid influx of Londoners could never regard town development as a success. Someone who moved to the town from London and was

---

[1] *South East Study* (London: H.M.S.O., 1964) page 74.

therefore able to get a new house would be likely to hold the opposite view. The question needs to be refined. Firstly, which of the major participants seems to have gained most from the process? Secondly, were there any drawbacks to this success?

Town expansion brought clear benefits to Swindon. It enabled the town to gain a wide range of jobs, housing, and civic amenities. Much of this has already been documented — the rapid growth of owner occupation, and the improved supply of public housing, a new town centre, and a new road system. But there are other indicators as well — new schools, and a college of further education, the rapid development of a new hospital, and the effect of expansion on increasing rateable value (approximately a threefold increase, allowing for revaluation, between 1951 and 1966) which enabled the Council to expand and improve its services without incurring an unacceptably high rate burden. Comparisons of the level of prosperity in the town with and without expansion are obviously impossible, but the pressure of workers who were prepared to use the unions' strength to raise wage rates to near London levels helped to increase the prosperity of all who worked in the town. By 1961 average household income in the town was £1374, 3 per cent above the current national average, and the 1964 income distribution was very close to the national norm. Fifty per cent of all households were owner occupiers in Swindon and district, compared with the national average of 41 per cent; and 51 per cent owned a car, compared with the national average of 43 per cent. According to a marketing survey, 'Its social problems are significant only if you live there; if you are just selling in Swindon then it is simply a good market'.[2] The last half of this conclusion could hardly have been true without town development.

There is little evidence that the social problems referred to above really existed to any serious extent. There was, and is, a small group of rather vocal middle-class Swindonians who think that expansion has become a rather soulless pursuit of growth for its own sake. They feel that Swindon has become a one-class society with few of the cultural trappings of a more socially balanced town. We referred to the views of this group, which included the town's former Labour M.P., in the last

---

[2] 'Marketing Profile — Swindon'. *TACK Magazine,* March 1965, page 15.

chapter. They have not been influential in the sense that they have not been able to command mass support or influence policy, but they seem to be the only identifiable local group who feel that expansion is rather to be regretted, at least in the form in which it was carried out. This group may have been mollified by the opening of the first stage of a new civic centre which includes a first-class theatre and will incorporate a new concert hall and library. However they might find it difficult to admit that none of this would have been possible without the revenue generated by town development.

Yet while town development has saved Swindon from economic and physical stagnation or even decline, some costs have been incurred. Because the Council had to concentrate on development, other problems were ignored. For example, it was a natural tendency to focus the social development work on the young mothers and their children who lived on the new estates on the edge of town. So, for ten or more years after development started, most of the social capital, both in physical and human form, was invested in these areas. The problems of the growing numbers of elderly single and housebound people, in older and often inadequate housing in the inner wards of the town, was left until the tempo of town development slackened in the middle sixties. This was the key issue which provoked a reformulation of the Council's social development policy. It has now become a comprehensive attempt to intervene in the social changes that are taking place in the whole town rather than merely being a short-term attempt to ease the integration of newcomers into the community.

As we have seen, the constraints which had to be overcome by town development led to the adoption of a piecemeal, opportunistic strategy. One result was that the physical layout of the new development sometimes lacks the overall coherence that the opportunity for a phased implementation of a master plan might have provided. However, in the long run the effects of Swindon's inability to achieve the initially desired industrial pattern may have more serious consequences. For example, the town still had 47 per cent of its workforce in manufacturing industry in 1966, compared with a national figure of 38.5 per cent. However it could be argued that the town would always be likely to diverge in this direction from the national pattern. Furthermore town development was at least creating a far more diversified and balanced employment structure in the town, in the sense that a far wider choice of jobs was available to people with given skills than before, and a far wider range of careers was available for those leaving school than had been the case in the railway age. Nevertheless the growth prospects of many of the new industries have been heavily dependent on the expansion of exports. The recurrent crises in the British economy have particularly serious effects on such firms, and when recessions occur areas which become more and more dependent on these firms can expect to suffer heavily. In Swindon these effects have become more noticeable as the industrial structure of the town has changed. Another problem too is the lack of opportunities that such industries offer for unskilled workers.

Perhaps the most worrying feature of the new industries that have come to the town is the likelihood that they will offer a declining number of male jobs in future. Such a situation is likely to create problems while female wages are below male levels.[3] Of course, in itself, the far greater range and numbers of jobs available for women is a beneficial result of town development. The extent of this can be gauged from the fact that while male jobs in the town rose from 43 706 in 1959 to 67 543 in 1965, a rise of about 32 per cent, female jobs rose from 11 635 to 22 736 in 1965, a rise of about 100 per cent. Much of this increase occurred in the sixties, and this is another factor which differentiates the two periods into which the account of the town's employment growth has been divided. The acceleration coincides with the growth of service employment in the second phase. But towards the end of the period many of the more advanced manufacturing firms, such as the electronics concerns, were reducing their processes to a simple and semi-automated series of operations; they then substituted unskilled and semi-skilled female labour for skilled male labour, thus saving on wage costs. This national development was likely to affect Swindon, where such advanced industries were concentrated, particularly strongly. By 1965 the increasing difficulty of creating more male jobs in the town began to be apparent. This trend, if continued, could have serious effects on the prospects for further town

---

[3] Equal pay legislation may have some effect but, typically, jobs are downgraded as an employer switches from male to a female workforce.

development, as it is still generally the case that the man is the main breadwinner. Therefore most families are unlikely to consider a move from London unless the man's job is assured.

The effect of town development on diversifying the town's social structure fell short of the initial expectation as well. This is clearly shown by Table 8.1.

Table 8.1

Five-year migrants by aggregated socio-economic groups—Swindon Municipal Borough, 1966 (percentages)

Grouping	Immigrants	Emigrants	Swindon as a whole
Professional (SEGs 3, 4)	5.1	8.3	3.5
Managers (SEGs 1, 2, 13)	8.2	13.0	6.9
Non-manual (SEGs 5, 6)	16.9	21.7	14.4
Skilled manual (SEGs 5, 6)	37.5	37.5	44.0
Semi-skilled manual (SEGs, 8, 9, 12, 14)	20.8	12.8	20.8
Unskilled manual (SEG 11)	8.5	3.8	9.1
Others (SEGs 16, 17)	2.9	2.8	1.4

Source: *Census Reports.*

This table shows that expansion generated a significantly higher influx of professional workers and managers than an examination of its overall socio-economic structure might lead one to suppose. Also the former predominance of skilled manual workers was being reduced. But the pattern of differential out migration is of greatest interest. Professionals, managers, and non-manual workers were leaving the town in much higher proportions than they were coming in or were already represented in the overall structure. The reverse was true for semi-skilled and unskilled manual workers. Thus the town was losing a disproportionate number of its higher-income white collar workers and retaining a disproportionate number of lower-income manual workers. As outward and inward flows were similar (in fact there was a small net out-migration) it appears that the town was becoming more rather than less working class,[4] the reverse of what was originally desired.

This pattern resulted from the fact that the major opportunities for owner occupation were outside the Borough,

---

[4] Of course this conclusion ignores the possibility that substantial numbers of lower-income manual workers will be upwardly socially (and economically) mobile.

n the surrounding rural districts. Therefore town development has helped to generate a process of social polarization, analogous to that which is occurring in Greater London. This may only be a matter for concern if a concentration of working-class people in any one area is thought to be objectionable in itself. There is little evidence that the phenomenon has led to social malaise. For example juvenile delinquency, which it is often suggested is a feature of such areas, is not a serious problem in Swindon. A recent survey showed that the delinquency rate stayed well below the national average during expansion, and was very low indeed in the new estates which are the most working class part of the town.[5] In London it is argued that social polarization may lead to the growth of large areas of low-income families, unable to support a high level of public services. It might be argued that this could happen in Swindon, but the new local government arrangements in the area which merge the town and the Highworth Rural District have averted this possibility. Anyway, as the town is the main service and employment centre for the subregion there will continue to be an increasing demand for a wide range of facilities and social activities. This is unlike the situation in some areas of London, where the existence of alternative centres in middle class areas results in a lack of demand for these things in working class centres.

However, if those who carried through town development were asked what their greatest disappointment was, they would probably mention the failure to achieve a greater degree of political independence *via* town expansion. Closely linked with this is the fact that much of the new rateable value created by town development did not benefit Swindon until local government reorganization in 1974. For example, the Parsonage Farm and Greenbridge Estates were both outside the borough boundary. At the end of 1965 a total of over 600 000 square feet of factory space had been built as a result of the town development scheme, but only a little over 100 000 square feet of this was within the Borough and therefore paid rates to the Council. It was argued if the town had had this revenue a much earlier start might have been made on improving its amenities. Because of the overriding importance that was attached to growth Swindon was

---

[5] Information provided by the Probation Service to the Town Clerk.

prepared to develop outside its area, hoping to incorporate th
new areas into the town later. These hopes were frustrated fo
many years.

It was not true, as some opponents alleged, that the desire t
gain county borough status was the major reason why th
Council wanted to accept overspill. But this possibility wa
seen as an important byproduct of town development. As w
have seen, Swindon never managed to cut itself loose from th
County Council, who in the later years might even have bee
relieved if this had occurred. The reason for this situation ha
little to do with local politics; it was a product of the failure o
successive postwar governments to take decisive action t
reform the antiquated structure of local government. O
course all this was changed by the Redcliffe-Mau
Commission and subsequent 1972 Local Government Act.
Swindon, to its chagrin, became second-tier authority. Th
new authority boundaries now include all the forme
Highworth Rural District Council,[7] but the first-tier authorit
is a little altered Wiltshire County Council so it looks as if th
history of strained relations between the county and the tow
may continue in the future.

This seems like a formidable catalogue of costs incurred b
expansion. But the significant question to ask is, what woul
have happened without town development? Certainly the tow
would not have been as prosperous as it is today. It still ha
problems but, given the size, density, and wealth of the town
it is in a better shape to tackle them than a dying railway tow
would have been. To say that the town's original goals hav
not all been met is not to minimize the many and outstandin
achievements.

The conclusion must be that so far as the people of Swindo
and their representatives were concerned, town development
for all its drawbacks, was a very beneficial exercise. Howeve
this can only be one aspect of any assessment of the value o
Swindon's expansion. How beneficial was the scheme t
London? In the Introduction we mentioned that the overspi

---

[6] *Royal Commission on Local Government in England, 1966-*
(Redcliffe-Maud Report) Cmmd 4040 (London: H.M.S.O., 1969). Loca
Government Act, 1972.

[7] The new authority has been renamed Thamesdown but it is dominate
by the Swindon urban area.

olicy aimed to help the conurbations in two ways. Firstly, it
ould relieve their industrial congestion. Secondly it would
rovide a source of good housing for those living in the worst
onditions in these cities. Swindon has made little contribution
owards the first goal. As we saw, the flow of mobile industry
) the town from London was insufficient for its needs and it
oon began to look elsewhere for new jobs. However this is not
eally a serious deficiency for there is now concern that the
ecline of manufacturing industry in London is occurring at
oo rapid a rate. In order to try to stem this decline the
.L.C.'s 1969 Development Plan actually proposed to increase
ne amount of manufacturing floor space in the capital. In
nese circumstances it could even be argued that an expansion
heme which took population in housing need from London,
ithout drawing on its industry, was more valuable than the
najority of schemes which relied on London for population
nd industry. But was Swindon helping to achieve what is now
een as the major goal of London's overspill policy, relieving
ne capital's housing need?

To answer this we have to examine the complex pattern of
opulation flows into and out of Swindon during the
xpansion period. Many people came to the town through the
fficial channels of the town development scheme. This meant
nat they applied to the London councils for registration on
ne Industrial Selection Scheme and their housing and job
equirements were noted.[8] In due course, if they were lucky
nd still wanted to move, they were given a job and a local
uthority house in Swindon. Such people are the major group
hich a town development scheme is meant to benefit. They
re in housing need and are unlikely to gain early rehousing in
ne exporting areas. However new and expanding towns also
equire key workers. These are the skilled people that the new
ndustries require to form the nucleus of the new firms'
orkforce. As far as possible these people are also selected
om the pool of those in housing need on the I.S.S. However,
nany of the workers who have the requisite skills are not in

---

[8] The I.S.S. is an administrative scheme which links a central register of
the skills of would be movers to new·and expanding towns with the need
of employers in these towns. For a full account see Gee, F. *Homes and
Jobs for Londoners in New and Expanding Towns* (London: H.M.S.O.,
1972) page 1.

housing need. Eventually, if employers are able to get these men through the I.S.S., they are allowed to advertise generall in London. The people who then come to the towns as ke workers are still eligible for council housing. In Swindon thi policy was applied more liberally than elsewhere and, apar from these London key workers, there were also som immigrants from elsewhere. They came to the town eithe because employers were not able to get the people the required in London, or because they were employed by firm which moved from other parts of the country. Table 8.2 show the magnitude of the flows from London and elsewhere t Swindon during town development.

Table 8.2

Borough of Swindon: Housing Record 1953-1966

Financial Year	Total dwellings available	Families housed from other areas		Dwellings available for local needs etc.
		Greater London	Elsewhere	
(1)	(2)	(3)	(4)	(5)
1953/4	589	20	—	569
1954/5	700	279		421
1955/6	1003	514	24	465
1956/7	1537	878	70	589
1957/8	1228	591	193	444
1968/9	948	393	180	375
1959/60	1060	484	202	374
1960/1	1057	482	192	383
1961/2	1223	555	301	367
1962/3	825	237	80	508
1963/4	1121	264	62	795
1964/5	1404	308	69	1027
1964/6	863	282	59	522
	13 558	5287	1432	6839

Source: *Swindon—A Study for Further Expansion, 1968, page 145*

Column 2 shows the total of local authority dwelling available for letting during the period. This includes house available for reletting as well as new ones.[9] Column 3 show that 5287 families were rehoused from Greater London. Th total included people in housing need who came via the I.S.S and key workers who did not. Column 4 shows that a total c

---

[9] In fact a total of 7599 houses were erected or acquired during t period — the rest of those available were relets.

1432 families came from elsewhere. These are the key workers who had to be recruited from elsewhere, and people who moved with firms coming to Swindon from outside the Greater London area.

According to a recent article by Roderick, during 1961-2 Swindon drew 70 per cent of its migrant tenants from Greater London and 30 per cent from the rest of the country.[10] Columns 3 and 4 in Table 8.2 show that, over the whole period of the expansion, 80 per cent of the tenants came from Greater London and 20 per cent elsewhere. Examination of the figures shows that in the first few years a very high percentage came from London, although this reduced later as new firms arrived in greater numbers. It can also be seen that 1961/2 was an exceptional year for immigrants from elsewhere. As Roderick notes, these figures were associated with the move of a Solihull firm to Swindon with some of its workers, and a recruiting campaign carried out by Pressed Steel (who could not obtain the skills they required in Swindon) in the North East with the assistance of the Ministry of Labour.

It is also important to know what percentage of the immigrants from London were actually in housing need and came through the I.S.S., and what percentage were not in need but came as key workers. No consistent record was kept of these figures, or at least none was readily available to the author. However, in the course of the lengthy correspondence between the respective Clerks to the L.C.C. and the Borough in 1963, which was referred to in the last chapter, the L.C.C. produced figures to show that, of the 2277 applicants housed from the L.C.C. areas from 1953 to 1963, 1570 or 60 per cent came through the I.S.S. Lacking a detailed breakdown of figures from the fifty-six other authorities in the Greater London area which exported population to Swindon during the period (and which, in 1965, together with the L.C.C. became a part of the G.L.C.), we can only suggest that it is reasonable to assume that from 1953 to 1966 60 per cent of the total inflow from Greater London came through the I.S.S., and that 40 per cent were key workers. So the complete pattern is as shown in Table 8.3.

---

[10] Roderick, W. P. 'The London New Towns — Origins of Migrants from Greater London up to December 1968'. *Town Planning Review*, vol. 42. no. 4, pages 232-341.

Table 8.3

Borough of Swindon: Immigrant flow of Local Authority Tenants 1953-66

Families housed from Greater London through I.S.S.	3172 (47.2%)
Key workers from Greater London	2115 (31.4%)
Key workers from elsewhere	1432 (21.4%)
TOTAL	6719 (100%)

These figures suggest that the town was more effective than the London-linked new towns in relieving housing needs in London, but less effective than some of the town development schemes over which the L.C.C. had a greater degree of control.[11]

It is interesting to take the analysis a stage further and examine the areas of origin of the London migrants. As Roderick has shown,[12] using data on the origins of migrants to Swindon from London in 1961-5, the pattern is strongly sectoral. His conclusion was that this was because Swindon naturally drew its migrants from these areas which were closest to it, rather than because of the effect of the sectorally based administrative arrangements that were in force for a short period in the fifties. This conclusion may underestimate the effect that individual housing departments can have on the extent to which people in housing need are steered towards solving their problems by a move out of London. Interviews with G.L.C. officials suggest that housing departments vary greatly in the extent to which they make use of this possibility according to quite subjective views about, and experiences of the Industrial Selection Scheme. It may well be that housing departments in the sectors closest to Swindon, which were originally linked with the town, retained the knowledge tha

---

[11] The G.L.C. has suggested that only 10 per cent of those going to the new towns from London have gone through the I.S.S. Hall, P. *et. al. The Containment of Urban England, vol. 1* (London: Allen and Unwin 1974) page 339.

[12] The G.L.C. also suggests that two-thirds of the families going t expanding towns are Londoners in housing need. *See* Evidence by th Greater London Council to the House of Commons Expenditur Committee. Environment and Home Office Sub-committee. Ne Towns, (typescript, n.d.) *also* Minutes of Evidence (of the abov committee) Wednesday 6 February 1974 (London: H.M.S.O., 1974 Exhibit 10, page 359.

the town offered a solution to some of their problems for several years after the arrangement lapsed. It would be interesting to see whether there has been any changes in the spatial distribution of the origins of migrants to Swindon since the re-organization of London government in 1965. However, even if the administrative arrangements and attitudes of individual housing departments have more influence than Roderick seems to suggest, it is still likely that the bulk of movement to Swindon would be radial, as various studies have shown this to be the dominant pattern of movement out from a metropolis.[13]

Analysis of migrants to Swindon from Greater London in the period from 1955 to the first quarter of 1965 (the period is slightly shorter than the period being reviewed here because of inadequate data for the early years) shows the same strongly sectoral pattern referred to above.

Table 8.4

Local authority migrants to Swindon from Greater London by sector of origin 1955-65

Sector of origin	Number of migrant families	Percentage of migrant families
Sector 1 (Essex)	206	5%
Sector 2 (Part of Middlesex and Hertfordshire)	796	20%
Sector 3 (Part of Middlesex and Buckinghamshire)	538	14%
Sector 4 (Surrey)	• 270	7%
Sector 5 (Kent)	50	1%
L.C.C.	2038	52%

Source: *Swindon Borough Council records.*

Swindon was originally linked with sectors 2 and 3 and it can be seen that the bulk of non-L.C.C. immigrants did come from these sectors. More detailed examination of the data at a

[13] e.g. Boal, F. W. 'Social Space in the Belfast Urban Area'. *Irish Geographical Studies,* 1970, pages 373-93.

local authority level shows interesting differences in the numbers of people coming to Swindon from these areas. Thus 436 (54 per cent of the total inflow from sector 2) came from two areas, Willesden Borough and Harrow Urban District. Willesden was certainly an area of bad housing conditions, but Harrow was not. Yet the latter area sent far more people to Swindon than areas with great problems in the same sector such as Tottenham (who were the first authority actually to send people to Swindon). These findings do suggest that the influence of individual housing departments referred to earlier has been an important factor in determining the flow of population to Swindon. Further examination of detailed local situations might also show that there is a strong correlation between the existence of major housing problems within an area and a determination to solve them locally. Areas with few problems may actually prefer to export the ones they have rather than deal with them. However the greatest number of migrants to Swindon, over half, did come from the L.C.C. the authority which had the worst housing problem. In this respect Swindon was probably more effective than the new towns. It took 52 per cent of its migrants from the L.C.C. compared with 40 per cent taken by the new towns.[14] Nonetheless both the new towns and Swindon took many people from areas in outer London.

To summarize, Swindon fell somewhere between the new towns and the other expanding towns in its value to London as a source of housing for those in greatest need. Furthermore detailed analysis suggests that many of those in genuine need may have come, not from the hardest-pressed areas in the metropolis, but from areas which could possibly have done far more within their own area to solve their inhabitants' housing problems. Of course this latter conclusion is likely to apply to all London-linked overspill schemes, and responsibility for it belongs with the G.L.C. (formerly the L.C.C.) and London boroughs, not the new or expanding towns. However the over-all proportion of the immigrant flow into Swindon which came from London, and indirectly the proportion in genuine housing need, were at least influenced by the way in which the town carried out expansion. The policy of accepting most of the available industry, rather than a more restricted range of

---

[14] Roderick, op.cit.

small-scale firms relocating from London (as other expanding towns did) resulted in a very different industrial pattern in Swindon compared with those other towns. The new, expanding firms required a higher proportion of skilled workers than the older, smaller firms. However these were precisely the sort of people already earning good wages in London, and therefore already well-housed or at least able to look forward to being so reasonably soon. Housing need is highly correlated with unskilled or semi-skilled employment and Swindon had little of this to offer. Furthermore the willingness of the town to accept large numbers of key workers from elsewhere, which was a considerable inducement to employers to move to the town and thereby sustain rapid growth, reduced the overall percentage of workers coming from London.

So Swindon was not as efficient at relieving London's housing problems as some other expanding towns. However this statement must be qualified. Firstly, the scheme was so much larger than most of the other ones, and it progressed so much more quickly than they did, that in numerical terms it was of greater value to London than any other scheme. Secondly, unlike the other schemes which all had considerable help from the L.C.C., Swindon only asked for a housing subsidy for every Londoner that it took. Thus the scheme was a cheap one from London's point of view and was highly cost effective. This probably explains why the L.C.C., and later the G.L.C., continued to support it.

It is hard to see how the Swindon expansion could be regarded as either a success or a failure by the County Council. It neither sought the expansion of Swindon, nor felt that it had anything to gain from the scheme. It was forced to participate against its will because Swindon had the power and ability to bring about this state of affairs, secure in the knowledge that the government was also anxious to see a scheme in operation in the town. There can be no doubt that in 1952 a majority of the County Council would have been unwilling to attribute any good at all to town development. With the passing of time and changing personalities, this attitude has softened somewhat. It seems that the County would now regard the scheme as neither a success nor a failure from their point of view, but rather an inevitable development in which they should participate in order to reduce or remove any undesirable consequences. However there is one very concrete way in which town development can be seen to have benefited the County. The industrial and commercial development in the Swindon area has made a significant contribution to the expanding revenues available to the County Council. Some measure of this can be gained from figures produced in 1964, when the Borough sought to incorporate much of Highworth Rural District Council plus their existing area into a new county borough. It was estimated that if this happened the County Council rate would have to go up by 7d to maintain the same level of services throughout its area, even though it would no longer have any responsibility for the new county borough.[15] In other words Swindon was helping to finance services in other parts of the county. In contrast, if town development had not taken place it seems likely that the social and economic problems caused by the decline of the railways would not only have prevented this from happening, but might even have resulted in other areas in the County having to contribute to the maintenance of county services in the town. So far as the Ministry of Housing was concerned Swindon's expansion obviously made a contribution to their policy of relieving London's housing problems. To this extent the same judgement of the advantages of the scheme, and its drawbacks, must be made in its case as has been made for London. However this case study of Swindon does enable us to go beyond this rather obvious conclusion and evaluate the significance of town development, particularly in comparison with the new towns and the policy of planned overspill which both programmes represented.

Overspill policy

The Town Development Act has never achieved the significance of the other postwar planning acts which were referred to in the Introduction. Planners and policy makers would agree with Shaffer's recent judgement: 'Many of these schemes are little more than small housing estates added to an existing town. They are thus quite different in conception

---

[15] Borough of Swindon. *Local Government Commission for England, Southern General Review Area.* Answers to Questionnaire. 1965, **page** 36.

from the new towns and even the few larger schemes that were started in the 1950s are, in the opinion of many, well below the standard of achievement in the new towns'.[16] It is obvious that the Act has failed to make a substantial contribution to solving the problems of urban congestion. However, the expansion of Swindon was one of the very few cases where the Town Development Act was used on a large-scale project, so a discussion of its value to the Ministry enables us to explore the limitations in the impact on national and regional policies of the type of overspill policy contained in the Act in one of the few cases where the Act was implemented in as vigorous a way as its initial sponsors must have envisaged.

As Rodwin pointed out in his pioneering study, the plans for the new and expanded towns did not form a part of a comprehensive and co-ordinated series of regional strategies which, in turn, fitted into a national plan.[17] Of course there was a regional plan for the Greater London área. This was first formulated in the 1944 Abercrombie Plan and elaborated in the 1951 County of London Development Plan. The strategy was to decentralize population and industry to a ring of new and expanded towns, most of which would be within fifty to seventy miles of London. But this objective existed uneasily alongside a national strategy of moving industry and population much further afield to the development areas. It is conceivable that the two policies could have operated side by side, but only if Britain's economic growth rate had been higher in the postwar era, if there had been a large supply of firms able and willing to move long distances, and if their workers had been willing to move as well. However neither the economic nor the social facts fitted the plan. Central government found itself trying to maintain a balance between two competing parties for industry and population. It proved to be an unpopular role for, while most mobile firms and workers would probably have preferred to go to the new and expanding towns, the very serious problems of the development areas made it necessary to persuade or cajole many of them into moving further afield.

---

[16] Schaffer, F. *The New Town Story* (London: MacGibbon and Kee, 1970) page 229.
[17] Rodwin, L. *The British New Towns Policy* (Cambridge, Mass.: Harvard University Press, 1956) page 71.

In national politics the policy of redistribution to
development areas had the most political support, and the
programme for the new and expanded towns had to take a
secondary place. So far as the relative weight of these two
latter policies was concerned, it seems clear that the Ministry
always regarded the new towns as the more important
programme. It is not entirely clear why this should be so, but
we have already suggested some reasons. The New Towns Act
involved government directly in the planning and building of
new communities. Because the towns were financed by the
Treasury, all items of expenditure were subject to
governmental approval. This unusual opportunity for the
Ministry to get directly involved in development generated an
able and enthusiastic band of Civil Service administrators who
were committed to promoting the new towns programme. In
contrast, the expanding towns were a responsibility of local
government with a minimum of direct state intervention. The
differing priorities that the Civil Service appeared to attach to
the two programmes was discussed at a recent seminar; 'It was
suggested that inequality between new and expanding towns
was also recognized at national level where it was felt that
while the New Towns division of the Department of the
Environment was very effective, the equivalent branch for
Town Development "went along on a shoestring" and was very
much diffused in terms of responsibility'.[18] Shaffer's view of
the expanding towns probably reflects the departmental
attitude regarding the respective merits of the two
programmes quite accurately, as he was a senior civil servant
with a career in new towns administration. Apart from this
personal involvement, the fact that the Minister was
responsible to Parliament for the new towns, but not for the
expanding towns, must have added to their importance in
official circles.

After an initial phase, when the town development policy
was new and had a measure of active interest and support
from the politicians, the Civil Service probably regarded it as a
rather minor part of their responsibilities. Although
individual civil servants were enthusiastic about Swindon and
admitted that it was a success, this in itself had no effect on

---

[18] Centre for Urban and Regional Studies. *Social Development in New Communities,* (Birmingham: CURS, 1972), pages 26-7.

their overall attitude to the policy. Indeed there is even evidence from the comment of a former Minister mentioned in the last chapter, that some civil servants were irritated by the success of Swindon and its council's wish to expand still further.

The conclusion must be that the major beneficiary of Swindon's development was the town itself. Most of the other bodies involved would either have preferred the scheme not to have occurred, or regarded it as a successful example of the implementation of a rather minor and defective element of the postwar planning strategy. This rather harsh judgement does not reflect on the particular way the scheme was run in Swindon. Even if the town had been willing to tie itself far more closely to London, and restrict its intake to those in housing need (and this would have cost London far more in terms of lost industry and subsidy) the impact of the overspill programme was insignificant compared with the magnitude of the housing problem which it was originally supposed to play a large part in solving. By 1966, the London ring of new towns had increased their population by approximately 275 000 in the twenty years or so since the programme began.[19] This figure includes the natural increase of the resident population in these towns, but on the other hand it overlooks the large number of people who moved out of London to these towns, and then moved on. However the overall achievement, even allowing for these two opposing factors, is not outstandingly important when compared with the size of London's continuing housing problem. Only about 10 per cent of those who went to the new towns were in real housing need, and this serves to diminish the importance of the programme, when judged by its *original goals*, even further. By 1967, the London-linked town development programme had provided houses for approximately 100 000 people. Of course this total is subject to the same factors as the new towns total mentioned above.[20] So numerically the expanding towns had achieved less than the new towns.

However, 70-80 per cent of those who moved to these towns were officially defined as being in housing need. Therefore this programme, which has been a poor relation to the new

---

[19] Figure derived from 1966 Census Usual Residence Tables, Table 1, and *Town and Country Planning*, vol. 38, no. 1, 1970, page 43.

towns policy, has a better claim to have fulfilled its aim than the new towns. However even the efforts of the expanding towns are minor in comparison with the size of London's problem for there was an estimated deficit of 326 000 houses in 1966, equivalent to 12 per cent of the total number of potential households in the city.[21]

In an influential article Foley has argued that British town planning has a flexible ideology which is easily adapted to take account of changing facts and pressures.[22] This is confirmed by the fact that supporters of the new towns gradually abandoned the claim that these towns were making a major contribution to solving London's housing needs as it became clear that this was not happening. The following extract from the journal of the Town and Country Planning Association, the main pro-new town pressure group, illustrates this switch clearly: 'A possible nemesis for the new towns has existed ever since their development became closely dependent on the public housing lists of the great cities. In itself this connection is just and humane. It is an expression of the social need to rehouse low-income workers in a better environment. But as a full *rationale* for the creation of new towns the concept is disastrous. It reinvokes a new if more welfare minded version of Disraeli's picture of the two Englands'.[23]

Of course the T.C.P.A. had supported new towns for many years before they became a part of national planning policy. But for this private ideal to become a national priority, and for there to be large sums of taxpayers' money devoted to it, it has to be believed that it is an essential part of a policy to improve the living conditions of the working class in the major

---

[20] Figures derived from *Town and Country Planning*, vol. 36, no. 1, January 1968. Town Development Act Progress to 30 June 1967. This table shows that 29 378 houses had been built for overspill in the London linked expanding towns. A factor of 3.4 persons per house was used to produce the population figures. Whilst this conversion factor is based on Ministry estimates these are only for the latter years of town development. Consequently the figure of 100 000 can only be a rough approximatiion.

[21] *London's Housing Needs up to 1974* (London: Ministry of Housing and Local Government, 1970) page 7, para. 16.

[22] Foley, D. L. 'British Town Planning, One ideology or Three?' *British Journal of Sociology*, vol. 11, no. 3, 1960, pages 211-31.

[23] Self, P. 'A New Vision for New Towns'. *Town and Country Planning*, vol. 38. no. 1, 1970, page 4.

conurbations. If this contribution is not forthcoming, and on the past record we must doubt whether this is so, the whole concept and the national investment in it is open to question.

In contrast the expanding towns continue to serve their original aim. The current attitude, that they will continue to play a small but useful part in helping some of those in need to find decent housing, seems sensible.[24] It might be argued that an extension of this programme would be useful but this is doubtful. The problem is the mismatch between the skill requirement of the expanding towns (and the new towns for that matter) and the skills of those in greatest housing need in London and other major cities. With a far more determined effort by the Government to provide retraining facilities, many of these people may eventually be able to make the move to a new community. However there will still be many who for reasons of age, lack of ability to learn new skills and family and community ties, will not want or be able to take up this opportunity. For these people solutions have to be found within the city.

The second problem is the difficulty of finding more towns which are prepared to expand. In 1967 Evelyn Denington outlined the main elements which were present when a scheme was successfully carried out.[25] For large-scale expansion the town needed to have a strong and capable body of expert officers. The main motive for expansion was usually a need to strengthen the economy of the town. Two further factors were also crucial. 'To make real progress a scheme must be wanted and supported without reservation by both partners. Party politics must never enter into the issue at all. Wherever there has been real success, certain key figures stand out among both members and officers as the personalities who made the scheme go'.

We saw how, in the case of Ashford, many of these elements were missing. As a consequence no progress was made with the scheme for a number of years. But in Swindon all these factors 1 we analysed the previous history of the town, and discovered

---

[24] This, for example, was the role suggested for them by the G.L.C. at the Greater London Development Plan Inquiry.

[25] Denington, E. 'Town Expansion. An Exercise in Mutual Aid' *Report of Housing Review—Special Feature*, vol. 16, no. 6, Nov-Dec 1967.

why and how both political groups became committed to expansion. In Chapters 3, 4, and 5 we showed how the officials and councillors skillfully negotiated the problems posed by such complex matters as land acquisition, social integration, the attraction of industry, and the management of a balanced programme of housing and job production. In Chapter 6 we showed how the staffing, organizational, and financial requirements of expansion were met. In Chapter 7 the crucial importance of the political process was identified.

If the town development programme was to expand, existing schemes will have to exceed their presently agreed overspill targets. Alternatively, new schemes must be started. In this case the newly participating towns must contain most of the elements that were present in Swindon and which Denington identifies as necessary for success. It is difficult to find towns where these conditions exist together. A town may, from the point of view of an outsider, be ideally suited for town development because of its size, location, and economic structure, but the political and personal factors mentioned above may be missing. As Denington recalls, of the nineteen towns which the Ministry originally thought would be suitable for expansion, only six finally agreed to participate. Even then it took many years for some of these to become operative, Ashford being a case in point. On the other hand there are some towns with a desire to expand, but which are too small, or which require too great an investment in the infrastructure to make the project feasible. Referring to this, a G.L.C. official mentioned a number of towns where his authority would have had to put too much money into, for example, flood protection works to make them candidates for expansion. Although the G.L.C. supported expansion in towns as small as Thetford, which had a population of only 4500 when the scheme started in the early fifties, it is no longer their policy to enter into agreement with towns of this size. They prefer to find places with at least three times this population because these have at least the rudiments of a full local government organization, and a reasonable financial base.[26] The problems of the really small towns are highlighted by Denington in an anecdote about Thetford. She recalled the consternation that

---

[26] What effect the new local government structure will have on the policy remains to be seen.

the Council experienced when they required another dustman, because it would have cost them a 6d rate!

Given the multi-dimensional nature of the criteria that have to be met before successful town development can take place, it is hardly surprising that the original hope that town development would bring major housing relief to the conurbations has not been met. A further implication is that the future contribution of this programme to the country's housing needs can only be a modest one, depending on the number of towns available for expansion. Furthermore it seems unlikely that, given the wholly voluntary nature of the legislation, there can be any decision by central government or by the conurbations acting alone to increase the scale of the programme.[27]

The future

This book has been mainly concerned with events that occurred in the fifties and early sixties. By 1965 the first phase of expansion was nearly over. In this year a firm of consultants suggested that the town be expanded to an ultimate size of 400 000.[28] This began a second phase of growth under the Town Development Act. The origins and progress of this new scheme are analysed in detail elsewhere, but a brief outline of progress to date seems appropriate.[29] The new scheme was foreshadowed by two previous reports. In 1963 the Borough Council had commissioned a firm of planners to prepare a study of how the town could be expanded to about 230 000.[30] It was about to use this as the basis of an approach to the L.C.C. and the Ministry when the first comprehensive review of regional policy in the South East, and the first major re-appraisal of the Abercrombie strategy, was announced by the government. In 1964 the South East Study recommended that

---

[27] Outside London there was never as much enthusiasm for the Act as in the capital anyway. In recent years, as the population of these other conurbations fell by voluntary migration, support for town development and the new towns has waned still further.

[28] Llewellyn Davies, Weeks and Partners. *A New City* (London: H.M.S.O., 1966).

[29] Dr P. H. Levin is preparing a major study of Swindon's new growth to be published shortly.

[30] Vincent, L. and Gorbing, R. *Swindon, A Plan for Expansion.* (Swindon: Swindon Borough Council, 1963).

a major overspill development should be sited in the Newbury/Swindon/Didcot area. Naturally Swindon wanted to be chosen. As mentioned above, in 1965 a further report came to such a conclusion.

Not surprisingly, the County Council and the rural districts objected to a scheme on the scale proposed by the consultants, so the Minister reduced the proposed size of the development to about 250 000, very similar to the size that the Borough's consultants had originally suggested in 1963. The next step was to set up a joint team of officers from the Borough, the County, and the G.L.C. to examine the details of the proposed development, and a parallel steering committee of councillors from the three authorities. Their physical, social, and economic appraisal was published at the end of 1968. It was approved by the Minister, subject to satisfactory arrangements being made to execute the scheme, in the following year.[31]

The contrast between the first stage of expansion and this latest phase is striking. In the early fifties it took little more than two years to conclude the preliminary negotiations, acquire land, and start building. In the sixties, seven years elapsed from the first consultant's report to the Minister's approval. In the fifties Swindon had been careful to exclude the L.C.C. and the County Council from any detailed influence over events. In the sixties they were both deeply involved in the planning process. The slow progress on this later scheme has resulted from several factors. The endemic national economic problems have made it much more difficult to launch a major new scheme. The advent of regional planning has meant that the government has become far more involved in decisions about the location of major schemes. This adds another complexity to the planning process. The scale of investment required, and the refinement of planning techniques, demand far more careful and lengthy planning. This has also meant that Swindon was bound to accept that the County Council and the G.L.C., who were being asked to contribute a great deal under both these headings, should become partners in an undertaking that, in any other town, would probably have been entrusted to a development corporation.

---

[31] Swindon Expansion Project. Joint Steering Committee. *Swindon. A Study for Further Expansion.* (Swindon: The Committee, 1968).

The involvement of the other two authorities created a number of problems, some of which have not yet been resolved. In the light of its concern about the outflow of industry and population, the G.L.C. has been re-appraising its support for overspill agreements. It has been unwilling to be committed to the maintenance of long-term support for any new scheme, preferring to sign a series of interim agreements. This obviously creates some uncertainty about Swindon's future. But the major obstacle to progress has been the thorny question of who should control and execute the scheme. Swindon wants to keep control, but the County (and to some extent the G.L.C.) wants to share it.

However all these problems may be insignificant so far as the continuing growth of the town is concerned. Events have not waited for the politicians to resolve their difficulties. Since 1965 housing, industry, and commerce have continued to expand. The first stage of the new civic centre has been built, and a massive new shopping centre is nearing completion. An interim overspill agreement has been concluded with the G.L.C., and two new neighbourhoods, housing about 13 000 people, are being added to the town, and the obvious locational advantages of the town, and its accumulated expertise in attracting new jobs, results in a pressure for growth which is no longer dependent on the existence of a town development agreement.

Swindon's future seems bright; however the legislation and policies which enabled it to expand are increasingly in doubt for reasons which have already been considered. But could new and expanding towns policy be altered so that it could play a more useful role in future planning strategies? As we have already suggested, the expanding towns can continue to offer an opportunity to a relatively small number of young skilled or semi-skilled workers to escape from the difficulties of the housing market in the cities. More retraining schemes could improve the chances that the unskilled have to move out. There are also a number of detailed improvements possible in the administrative arrangements, especially the Industrial Selection Scheme.[32]

However town development could make an important contribution to thinking about the political and organizational forms that the development of new communities should take. The expansion of an existing town has two major

advantages over the building of a green fields new town.
The first is that an existing settlement of any size is likely
to be sited strategically with respect to communication;
it will also have a nucleus of social and recreational facilities
and can thus provide some of the necessities of life from the
time that the first overspill family arrives. Compare this with a
new town where completely new transport links may be
required, and there are no pre-existing social and recreational
facilities. Of course the validity of this argument has been
partly accepted as most of the new towns of the sixties are
based on existing towns, some of them as large as Swindon.

The second lesson that can be drawn from the expanding
towns is a more controversial one. It is that the control of new
communities   by   local   government,   rather   than   by
development corporations, may offer a more democratic and
satisfactory way of ensuring that growth occurs. The
development corporation is an *ad hoc* body, appointed by the
Minister and accountable only to him. It offers local residents
no opportunity *as of right* for influencing what is happening to
their town. In the era when green fields new towns were the
common form of development, such a body might have been
defensible. However, most future new towns are likely
to be expansions of large existing settlements. In these
circumstances the exclusion of local politics from a vast area of
decision-making which radically affects the form and future of
the town is questionable. Furthermore, as the plans for new
towns become more and more ambitious, involving the
development corporations in large-scale intervention in social
and economic as well as physical planning, the gap between
the goals of the corporations and their power to implement
these goals gets wider. They are becoming more and more
dependent on the co-operation of the local authorities who are
the major providers of many of the services for which the
corporations need to plan. The mechanism of local politics
can provide a far more effective device for the determination

---

[32] See Gee, F. op. cit. Also the London Borough of Lambeth used their
Housing Advice Centre, in conjunction with Peterborough New Town, to
publicize the advantages of a move to that town out of London. Special
efforts were made to reduce the lengthy wait that I.S.S. applicants
usually experience. A sharp increase in the number of movers resulted
from these efforts.

of priorities, co-ordination of action, and resolution of disputes, than the uneasy combination of corporation and council, with their differing ideologies and sources of accountability.[33]

Of course towns which are only the initial size of Stevenage or Hemel Hempstead could not have carried out the tasks that their development corporations subsequently executed. However, as we have already stated, the future new towns are likely to be based on far larger towns. Our examination of Swindon shows that these larger towns are capable of carrying out development on the new town scale. There seems no reason why this pattern should not become the norm with the reform of local government and the emergence of larger units. Of course there might still be occasions when a development corporation would be needed, but even in these circumstances there should be statutory provision for local government to be represented on the corporation, and for its influence to grow as the new town grows. Where local government undertakes the task alone, there would obviously have to be adequate arrangements for the government and the other involved bodies to play a part in the decision-making process. This is not impossible to arrange. The example of Basingstoke, where development has been controlled by a joint committee of the Town Council, the Hampshire County Council, and the G.L.C., might be a model for many schemes. The limited experiment in partnership at Northampton is another example.[34]

However, is it worth creating more new and expanding towns at all? They can only make a marginal contribution to

---

[33] For an expanded version of these views see M. Harloe, 'Milton Keynes Final Report (review article). *Environment and Planning* vol. 2, pages 357–62, 1970. Ruth Glass has referred to these problems. She suggests 'there are . . . distinct advantages in giving the new planning functions to established government agencies: indeed, it often seems that the advantages outweigh the disadvantages. That was the conclusion which we reached after our own comparison of the planning work of the new agencies—the new town development corporations—and that of established institutions—the counties and county boroughs, which are the local planning authorities. The new agencies seem to have the defects of the old ones often in an accentuated form, and without the compensating virtues'. Glass, R. 'The Study and Practice of Planning'. *International Social Science Journal*, vol. 11. no. 3, 1959, page 398.

[34] See Schaffer, op. cit., pages 283–4 for details.

the relief of housing need, and will probably never offer a solution to the hard core of need in the conurbations. The expanding towns can continue to play a useful, if minor role, and the programme has the advantage of regenerating the town where it takes place. New towns will continue to have their uses as well because they are often designated for reasons other than to relieve housing need in the cities,[35] for example as elements in a regional economic strategy, such as the proposed Central Lancashire New Town, or to provide housing for a major new development such as the new town which was to be built near London's proposed third airport at Foulness. But little of value remains in the claim which, more than any other, inspired the adoption of the overspill programme by the national government after the last war, namely that new and expanded towns could play a strategic role in the relief of industrial congestion, poor environment, and housing need in the major British cities. The solution to these problems is far more intractable than the optimistic postwar generation of planners and politicians believed. To some extent this has been realized, as urban policy and research has increasingly concentrated its attention on the need to find solutions to the problem of the conurbations which do not merely result in the most active and skilled elements of the population being creamed off or forced out by rising housing costs, leaving the old, the poor, and the transient to share a deteriorating urban system, while those who have the money are able to avoid problems such as declining public transport, inadequate housing, and diminishing job opportunities, and are able to enjoy the positive aspects of city life. To solve these problems requires more understanding of urban processes, a commitment to the ending of the social and economic inequalities that underpin these processes, and the power and determination to act. Overspill policy as it has been carried out in Britain in the post war era has contributed to the evasion, rather than the solution of these problems.

---

[35] But in the light of Foley's article, it is interesting to note the shift in official justifications of the value of individual new towns as the need to help the housing situation by means of overspill in some of the major conurbations appears to recede.

Index